Tent City, Seattle

Tent City, Seattle

Refusing Homelessness and Making a Home

Tony Sparks

University of Washington Press Seattle

Tent City, Seattle was made possible in part
by the University of Washington Press Authors Fund.

Copyright © 2024 by the University of Washington Press

Design by Mindy Basinger Hill

Composed in 10/14 pt Minion Pro

All rights reserved. No part of this publication may be reproduced
or transmitted in any form or by any means, electronic or mechanical,
including photocopy, recording, or any information storage or
retrieval system, without permission in writing from the publisher.

Photographs by the author.

UNIVERSITY OF WASHINGTON PRESS   uwapress.uw.edu

LIBRARY OF CONGRESS CONTROL NUMBER 2023054309
ISBN 9780295752600 (hardcover)
ISBN 9780295752617 (paperback)
ISBN 9780295752624 (ebook)

∞ This paper meets the requirements of ANSI/NISO Z39.48-1992
(Permanence of Paper).

Contents

Acknowledgments *vii*

Introduction *1*

1. Home and Homelessness in a Settler Colonial City *27*

2. The Making of Homespace *47*

3. Becoming a Good Camper *69*

4. Seeing Like a Tent City *93*

5. Community, Recognition, and Encroachment *118*

6. Home beyond Property *137*

Notes *157*

Index *177*

Acknowledgments

I would never have been able to write this book without the generous inclusion offered me by Tent City 3 residents and SHARE/WHEEL staff. Much of this book is about creating a sense of home amid the stress and struggle of ongoing displacement. I am deeply grateful to the residents of Tent City 3 and the staff of SHARE/WHEEL for including me in this effort and sharing their time, thoughts, and companionship. In this vein, special mention goes to Michelle Marchand, whose tireless patience, compassion, and advocacy are an inspiration.

This book has been a long time coming. It began at the University of Washington, where I was extremely fortunate to have the opportunity to learn from incredible teachers, mentors, and peers. In particular, I owe the most profound debt of gratitude to Vicky Lawson for challenging my thinking and allowing space and time for me to grapple with those challenges. Her unwavering and ongoing mentorship, support, and example have greatly informed this work as well as the academic and person I am today. I am thankful as well to Steve Herbert, Arzoo Osanloo, and Matt Sparke, who helped design the research and shepherd it through its early phases.

I am grateful for the support, encouragement, and patience of the people at the University of Washington Press. I can't thank Andrew Bersanskis enough for his encouragement and the many conversations that enabled me to finally develop my research into a full-fledged draft. I also want to thank the two anonymous reviewers, who offered thoughtful and insightful critiques; such uncompensated labor makes academic publication possible. I feel lucky also to have worked with Mike Baccam, whose thoughtful comments and insights made this a better book and me a better writer.

Many people have significantly shaped the development of this work and my thinking since I began my engagement with Tent City 3. Sarah Elwood, Ananya Roy, David Boarder Giles, Monica Farias, Eric Sheppard, Frances Fox Piven, and all the members of the Relational Poverty Network have left a deep imprint on my work through their inspiring models of politics and thought. Maggie Ramírez, Chris Herring, Jessie Speer, Steve Przybylinski, and Eric Goldfischer continue to push me through their scholarship and conversation to think more deeply about the themes and issues explored here. Martha Bridegam and Tim McCormick were kind enough to read and provide incredibly thoughtful and helpful comments on early drafts. Liz Brown, who has been part of this project from the very beginning, has read every draft and has unfailingly provided thoughtful, insightful commentary that has improved nearly every aspect of this book—and also makes my life brighter and more enjoyable in every way. I am deeply indebted and profoundly grateful to you all.

Tent City, Seattle

Introduction

The first time I really felt at home in Tent City 3 was the day of what I have come to call the ankle incident. It was late April 2006. The camp was conducting one of its periodic moves to a new host site. This move was from the grounds of Saint Mark's Cathedral in the posh North Capitol Hill neighborhood, to a vacant lot adjacent to Cherry Hill Baptist Church in Seattle's Central District, about five miles away. For the most part, moving days sucked. The process of taking down a city of almost a hundred residents with their possessions, packing it up on borrowed trucks, and moving it across town, only to set it all back up again, was a daunting task. By the end of moving day, bodies were tired and nerves frayed. In hindsight, this exhaustion is what likely initiated the ankle incident.

This particular moving day had gone more smoothly than most, and I was eager to be done. The weather was nice. Everybody's things had arrived together and intact. By late afternoon, most of the communal tents were up. A group of about twelve of us had just finished wrestling the "MASH," a giant military surplus tent that served as a men's dormitory for new arrivals, into an upright position. Tradition dictated that personal tents went up last. I had the poles in place on my own tent and was ready to attach the clips when—CRACK!—the pallet on which I had been setting up my tent suddenly gave way. I lost my balance and fell. A searing pain shot from my ankle. My memory is a bit blurry on this part, but I clearly remember that Mel, an older man who had become a friend and mentor in the month I had been living in the tent city, raised one eyebrow, shook his head, and said, "Uh, I think you better take that to the ER."

Three hours later, I hobbled unsteadily back into the now completed Cherry Hill version of Tent City 3. "Welcome home!" called Mel from somewhere near the executive committee desk. "We thought you wouldn't wanna come back!"

"You can't get rid of me that easy," I replied. Despite my attempt at lightheartedness, I wasn't in any mood to chat. My foot hurt, my arms ached from the move and the new crutches, and I was groggy from the pain meds administered at the hospital. That moment was probably the closest I came to giving up during the seven months I spent living in Tent City 3.

Instead, I gave a general wave and hobbled toward my tent on the uneven ground. I just wanted to go to sleep. When I arrived at my tent, I noticed two sets of crutches waiting on the pallet beside my door. Inside my tent, there was an odd contraption made of duct tape and foam and a small wicker basket with three prescription bottles, each containing a couple of pain pills and a "break and shake" ice pack. As I eased myself onto my sleeping pad, I heard Melanie's voice behind me: "It's for your foot."

"Huh?" I replied, barely turning around.

"That," she said, pointing to the contraption. "I made it so you could keep your foot elevated."

"Thank you so much," I said wearily as I hoisted my foot onto the surprisingly comfortable platform.

"And the pills are from all of us," she said. "We didn't know if you had allergies, so there are different ones in there."

"Okay. Thanks, that's really nice," I said as I laid my head back onto my pillow.

"No worries—we have all been there."

At that point, I must have dozed off, because when I awakened to a whooshing knock on the soft nylon of my tent door, I opened my eyes on mostly darkness. Paul, who was one of the first people I had met when I moved to the tent city and who was now my neighbor, was standing there awkwardly, holding a plate with three pieces of pizza in one hand and a soda in the other. "The Cherry Hill folks brought over pizzas and, well, we thought you might be hungry."

"Hey, that's awesome," I uttered groggily, sitting up to take the pizza.

"Well, uh, I'll leave you with it," mumbled Paul, who was not much for conversation, as he backed away. "Feel better."

I don't know if it was the drugs or the exhaustion from the move, but as I sat eating my pizza in my little four-by-eight-foot section of Tent City 3, I teared up. At that moment, in a flimsy tent in a vacant lot, I felt at home. At the time of the ankle incident, I had been living in Tent City 3 for a month. Although that was the first time I really felt completely and totally at home there, I had felt and experienced the intentional making of the camp into a homelike space from my first day.

Indeed, from the time I arrived at the tent city, every small task was an act of homemaking, a reminder that the ability to be at home is a collective and participatory project. When I think back to the day of the ankle incident, I recognize that my own homey feelings arose from a confluence of many factors. Of course, the caring and compassionate reactions from my fellow campers were foremost. Their actions made me feel both cared for and included in a way I had not expected. But that wasn't all. I was hurt and tired. The camp itself and the personal space of my tent provided the ability to just lie down and feel safe, which allowed me to be "at home" at that moment.

This is a book about home. Specifically, it is about how an ever-changing group of people forges a space of home—a homespace—in a rough assemblage of tents that moves every thirty to ninety days, from neighborhood to neighborhood throughout the city of Seattle. This assemblage, called Tent City 3, is the third incarnation of a peer-managed, self-governed tent encampment located in Seattle, Washington. Enabled by a 2002 consent decree to operate by the host's permission on privately held land for up to ninety days, later modified by city ordinance in 2010 to remove this time limit when the camp was hosted by a religious organization, the camp's persistent peripatetic existence has over the last twenty-three years become a regular feature of Seattle's neighborhood landscape. It has also, for its residents, served as a space they can call home.

But what is home anyway? Home refers to a place, of course: a place that shelters one from the elements. But home exceeds mere shelter. It is more than just a place where one has permission to live. For liberal political theorists, the physical boundaries of home form the basis of our political system. For them, the space of home is both the physical embodiment and protector of individual freedom and autonomy.[1] It is the place from which we come and go freely and within which we exercise a reliable level of privacy and control. For Western (mostly white male) philosophers, the bounded physicality of the home functions as an extension of the self and a metaphor for the relationship between our conscious and unconscious minds.[2] Others, primarily feminist and postcolonial scholars, have argued that these ostensibly universal invocations of the relationship between home and identity naturalize a specifically classed, raced, gendered, and placed norm while masking the power relations through which these norms are maintained. Here, the physical boundaries of the home are not simply an insulated, isolated space for self-realization, for intellectual and social becoming, but also power-filled sites of intimacy, violence, liberation, imprisonment, social reproduction, unpaid labor, and capitalist efficiency.[3] Yet one thing all of these theorizations have in common is the notion that home is an essential part of the human experience. It is through our relationships with home that we come to understand ourselves, our place in the world, and our relation to others.

Homes are important physical spaces, yes. But they are not simply physical spaces. Even beyond trite clichés like "Home sweet home" and "Home is where the heart is," the importance of our homes clearly goes far beyond their ability to provide simple shelter from the elements. Home is a conflicted space of care and belonging. It is a place in which we practice care and are cared for, a place of intimacy and connection where we recognize ourselves as a constitutive part of a homely whole.[4]

For many Americans, the COVID pandemic brought new attention to the spaces and relationships of home. School closures and stay-at-home orders had many spending far more time within the confines of their homes. In these confined, sometimes newly crowded spaces, people became acutely attuned to the complex relationship of bodies, personalities, objects, and spaces that constitute the places we call home. For many, the process of homemaking has become a bit of an obsession. Even before the pandemic, entire cable and internet channels, as well as countless blogs and social media accounts, were devoted to home improvement, home decorating, and home buying and selling. This obsession also clearly translates to our consumer habits. Home appliances, decor, furniture, security systems, and electronics, not to mention homes themselves, make up an enormous portion of our consumer landscape, which grew exponentially during and even after the COVID lockdowns kept us all indoors. When we refer to home—be it our residence, our hometown, or our homeland—we speak of something that transcends mere spatial categorization. The language of home is imbued with deep meanings, responsibilities, and attachments; it's where our identities are formed and needs met. The home speaks of ourselves, our aspirations, our insecurities and anxieties, our links with others—intimate, familiar, and ongoing.

As our shopping, decorating, and improving habits suggest, home is not purely spatial or emotional. It is temporal. It unfolds in time. It is a process, a making. There is no preexisting home that one can walk into. Home is not ready-made and waiting, but rather the outcome of a process of homemaking that is forever under construction. As anthropologist Mary Douglas famously argues, home is a temporal as well as a spatial product. It is a site of routinization, familiarity, and control where practices of mutual aid, familiarity, and intimate sociality occur.[5]

Indeed, the actions and spaces that made possible the privacy, safety, belonging, and care I felt after I returned to Tent City 3 from the hospital after the ankle incident were neither exceptional nor accidental. Rather, they were the outcome of ongoing practices of care, commoning, and collectivity that, over time, knit the relationships between people and the spaces they inhabit into a place called home. These acts do not occur in a vacuum nor are they a manifestation of innate drives or a priori notions of what home should be. Rather, the homespace of Tent City 3 was forged within and against the social, political, and material realities of being homeless in the United States. In this book, I explore how residents of Tent City 3 create and sustain a sense of home in the context of the displacement and exclusion we often refer to as "homelessness." I argue that the homemaking practices of Tent City 3 residents engender ideas of self, home, and belonging that are ongoing, fluid, and relational in ways that challenge the conceptions of private/public, self/other, and home/homeless that justify and emanate from the normative boundaries of private property.

The homespace of Tent City 3 is articulated and embodied in both its operational structure and physical layout. In contrast to the vast majority of officially sanctioned spaces and services for the unhoused, Tent City 3 prides itself on being a self-managed, self-governing, and largely self-supporting encampment aimed at allowing those seeking shelter to stay "together and safe."[6] In practice, this means that in addition to abiding by the camp's code of conduct, every person who stays in the camp must agree to participate in camp governance and operations as well as performing a small amount of community service. Encampment governance revolves around weekly meetings. In these meetings, residents nominate and elect their own officials to the executive committee, as well as other functionaries who serve in various coordinator and organizational positions. During meetings residents also share news and vote on rule changes and upcoming activities.

One of the duties every camp member must perform is security duty. This entails not only serving in a security detail inside and outside the camp but also keeping the camp clean and the water, supplies, and toilet paper refilled; alerting camp members of visitors or phone calls; and receiving donations. Each camper is required to work between two and five four-hour shifts per week, depending on camp population. Volunteers elected at each meeting perform other duties, such as kitchen help, donations coordination, tent repair, and all other miscellanies necessary to make the camp function. The day-to-day operations of the camp are overseen by an executive committee (EC) of five individuals, of whom one must be on duty at all times. The EC is responsible for staffing the front desk, supervising security staff, making sure sign-up sheets for various tasks are filled, assigning "bars" (temporary or permanent banishment orders), mediating disputes, performing intakes, greeting visitors, and countless other duties.

Tent City 3 is operated by the Seattle Housing and Resource Effort (SHARE) organization, which, together with its offshoot, Women's Housing Equality and

Enhancement League (WHEEL), serves as of 2023 as the umbrella organization for eleven indoor shelters and two tent cities. Each shelter or tent city is managed and maintained entirely by its residents. The SHARE/WHEEL organization operates as the fiscal manager of all the shelters and tent cities, collecting and disseminating funds, support, and resources.[7] In the tent cities, this means providing restroom facilities (porta-potties), waste removal, laundering of bedding, and bus tickets for residents. Each camp has one SHARE employee who serves as camp coordinator. The camp coordinator's duties include serving as liaison among the camp, the SHARE organization, and the host organization. The SHARE organization, through the camp coordinator, also negotiates with and secures host sites for the camp, as well as arranging bus tickets and trash, porta-potty, and laundry service. In collaboration with camp residents, the camp coordinator arranges community meetings, camp visits, and sometimes donations. Lastly, the camp coordinator prepares the agenda for meetings and attends all meetings but does not live in the camp and cannot vote on camp affairs.

The physical layout of the tent city is striking. It is at once city and household. The two functions blur, shift, and intersect as one's perspective, mood, and purpose changes. As one approaches the camp entrance, the first thing one encounters is the EC tent. This open, three-sided tent is the first and often last stop for visitors, donations, and new residents. As such, it functions as a combination front door, border, and administrative area that physically and functionally separates camp space from its immediate surroundings.

Although the exact arrangement varies slightly from site to site, once inside the camp, one is likely to enter directly into an area with an amalgam of salvaged folding tables and white plastic patio chairs that serves as a communal eating, meeting, and hanging-out space. Somewhere adjacent to the communal area will be the kitchen tent, a large, open tent containing numerous coolers, a varying supply of food, a microwave, two five-gallon water jugs, and a large coffee urn, all placed on or under three-by-six-foot folding tables arranged along three sides.

During my stay at Tent City 3 there was, when space and electricity were available, a TV room near the kitchen tent, containing several chairs, a large TV, a VCR, a DVD player, and a small collection of found or donated movies and books, all arranged on a series of milk-crate shelves. Today, this space is likely to be more flexible and used for computer phone charging. Movies have largely moved to personal devices, rendering the TV redundant. On the outskirts of this arrangement, usually near the EC tent, will be some low, small, closet-like tents containing extra supplies and recent donations.

Tent City 3, executive committee (EC) desk, circa 2007. The EC desk was both front desk and administrative center of the camp.

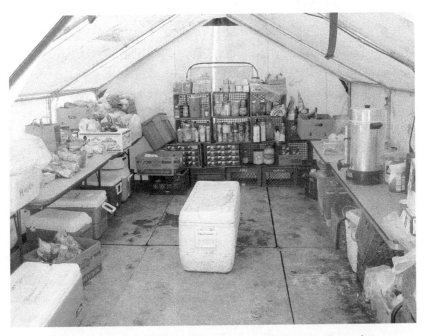

Kitchen interior, circa 2007. In this image, the approximately twelve-by-twelve-foot communal kitchen is fully stocked with donated food for one hundred people. Although common, this amount of food was not always available.

TV room interior circa, 2007. At the time, the camp relied on donated VHS and DVD tapes, and viewing was shared. Today, this is mostly a place for books and phone charging.

Beyond these public commons lies the more private residential zone. In this space, two large communal tents, one for women and one for men, stand alongside ten to forty single tents (most often small domed tents) and larger couples' tents, which are generally larger domes or square canvas tents. While the number of single and couples' tents vary according to camp population, the larger shared tents are a constant presence in every iteration of Tent City 3. The largest communal tent is the men's tent. Referred to alternately as the Hilton or the MASH, this tent is a huge military surplus tent capable of housing up to thirty individuals. The women's tent, sometimes referred to by residents as the Queen Dome, was during my time at the camp a large, twelve-person dome. The relative size of the men's and women's group tents reflects the general gender disparity in the camp. Somewhere near the edge or at the back of the camp are the bathrooms. When the camp is at or near capacity, the bathrooms consist of six porta-potties— generally three for men and three for women—and two portable sinks. Although the specific layout and number of tents and bathroom facilities vary by camp

A typical Tent City 3 layout, circa 2007, with single tents in the foreground and couples' tents behind. Single tents housed one person and made up the bulk of the residential space. Couples' tents were significant because few shelters allowed couples to stay together. This picture was taken during the summer. During the rainy season, all tents would likely be covered with blue plastic tarps.

A large communal tent known as the MASH due to its military surplus origins. The MASH served as a communal men's tent and could house up to thirty men on cots. Most new arrivals stayed in one of the communal tents until a private tent was available.

The communal women's tent, often referred to within the camp as the Queen Dome, circa 2007. Although the tent itself changed, the Queen Dome held between ten and twelve individuals on cots.

population and size of the site, this general layout remains remarkably constant over time and from one location to the next.

With its clearly defined division among administrative, public, and residential spaces, Tent City 3 recalls the structure of a small city. Yet inside the camp the resemblance to a typical American household is undeniable. There are the immediately recognizable spaces of kitchen, living room, office, bedrooms, and bathrooms, with communal and public spaces near the front and more private sleeping and bathroom spaces toward the rear. None of this, neither physical nor organizational structure, was planned, prescribed, or purely ad hoc. Rather they were the outcome of a long and ongoing set of choices about how residents wanted to live and why. As I explore in chapters 3, 4, and 5, every spatial and social relation in the tent city is an effort to create a space of collective inclusion, agency, and belonging—in short, a home.

Porta-potties, circa 2007. The number of porta-potties and handwashing stations varied by population. When this photo was taken, the camp population was around ninety people.

Yet Tent City 3 is not just any home. It is a home forged within and against the experience of homelessness in the United States. Despite the importance of home in our lives, my own homey feelings on the day of the ankle incident, and the ongoing homemaking efforts of Tent City 3 residents, home in the affective sense seldom appears in conversations about homelessness in the United States.[8] Instead, when we discuss homelessness in the United States today, we speak almost exclusively of one's relation to a particular kind of space in a particular relation to private property to which the name *home* can be attached. For instance, the official federal definition of homelessness identifies as "homeless" an "individual or family who lacks a fixed, regular and adequate nighttime residence [or whose] primary nighttime residence is a public or private place not meant for human habitation."[9] By this definition, to be homeless refers entirely to one's lack of possession, or access to, a specific kind of physical space.

Introduction 11

But what kind of space? And what does it mean to be "not fit for human habitation"? In the next chapter, I delve into the complex histories of how we come to recognize a particular home as one that is "fixed, regular and adequate." Here, however, I want to focus on the second part: to think about what kind of home renders one homeless. The statute is curiously silent on what constitutes a habitation fit for human habitation but is remarkably specific on what is not. For instance, it names "car, park, abandoned building, bus/train station, airport, or camping ground" as places not fit for human habitation.[10] Yet the common thread among these unfit spaces is not their inadequacy but their ubiquity as spaces of human habitation.

Indeed, these places are explicitly mentioned precisely because they are commonly used as dwellings of last resort. What renders these places unfit is not their physical characteristics but their relationship to private property, ownership, and access. Home, as it is framed in the federal government's definition of homelessness, is not simply the taken-for-granted living spaces of apartment buildings and single-family homes. Rather, it is a specific legal construction of home that is the product of building and zoning codes governed by the rules of private property. In a property-based system such as the United States, the very idea of housing presupposes and relies upon both the existence of and access to private property.

Access to property that is owned, either by government entities or private individuals in the United States, is what gives shape and permanence to the notions of both home and homelessness. *Property* as term and concept refers to state or social recognition of places and objects that are proper to an individual. Property is not an object in and of itself. Contrary to popular usage, cars and houses—or anything, for that matter—are not in and of themselves property. Rather, property refers to a bundle of rights that defines one's relation and access to places and things. In the contemporary United States, property is generally considered a relation between individual and state.[11] Property can be common (held by all), public (held by government), or private (held by individuals). However, as property scholar Nicholas Blomley notes, the dominant form of property in much of the world is by far what he calls, borrowing a term from Jeffrey Singer, the "ownership model," which "assumes a unitary, solitary, and identifiable owner, separated from others by boundaries that protect him or her from nonowners and grant the owner the power to exclude."[12]

In the ownership model, having a home and being homeless are not mutually exclusive. Rather, in property-based societies like the United States, the homeless only exist in negative relation to property, as those who lack regular uncoerced access to at least one place governed by a private property rule.[13] Conversely, one might say that people who have homes are those who have fixed and regular access to at least one place governed by private property. To be homeless in the United States does not refer to being without shelter, or without a home in a broader sense, but instead to a lack of access to a specifically defined type of shelter that is legally recognized and regulated as private property.

In his invocation of Singer's concept of the ownership model, Blomley calls attention not only to the ubiquity of the model but to how the presumption of its universality erases the complexity of the spaces we call home, flattening a world of infinite difference into a binary of norm and deviance—home and homeless. Referring to someone who lacks access to private property as homeless is what we might call a malign misnomer. It is a misnomer in the sense that it is simply inaccurate, as this book and many others attest, to assert that those without access to property do not have homes. The malignancy of the term *homeless* arises from the realization that the inability of those without access to private property to be at home in the United States arises not from a lack of housing but from our collective political, social, and legal responses to the visible presence of those who lack access to private property and how we assign meaning to them. Homelessness is not a status; it is a production.

Very early in my research, it became apparent that Tent City 3 wasn't just a home for people with nowhere else to go. Rather, residents actively produced ideas and spaces of home in the tent city directly in relation to their experiences of being recognized as *homeless*. As I explore in chapter 1, the term *homeless* has never simply been a signifier of one's housing status.[14] Rather, both the term itself and its connotations evince a complex set of beliefs about the nature of home, care, and belonging that give shape to a moral semiology of inside/outside and self/other in which unhoused people exist only in negative relation to these concepts.[15] In this context, one's recognition or identification as homeless is itself an exclusion or displacement couched as technical classification. Although those considered homeless might meet the official definition of homelessness, they are commonly identified not by their lack of authorized housing but by their visible presence in the public spaces of the city.

For most of us, homelessness is something we can see. It is not a housing status at all, but an aesthetic, racialized category where a body is recognized in its visible difference and presumed deviance from a normative homed subject.[16] The classification of humans as homeless thus performs a dehumanization, or as Samira Kawash puts it, a "constitutive violence," which transforms the person without housing into "the homeless body," a deviant, defensive, and vaguely threatening figure that marks the constitutive outside of a homed norm.[17] For these reasons, when I use the term *homeless* in this book, I use it only to refer to an abstract yet embodied subject that is produced socially, politically, and legally as the constitutive outside to a homed norm. When I refer to tent city residents or their counterparts, I use the more accurate and precise terminology of *those who lack access to sanctioned housing, those who lack housing*, or simply *unhoused people*.

Over the course of my ethnographic engagement with Tent City 3, two ubiquitous themes emerged. On the one hand, the people I interviewed nearly unanimously felt that existing both on the streets and in current systems of homeless management (referred to by more than one interviewee as the "homeless industrial complex") were uniformly dehumanizing. Many referred to feelings of being treated "like children," as "idiots," or as one woman tellingly described it, as "a lesser breed." On the other hand, the tent city enabled a space of refusal where residents could escape what they felt was a dehumanizing system of homeless management and reclaim what was commonly described as the "dignity, freedom, and respect" that otherwise seemed to disappear with the loss of housing.

The Tent City 3 residents I spoke with aren't alone in feeling that systems of homeless management are dehumanizing. As I discuss in some depth in chapter 2, people who lack access to housing are subject to an endless array of negative assumptions and disciplinary practices through their interactions with shelters: policies that seem designed to punish them and make their already incredibly complicated lives more difficult, casual insults from or being made to feel invisible by passersby, and media coverage that many felt blamed them for simply not having enough money for housing in an increasingly unaffordable housing market. For almost everyone I spoke to in the six months I spent in the tent city, the weight of homeless stereotypes was ever present. Some people embraced them, some rejected them, some ignored them, and still others chose to locate the stereotypes in others. But the weight was there. All the time. While residents sought to create and maintain a sense of home in the tent city, they did so within and against the material context of their own displacement and exclusion.

Outside the legal exclusions and protections of private property, those who lack access appear as invasive interlopers in urban public space.[18] Here, people without housing appear and are recognized by many city dwellers, as well as in urban law and public policy, as disorderly, out-of-place objects to be removed, managed, or quarantined to preserve the "quiet enjoyment" of the city's properly propertied residents.[19] The lack implied by the term *homeless* is self-evident. For those displaced from sanctioned property, there is no place where they can be at home.

In the context of the ownership model and the deviance of homelessness, the practices of homemaking that give shape and substance to Tent City 3 become political, subversive, unsettling even. In this book, I dwell in the spaces created by post-, anti-, and decolonial scholars to argue that the practices of care, commoning, and collectivity that enabled me and my campmates to feel at home in Tent City emanated from both a refusal of homeless subjectivity and a "reworking [of] settler colonial and racial capitalist relations of contemporary urban life and re-assembling around mutual relations and collective forms of thriving."[20]

This is a settler colonial story. Homelessness is seldom considered in accounts of settler colonialism. Yet settler colonialism shapes every aspect of our contemporary understandings of who can be at home and how in the settler state. Understanding Tent City 3 requires an accounting with settler colonialism.

The term *settler colonialism* is commonly used to refer to a condition or location of colonial conquest where the colonists claim permanent dominance and control over space. Settler colonial societies include Australia, Israel, Canada, Latin America, and the United States. Settler colonialism represents not a period in time but an ongoing process of dispossession, exclusion, and erasure of Indigenous and nonwhite bodies, spaces, and ways of being with the goal of permanently eliminating and replacing nonsettler bodies and knowledges and replacing them with a permanent settler society.[21] In short, settler colonialism refers to the ability of settler bodies to claim, make, and define home through property, law, and policy, thus enabling and justifying the displacement, erasure, and criminalization of Indigenous people, communities, and lifeways.[22]

The production of homelessness is fundamental to settler colonial conquest and erasure. Far from simply a project of land acquisition and racial apartheid, settler colonialism in the United States rests on the imposition of an explicitly Eurocentric spatialized imaginary of civilization that "is grounded in racialized and gendered knowledge systems and [where] the norms of liberal individualism legitimate private property rights."[23] This imagined civilization is famously embodied by John Stuart Mill's definition of civilization as "a dense population, therefore, dwelling in fixed habitations, and largely collected together in towns and villages." Mill juxtaposes this against the "savagery" of "a handful of individuals, wandering or thinly scattered over a vast tract of country."[24] In the settler

Introduction 15

colonial "logic of elimination," property itself and one's relationship to it become a proxy for one's civilized humanity.[25]

Since the arrival of Europeans in North America, the imposition of Western juridical property regimes, as both a right to exclude and a practice of boundary-making, have been a primary justification for Indigenous erasure and the vernacular through which colonial territoriality is inscribed on the landscape.[26] As Evelyn Nakano Glenn explains, "Settlers sought to control space, resources, and people not only by occupying land but also by establishing an exclusionary private property regime."[27] In this context, the American city stands as the civilized endpoint whereby "land is remade into property and human relationships to land are restricted to the relationship of the owner to his property." All other understandings of land, home, and space are "interred, indeed made pre-modern and backward. Made savage."[28]

In what Penelope Edmonds refers to as the "syntax" of propertied civilization, Indigenous spaces and bodies are displaced, erased, and contained through physical violence legitimated by the legal violence of property enactment.[29] As Blomley notes, settler boundary-making, in the form of the frontier, cadastral survey, and urban grid, legitimizes the spaces of white settler coloniality predicated on Indigenous absence and removal.[30] As Patrick Wolfe succinctly puts it, these enactments of settler territorialization "destroy to replace" Indigenous lands, bodies, and social orders through the spatial enactment of white propertied personhood.[31] In the European settlement of the United States, property was used as a supposedly rational cudgel to expel Indigenous populations and to control and dehumanize Black and Indigenous and other nonwhite people. As the nation's border closed and the country began to rapidly urbanize, access to property increasingly formed the boundaries between inside and outside, order and disorder, self and other, homed and homeless. It is within liberal settler normativity that the modern concept of homelessness becomes the internal outside to propertied conceptions of civilization.[32]

By placing homelessness in the United States into a settler colonial context, I do not intend to equate homelessness with the continuing experience of colonial violence and erasure of Indigenous bodies and lands. Rather, I situate the production of homelessness as a fundamental part of an ongoing settler colonial process. As the word *civilization* implies, settler colonialism is not an event or fixed structure but a process, which Anne Bonds and Joshua Inwood evocatively describe as "a kind of permanent occupation that is always in a state of becoming."[33] Colonialism in the United States implies not only the manifest destiny imperative of "taming the land" but a never-ending process of rendering the land and its inhabitants legible within an urban cartography of civic and civitas premised on the exclusion and erasure of racialized bodies, spaces, and lifeways. Through these colonial cartographies, the social differentiation and exclusion of marginalized bodies are written into the landscape and rationalized as normal and inevitable. Homelessness appears not as the seemingly natural opposite of propertied housing, but as a racialized process of settler colonial exclusion and erasure that deprives the propertyless of the ability to be at home in their dwellings, hometowns, and homelands.

Viewed through the lens of settler colonialism, homelessness is about neither housing nor personal character but rather a struggle over who can be at home in the city and who cannot. A documentary that aired in 2019 on the Seattle ABC affiliate KOMO, titled *Seattle Is Dying*, offers an evocative example.[34] The video opens with an aerial shot of a garbage-strewn encampment on a tree-darkened hillside near the area where the city's last public housing had been destroyed just a few years earlier. As the camera rises, the shot brightens, and Seattle's central business district slowly comes into view, framed by the picturesque backdrop of Puget Sound, with the Olympic Mountains in the distance. The camera holds on the familiar Seattle skyline for about one second before cutting to a graphic that announces "SEATTLE IS DYING" in all caps over an iconic image of the Space Needle, its base transformed into exposed tree roots. Over the exposed roots, words like *safety*, *innovation*, *incarceration*, and *leadership* float and disappear as if fleeing the dying city. The imagery suggests imminent invasion, the enemy at the gates.

Over a series of graphic images of obvious human pain and destitution, narrator Eric Johnson speaks for viewers "who no longer feel safe. No longer feel like they are heard. No longer feel protected." He tells his audience, in a nod to Seattle's nickname of "the emerald city," that "this is a story of a jewel that has been violated." In both image and perspective, *Seattle Is Dying* engages in what Chris Herring calls a "politics of visibility" in which "the media's gaze simultaneously stokes the insecurity of local residents and reveals the social problems unaddressed by city administration."[35]

Certainly, the presence of seemingly disorderly, disheveled poverty amid Seattle's gentrified prosperity appeared to many commentators and residents alike as unacceptably out of place. At the time this video aired, media reports and social media posts highlighting the danger and disorder of visible homelessness provided the daily drumbeat of my newsfeed. *Seattle Is Dying* is far from a fringe phenomenon. Since its first airing in spring 2019, the video has racked up over twelve million views on YouTube. While critics have decried its hyperbole, shoddy reportage, and shallow partisanship, the popularity of the program and the high volume of media response show it reflected widespread frustration with visible poverty in gentrified cities. Its opening imagery of invasion, exposed roots, and thinly veiled sexual violence captures commonly expressed feelings about the informal habitations of the visibly poor: their presence is both abomination and invasion. They are "violations" of a particular normative view of urban life in which homelessness and poverty have no place.

Tent encampments and other habitations of the poor disrupt normative visions of propertied prosperity by troubling the settler colonial relationship between home and property ownership. In this troubling, they become troublesome. The dual movement of erasure and reclamation embodied by the removal of homeless habitations and the relocation of unhoused bodies into acceptable disciplinary quarantine mirror the colonial process of which they are a part. While viewed as perhaps worthy of pity, scorn, or moral outrage, the dwellings and bodies of the urban poor in the United States are often seen as alien to the postgentrification city, as is the poverty they embody and symbolize. The urban poor can be in but not of these places. Their removal, quarantine, and erasure right the balance of twenty-first-century settler colonialism.

In the chapters that follow, I illustrate how residents of Tent City 3, like their peers dwelling in encampments, squats, and tent cities throughout the United States, both refuse homeless subjectivities and attempt to produce and reclaim a sense of home in the context of their own exclusion.[36] Much of this work draws on research I conducted between December 2005 and July 2006, over the course of seven months living and doing interviews in Tent City 3. Additionally, I conducted follow-up interviews with encampment residents, homeless activists, advocates, and city and county officials in 2007, 2008, and 2017.

During the time I lived in Tent City 3, the camp was sited in four different locations. From December 2005 to February 2006 it was located on the lot of an abandoned motel in a semirural area at Seattle's southernmost border. From February to April the camp was hosted by Saint Mark's Cathedral in Seattle's Capitol Hill neighborhood, where it was erected in the church parking lot. In May, we moved to a vacant lot adjacent to and owned by Cherry Hill Baptist Church in the ethnically diverse and primarily working-class Central District neighborhood, where the camp was located until the end of June. Following the tenure at Cherry Hill, we once again returned to the affluent and mostly white

North Capitol Hill neighborhood in July, where the tent city resided on the paved playfield of Saint Joseph's Catholic Church for the remainder of the summer. Living in the camp at these various locations allowed me to better grasp the ways tent city residents negotiated changing populations and environments, and how these changes were reflected in the demographics, internal organization, and daily practices of the camp residents.

During the time I conducted research, the residents were a fairly representative cross section of the US unhoused population at the time. According to an internal survey conducted by the SHARE/WHEEL collective in 2005, the tent city was composed of approximately 75 percent men and 25 percent women.[37] In terms of ethnicity it was primarily white (44%), followed by African American (15.4%), Latinx (14.8%), Native American (5.7%), African (3.5%), Pacific Islander (0.3%), and Asian (0.3%). Those who identified as multiethnic (6.3%), other (5.7%), and unknown (3.5%) composed the remainder. Tent city residents ranged in age from eighteen to seventy-two, although the majority reported being in their forties (37.1%), with an age range between twenty and fifty representing the vast majority of residents (91.4%).[38] Overall, these numbers are fairly representative of national averages. That same year HUD reported a gender ratio of 65.3 percent men to 34.7 percent women and a heavy age concentration in the eighteen-to-fifty range for the US population of people identified as homeless. Likewise, national trends document a racial disparity similar to that of the tent city, reflecting national and local processes of racialized dispossession. For instance, according to the HUD report, Black, Indigenous, Latinx, and Pacific Islander populations composed approximately 31 percent of the total US population in 2006 while accounting for nearly 59 percent of the homeless population. In Seattle, those who identify as BIPOC made up approximately 33 percent of the total population in 2006 while accounting for 46 percent of the tent city population.

While living in the camp, I participated fully as a camp resident—or "camper," as residents often referred to themselves. This meant that I performed all the duties necessary to maintain my residency, including cleaning chores, security detail, attendance at mandatory meetings, and performance of community credits. In addition, I frequently participated as a tent city resident in community outreach meetings, meetings with city and county officials, and political strategy sessions. I also served on the SHARE/WHEEL board of directors as camp liaison from mid-April to June. This level of in-depth ethnographic engagement allowed me to gain detailed insight into the daily life of the camp and its residents.

In addition to participant observation, I conducted fifty interviews with camp residents. These interviews ranged in length from forty-five minutes to two hours, in which I asked residents several broad, open-ended questions about their experiences in the tent city, their experiences with other shelter providers, and their impressions of the structure and modes of governance in the tent city. While I originally set out to interview everyone who stayed at Tent City 3 during my residence, I quickly realized that the mobile nature of homelessness and the tent city itself meant that the population was continually changing and replenishing itself with new faces. Therefore, I tried to interview representative samples of new members, members who had been in the camp between one and three months, those who had been there between three and six months, and "old-timers" who had been in the camp anywhere from six months to multiple years.

In this book, I draw three conclusions from this ethnographic research. First, residents of Tent City 3 continually strive to build a sense of home both against and within the context of settler colonial exclusion. These acts of building and dwelling, I argue, constitute consequential acts of refusal. As I explore in the following chapters, Tent City 3 residents overwhelmingly felt the conditions of being without housing as demeaning and dehumanizing. This was particularly true of their experiences in shelters and with other homeless services. Much of the production of space and subjectivities of the camp occurred directly in opposition to these experiences.

Tent City 3 residents are not unique in their feelings about shelters. For example, an analysis of data provided by Seattle's navigation team in 2019 suggests that only around 8 percent of encampment dwellers engaged by the team accepted temporary shelter offers.[39] Seattle is by no means an outlier in this regard. Cities throughout the American West cite a similar intransigence on the part of encampment dwellers.[40] The reasons for these refusals are well documented and consistent. The most common reasons people state for refusing offers of shelter or services relate to feelings of danger, dehumanization, and temporal precarity created by many shelter situations.[41] For Tent City 3 residents and many other encampment dwellers in the United States, the encampment serves not simply as a way to escape a dehumanizing system but as a way to reclaim what was most commonly described as the "dignity, freedom, and respect" that residents felt had been denied them as a consequence of the loss of financial and housing security and social networks that accompanied their becoming homeless.[42]

It is not uncommon today to frame the refusal of shelter by those who lack housing as a justification for encampment sweeps, punitive trespassing and stay-away orders, and even a reason for forced commitment or incarceration.

Those we recognize as homeless seem to constantly refuse: refuse to go away, refuse to accept shelter, refuse to accept their status as homeless. Tent City 3, I argue, is built on such refusals. The residents refuse to be recognized as homeless subjects. They refuse to consent to the stereotypes, the presumed dependencies, pathologies, and irrationalities that are imputed to them because they lack access to private property. They know they are not these things, and therefore they refuse to consent to offers of shelter, services, or other implicit demands to acknowledge that they are anything less than fully equal citizens.[43] Residents of Tent City 3 refuse and, in their refusal, become unsettling.

Second, operating in the space of possibility opened by homeless refusal, homemaking in Tent City 3 was enacted through intentional, specific, and ongoing practices of care, commoning, and collectivity through which residents created a homelike space of safety, belonging, and agency. These acts did not emerge from any communitarian ethos or utopian ideal but were specifically enacted in relation to reclaiming traditionally liberal rights of autonomy, privacy, and citizenship, which they felt were fundamental aspects of being human that were denied them as a result of their loss of formal housing.

Refusal is relational. We are co-constituted by what we desire and what we refuse to inhabit. Thinking of Tent City 3 as a space of refusal or opposition does not imply that it occupies a space external to the laws and logics that produce it. The space of the tent city, as with all encampments and other informal dwellings, does not exist outside legal regimes of property ownership. All such places are produced and shaped by formal property regimes as illegal, informal, and illegitimate spaces of home. Tent City 3 dwellers draw upon culturally produced norms, experiences of exclusion, and the structured space of informality to inform their ideas of home and homemaking. However, within the informal space of the tent city, individualized and property-based conceptions of autonomy, privacy, citizenship, and belonging underwent a transformation. In the absence of formal property-based state protections, these concepts were reimagined as collective, adaptable, and flexible processes.

My third conclusion is that the homemaking processes and practices I explore in this book do not occur simply within and against settler colonial norms; rather, they are in excess. Refusal, as Audra Simpson tells us, is a technique, "a symptom, a practice, a possibility for doing things differently, for thinking beyond."[44] During the time I spent in Tent City 3, not only was the tent city itself forced to move every few months, but the population was continuously in flux. People came and went, bringing with them an infinite variety of personalities, proclivities, habits, triggers, joys, and sorrows. Accordingly, ideas and practices of home and homemaking never remained static; they were always in motion, adapting and experimenting. These practices occurred in reference to past experiences and beliefs, yet they weren't contained by them. They were excessive.

In this book, I illustrate how the homemaking of Tent City 3 occurred through an ensemble of overlapping processes of commoning, subjectification, and governance. Through these processes, camp dwellers coproduced the camp as homespace, themselves as homely subjects proper to that space, and an art of governance that maintained domestic norms while adapting to the needs of an ever-changing population. In contrast to the fixed distinctions between inside and outside, public and private, self and other that underwrite the settler colonial project, these categories within the tent city were always, as Judith Butler notes in relation to gender, "in process, a becoming, a constructing that cannot be rightfully said to originate or end."[45] In the space of Tent City 3, the process of what I refer to in chapter 4 as "becoming together" manifested as a contextual understanding of home, self, and others that laid the groundwork for forms of caring, commoning, and collectivity that are not captured by propertied discourses of home and homelessness.

Based on these conclusions, I argue that Tent City 3, through its continued existence in the gentrified spaces of Seattle, Washington, brightly illuminates the limits of settler colonial narratives of a normative propertied order. Settler imaginaries of totality or completion rely on the absence, implausibility, and irrationality of other narratives. Borrowing again from Audra Simpson, I assert that Tent City 3 "is a sign, also, of colonialism's ongoing existence and simultaneous failure."[46] That colonialism survives in a settler form is evidenced by the ongoing attempts to displace, erase, quarantine, and absorb Indigenous, racialized, and nonconforming bodies and space "into a white, property-owning body politic."[47] From this perspective, the habitations of the unhoused step out from the shadows of settler colonialism's threatening other and emerge as an insurgent space of agency, creativity, and commoning.[48] As such, the homemaking practices of tent city residents call attention and speak back to the everyday violence, erasure, and exclusion inherent in propertied notions of home and homelessness in the United States.

In approaching the tent city in this way, it is not my intention to romanticize life in tent encampments. Indeed, life in an encampment is hard. Tent life is incredibly cold in the winter and unbearably hot in the summer—and, in the notoriously rainy climate of Seattle, soggy a great deal of the time. Living in close quarters with virtual strangers is difficult in any context. Add to that the incredibly burdensome stresses and difficulties of losing housing, navigating life outside the formal housing system, and managing the mental and emotional toll that these stresses take, and you have a recipe for intense and ongoing conflict. These were all aspects of life in Tent City 3. Yet, although I touch briefly on these aspects of tent life, by focusing on the practices of care, collectivity, and commoning practiced by tent city residents in their attempts to create a home in the context of homelessness, I attempt to loose these concepts from their settler colonial moorings and think instead about home as a site of open-ended inclusion and experimentation.

Chapter 1 places Tent City 3 in the spatial and temporal context of Seattle's long-standing encounters with housing informality to illustrate (1) how settler colonial linkages among home, property, and personhood inform contemporary ideas of home and homelessness; (2) how these logics have been applied to informal dwellings, shantytowns, and squatter camps to narrow the universe of home and belonging in the United States according to a propertied middle-class white heterosexual norm; (3) how these norms serve to systematically displace those without housing from the spaces, connections, and freedoms of home; and (4) how these historical processes enable an understanding of Tent City 3 as both a spectacular symbol of settler fragility and a space of refusal where residents can resist and rework their status as homeless subjects.

Against this backdrop, I argue that Tent City 3 offered a safe space of self-imposed and self-determined refuge. Yet it also became more. Through the everyday practices of dwelling, the tent city became for its residents a home crafted within and against settler logics of normative property relations. Through practices of care, commoning, and collectivity, residents produced Tent City 3 as an urban commons in which they felt they could be full citizens and a participatory collective of which they could be a part. In chapters 2, 3, and 4, I focus on these practices of reclamation and inclusion.

Chapter 2 explores the production of a homespace crafted within and against settler norms of private property. Drawing on liberal conceptions of home as property, which serves as the prerequisite to and protector of the natural rights of liberty, freedom, and autonomy, I argue that the strict division between public and private that makes possible liberal conceptions of these rights is, in practice, held in place by the juridical production of private property as a right to exclude. By contrast, the homemaking practices undertaken by Tent City 3 residents in the context of propertied exclusion take place through a series of acts of commoning that challenge and disrupt a settler colonial linkage among property, home, and personhood.

Chapter 3 examines how the shared experience of being without sanctioned housing and the practical necessities of encampment life combine to create unique forms of subjectivity and belonging. In their refusal of propertied exclusion, residents created and negotiated the normative boundaries of inclusion in the homespace of the tent city through ongoing practices of care. Drawing on the conception of "feeling citizenship," this chapter explores how residents negotiated ideas of self and belonging in relation to caring labor and collective well-being. In the context of the camp, I argue that care work performs a normative and performative function in the production of collective belonging that reconfigures citizenship and home, against the logic of coloniality, as spaces of caring, commoning, and collectivity.

Chapter 4 turns to management and governance in the tent city. This chapter examines the everyday management and maintenance of the space and population of the tent city through the lens of urban governance. Taking as my starting point the tent city as a particular form of informal urban jurisdiction, I situate governance of the tent city within broader theories of government and management of urban populations. I explore how residents developed structures and practices of governance that both fostered and enabled a political culture of inclusion and contextual flexibility to flourish and persist in the context of a mobile encampment and a highly fluid population.

In the final two chapters I turn to Tent City 3's relationship to the city and spaces it occupies to illustrate how the camp operated simultaneously as a space of incursion and of containment. Here I argue that the persistent presence of the camp and the ongoing interactions among the camp, its hosts, and its neighbors served to normalize the camp and disrupt homeless stereotypes. Yet the legalization of encampments that occurred in 2015 also rendered the encampment a tool for securing the contemporary settler city in the face of a growing homeless "crisis." The tension that arises from this encampment trajectory evidences not a homeless crisis but a crisis of settler colonial urbanism. In the face of this crisis, I suggest ways we might conceive of a home beyond property.

In chapter 5, I focus on the persistence of Tent City 3 through time and space and the relationships of the campers with their housed neighbors and (largely religious) hosts. In examining these interactions, I illustrate how, through their refusal of homeless stereotypes, tent city residents crafted a self-defined politics of recognition that contested hierarchies of propertied personhood. These efforts, while unsettling to some residents, ultimately—over time and through the camp's movement from neighborhood to neighborhood—allowed the camp and its self-crafted subjectivities to become normalized and in some cases transformative. I contend that although this acceptance is far from satisfactory, the normalization of self-managed spaces of informal housing suggests an enduring and slow-moving "encroachment of the ordinary" through which the informally housed can be recognized as both community members and full and active agents in their own lives.[49]

In the final chapter, I turn a post-pandemic lens on the contemporary landscape of homeless management. I focus on how Seattle has responded to its unhoused residents in the wake of the dual emergencies of growing homelessness and, later, COVID. I demonstrate how the crisis of the settler colonial imaginary of normative prosperity and propertied citizenship has produced a brutal necropolitics of erasure and quarantine of the city's poor and unhoused residents. Against these trends of eviction, erasure, and quarantine, I examine how a 2015 ordinance that legalized self-governed encampments in Seattle may have engendered a countertrend of expanded practices of care, commoning, and collectivity between housed residents and those dwelling in encampments. This dual movement, I argue, points to both the cruelty and the incompleteness of the hegemony of the settler colonial logic of propertied personhood. I conclude by introducing the idea of thinking home beyond the sanctioning of encampments as a way to imagine alternatives to the ongoing displacements and dehumanization produced by propertied conceptions of home. Drawing on preceding chapters, I use the concepts of commoning, care, and collectivity to open a conversation about how to rethink and undo propertied boundaries between home and homelessness, inside and outside, self and other that maintain settler dominance.

My hope and intent with this work is to unsettle settler colonial logics of propertied exclusion, quarantine, and erasure and make space for new and experimental claims to urban space.[50] Tent City 3 residents, like their peers dwelling in encampments, squats, and tent cities throughout the United States, attempt to produce and reclaim a sense of home in the context of their own exclusion.[51] In doing so, residents of these informal dwelling spaces join in a global struggle to remake and reclaim a home. As Leilani Farha writes in a 2019 report to the United Nations, informal settlements, regardless of global location, far from being simply urban abominations or coping strategies, are "an incredible accomplishment, a profound expression of individuals, families and communities claiming their place and their right to housing. They are 'habitats made by people,' who are creating homes, culture, and community life in the most adverse circumstances."[52]

Against the settler colonial assertions of invasion and decay exemplified in *Seattle Is Dying*, Farha argues that the informal dwellings of the poor should not be understood solely in negative relation to formal property relations. Rather, they should be understood broadly as "a set of relationships with respect to housing and land, established through statutory or customary law or informal or hybrid arrangements, that enables one to live in one's home in security, peace and dignity."[53] Instead of seeing the habitations of the poor as exceptional abominations in a sanitized urban imaginary, Farha views unhoused residents of the United States through a global lens where informal settlements are a norm, accounting for the habitations of nearly 25 percent of the world's population. In doing so, she decenters notions of American exceptionalism and settler colonialism.

Taking inspiration from Farha's words, I situate this work within a tradition of feminist and postcolonial thinking about home as a relational set of spaces and processes through which center and margin, normal and deviant, and self and other are constructed.[54] I adopt this perspective to ask, How do the everyday practices of tent city residents respond to common assumptions about home and homelessness in the United States? In answering this question, I illustrate how, in an ongoing series of acts of refusal and creative reclamation of spaces and subjects of home, Tent City 3 residents unsettle propertied normativity in what Lorenzo Veracini has called the "settler colonial present."[55] In approaching Tent City 3 as both a product and a refusal of settler colonial logics, this work seeks to contribute, in some small way, to the growing chorus of postcolonial, anticolonial, and decolonial scholars whose cumulative work exposes the fragility and fragmentation of colonial narratives of belonging, home, and personhood in the settler present.

1. Home and Homelessness in a Settler Colonial City

Narratives of normative prosperity and the invasiveness of poverty, like those presented in *Seattle Is Dying*, are exemplars of the ongoing process of settler colonialism. In stories the United States tells itself about itself, informal habitations have long functioned to demarcate racial, spatial, and temporal borders between normative settler space and its outsides. Constituted by, and constitutive of, property's frontier, the shantytown, encampment, and squatter settlement inhabit a space of disorder and quarantine. Here the visible presence of the poor and their makeshift habitations represents not simply an abomination but, as the *Seattle Is Dying* narrative suggests, an existential threat to the contemporary settler colonial city.

The original Tent City was created in the 1990s as a symbol of the ongoing exclusions produced by settler logics of propertied enclosure and, for its creators, a refusal of the normative dehumanization of these logics. A *Seattle Times* article chronicling the creation of the original Tent City sums up this dual function. The article opens by highlighting the spectacular and symbolic function of the camp's "conspicuous location," chosen to "awaken the city's better-off citizens to their plight." Founding SHARE member Mark Mullins is quoted as saying, "We want to say, hey, we've got a problem out here. We've got to erect tents to survive." "Mullins's emphasis on the spectacle of the camp is further supported by fellow SHARE member Howard Tenke, who tells the *Seattle Times*, "The individuals and corporations that value the bottom line of their ledgers more than people can't or won't let their properties be put to good use. They need a nudge to open them to the useful purpose of housing Seattle's homeless men, women, and children."[1] In the original incarnation of Tent City, the construction of a dwelling space by and for its unhoused residents spectacularly called attention to the injustice that made tent dwellings necessary.

The symbolic use of the camp to call attention to issues of marginalization and injustice is not unique to Tent City. When camp founders state that "we want to say, hey, we've got a problem" or argue that property owners "need a nudge," they are participating in a long history of symbolic occupation of public space by the poor.[2] Marginalized people and groups have long used temporary dwelling on public lands as a way to call attention to injustice and demand recognition and redress in the public sphere. This includes events such as the occupation of the Anacostia Flats by the Bonus Army in 1932, the Indigenous occupation of Alcatraz in 1969, the Occupy movement of 2011, and Seattle's short-lived Capitol Hill Organized Protest (CHOP) encampment, which emerged in the wake of the police murder of George Floyd.

Like these encampments, Tent City founders consciously sought to call attention to injustice through the spectacle of the camp. Yet, from its earliest incarnation, Seattle's Tent City was imagined by its creators also as a sanctuary from the dehumanizing treatment they encountered in Seattle's shelter spaces. In the same *Seattle Times* article, Howard Tenke is quoted as telling a group gathered to plan Tent City that "we are here because we want shelter that is not managed and staffed by religious organizations or social-service agencies that are overcrowded and dehumanizing. We are here because we want to manage our own lives and our own place in which to live."[3] Tenke's invocation of the desire to manage their own lives and spaces is no accident. Residents of Tent City 3, both past and present, found themselves entangled in a complex web of presumptions of deviance and imputed pathology that emerged from a relational conflation of character and habitation. For the founders of Tent City, the self-provision and self-management of housing in the form of tents offered them sanctuary from the demeaning treatment they received on the streets and shelters of Seattle's downtown. Although the symbolism of the camp served an important function for those who viewed it from the outside, for its residents, the promise of Tent City was also the possibility of creating a collective space of sanctuary and a site of refusal, where they could escape from and resist property-based presuppositions of deviance and dependency.[4]

Like many tent city residents I encountered in the course of my stay, Tenke believed that, from the very beginning, the symbolism and spectacle of Tent City was a means as much as an end. Although the tent city symbolically draws the public's attention to the lack of shelter and affordable housing, for the people who live there, it has been, since its inception, a space in which they can exercise some autonomy outside the patronizing and dehumanizing apparatus of law enforcement and social service organizations. By saying both "Hey, we have a problem here" and "We want to manage our own lives and our own place in which to live," camp founders sought to resist both the exclusion and the presumption of dependence that deny people who lack access to property the ability to maintain a home in the contemporary United States.

Seattle's Tent City is only the latest incarnation in a long line of informal habitations that have rendered visible the rough edges and displacements of settler colonial enclosure. Today, the assumption that a home in the United States is synonymous with both a particular sort of structure and a particular relation to private property is so deeply ingrained as to appear to be simply common sense. It is, one might say, settled.

Similarly, the propertied ideal of home looms large in the Anglo-American imagination. It is a space of intellectual becoming, a visible sign of one's capability for self-governance, and a signifier of a work ethic. By contrast, those who lack access to property are frequently assumed to lack its attendant character attributes. Framed this way, it becomes easy to imagine lack of housing as the result of personal failure, pathology, or chemical dependency rather than the byproduct of property owners' right to exclude. This view, however, makes invisible both the colonial violence that created private property and the ongoing displacements that normalize the propertied home.

In this chapter I situate Seattle's Tent City within the spatial and historical context of one American city. I illustrate how settler colonialism has produced informal housing settlements of the poor as both spectacle and sanctuary in the formation of Seattle's urban spaces. Through an exploration of Seattle's informal spaces and the city's desire to displace, erase, and dehumanize their residents, I demonstrate how the concept of homelessness becomes both a spatially defined subjectivity and a marker of deviance in the production of the settler colonial city. Through this lens, I trace how the creation of Tent City responds to a settler regime that is justified and enabled through the displacement of people who lack access to private property, not just from housing but from their homes, their hometowns, and their homelands.

Property, Informality, and the Settler Logic of Eviction and Replacement

Today, informal dwellings mark both the limit and the constitutive outside of the modern city. These dwellings embody this boundary not because they are objectively dangerous or disorderly but because they disrupt specific racialized, gendered, and classed understandings of property possession and dwelling.

Property is enclosure. Its purpose is to enclose. In enclosing, it enables some to be inside and forces others outside its boundary. In her influential work, "Settler Colonialism as Structure," Evelyn Nakano Glenn notes that settler colonialism proceeds in two movements. The first is to eliminate Indigenous people, lifeways, and spaces through the direct violence of forced removal and genocide; the second is the imposition of an "exclusionary private property regime."[5] This second movement lays the groundwork for settler perpetuity by transforming land into something that not only can be owned but *must be* owned to be considered civilized. Property, in enclosing, both produces and defines insiders and outsiders, us and them, domestic and alien. What we call urban order, or civility, in the United States today is a product of property-based exclusions.

Seattle has been both literally and figuratively at the frontier of struggles to define the proper spaces and subjects of home within the settler city. Inhabited by the Duwamish and other Coast Salish tribes from time immemorial, the city of Seattle was incorporated in 1869 as a settler colonial city in the unceded Northwest Territory. The city's incorporation was an enactment of territorial violence that both displaced and disenfranchised its Indigenous population through the state-led process of propertied land acquisition, cadastral mapping, and distribution of stolen property to white European settlers.[6]

Soon after Seattle's incorporation, the 1889 Washington state constitution prohibited "ownership of lands by aliens, other than those who in good faith have declared their intentions to become citizens of the United States"—an option not available to Indigenous or Asian people.[7] Yet while the practice of racial apartheid through propertied entitlement and enclosure was at least partially successful in removing official Indigenous and other nonwhite settlements to Seattle's periphery, the space of the city itself, owing in part to its frontier past, was home to large pockets of informal and racially mixed shantytowns located along its muddy coastline.[8]

The presence of widespread housing informality was not unique to Seattle. For much of the United States' first hundred years, shacks, encampments, and shantytowns were considered necessary, if at times undesirable, settler homespaces. Situated on the fringes—or occasionally in the heart of American cities—informal, self-constructed structures, often clustered together, have served as both shelters and social safety nets of last resort for those pushed to the edges by settler incursion and the upheavals of racial capitalism.

In Seattle, these early precursors to Tent City provided both shelter and sanctuary to the growing city's largely informal workforce. As Josephine Ensign notes in her book *Skid Road: On the Frontier of Homelessness in an American City*, Seattle's shantytowns were home to "urban Indigenous people . . . recent immigrants, migrant workers, and families who were too poor to afford other housing options in Seattle or who were excluded from housing due to their race or ethnicity."[9] Ironically, spaces of informal and collective dwelling were fundamental to the settler colonial project of Indigenous erasure. From the homespaces of labor, logging, mining, and railroad camps, immigrants, formerly enslaved people, displaced Indigenous people, and unpropertied white laborers constructed much of the nation's infrastructure.[10] Seattle's shantytowns, for instance, housed loggers, mill workers, railroad workers, miners, and trappers, as well as domestic workers. Living in informal camps and shantytowns like those on the Seattle waterfront, marginalized contract laborers were fundamental to the exploitation of natural resources that produced the nation's wealth and the railroads, factories, and buildings that allowed for its development, reproduction, and expansion.

Despite their colonial necessity for shoring up frontiers, constructing vital infrastructure, and sustaining low-wage workers, informal spaces of the poor were, by the mid-nineteenth century, increasingly understood as a threat to the propertied legitimation of settler colonialism and an untenable relic of a less civilized past.[11] Echoing national trends in the latter half of the nineteenth century, encampments along the shoreline, despite being home to hundreds of Seattle residents, including Chief Seattle's daughter Kikisoblu, were portrayed by both the media and Seattle's wealthy elite as dirty, dangerous, and immoral. Efforts were made to expel their residents or relocate them to newly built hospitals, asylums, and poorhouses.[12] The ideas that made these struggles important had to do with not only what constitutes the space of home, but its scale—who could be included in the spaces we call home, from the dwelling to the homeland.

Defining Who Can Be at Home in the Settler City

While the first few decades of Seattle's existence were spent expelling native others and, by extension, constituting the boundaries of civilized whiteness, by the turn of the twentieth century, the city's focus turned to internal boundary-making. Seattle was undergoing a period of rapid urbanization and population growth in its transition from colonial outpost to modern industrial city. During this time, the city's grid expanded from two small downtown grids, one running north–south and the other following the waterfront, to incorporate almost all the area within the current city boundaries. In the process, the city was neatly divided into private property parcels except for an elegant ring of parks and parkways designed by the Olmsted brothers in the City Beautiful tradition. Yet the expansion of the grid and the platted division of space into private property parcels also resulted in the massive displacement of Seattle's most marginalized people. Many of these local refugees ended up constituting a large informal encampment on Seattle's southwest flank that locals referred to as Shacktown.[13]

What newspapers referred to as Shacktown in the first years of the twentieth century was likely a continuation and outgrowth of the beachside shantytowns that housed Kikisoblu and other early poor residents of the fledgling city. With the population growth and the incorporation and platting of the city, white people who couldn't afford property and nonwhite groups—like Native Americans, African Americans, and a growing population of Chinese Americans, who were forbidden to own land—were pushed together into the waterfront shantytown without benefit of title or access to the sewer and water services that accompanied the city's street expansion.[14]

Linking belonging and residence with property in the early twentieth century not only displaced and contained the nonwhite population but also served as a bulwark against challenges to the hegemony of normative regimes of property and inclusion. Following the colonial script of Indigenous expulsion and quarantine on distant reservations, the anxieties produced by US urbanization were addressed through patterns of racialized banishment and purification.[15] With the increasing formalization of Seattle's urban spaces, Seattle boosters, real estate developers, and labor unionists joined a national chorus of settler colonial narratives of white propertied belonging set against a spectral backdrop of threat and removal directed at poor and racialized others.[16] This came to a head on February 7, 1886, when a mob of white Seattleites rounded up nearly every Chinese resident and marched them to a waiting steamer with the intention of shipping them to California. Although the governor intervened and called in the National Guard, which was able to defuse the situation on that occasion, very few Chinese people remained in Seattle. A few years later, the federal Chinese Exclusion Act survived constitutional challenge, thus ensuring their continued marginalization.

Although the city had very few Black residents at the time, those who did reside in the city were, like their Chinese and Indigenous counterparts, forced to work in menial jobs, excluded by covenant from owning property, and kept from many neighborhoods by racist policing practices.[17] Together, these property-based tools of exclusion fortified a racialized residential regime through which white supremacy was spatially constituted. By contrast, poor and racially excluded people, though necessary for low-wage labor, were pushed to informal shantytowns on the city's southern border, resulting in a north/south racial and class apartheid that continues to define Seattle's urban landscape.[18]

At the turn of the twentieth century, as Seattle's population increased and its spaces increasingly divided along race and class lines, ideas about what type of dwelling constituted a residence also shifted. In response to growing disease, overcrowding, and poverty in American cities, deeply racialized, xenophobic, and gendered discourses of health, safety and morality drove an explosion of building, land use, and nuisance codes throughout the United States.[19] These codes often reclassified traditional housing types such as the tent, shanty, collective shelter, or tenement house, and the bodies that inhabited them, as unhealthy and uncivilized.[20] By 1905, Shacktown, the oldest continually occupied section of Seattle, was deemed a public health hazard. In 1909 the residents of Shacktown were ordered to leave, and the structures were burned.[21]

The displaced inhabitants of Shacktown and the racialized poor populations who dwelt there did not disappear. However, when Shacktown reappeared twenty years later as a Depression-era Hooverville, the relationship of the inhabitants to the home had fundamentally shifted. Excised from "purified" spaces of the city, poor racialized bodies were shunted into spaces that city officials and the press deemed uninhabitable, backward, and dangerous, thus reinforcing both the project and justifications of settler colonial white supremacy. As a result, a specifically American white propertied ethnoclass was constituted along with and in opposition to a racialized nonpropertied other.[22]

Putting the Camp in Its Place: Defining the Proper Settler Subject and Its Others

As the exclusionary power of property narrowed the boundaries of who can be at home in the city, Shacktown dwellers emerged as the deviant and disorderly products of unfit home environments. Yet, even as Seattle was pushing Shacktown and its inhabitants farther to the margins, encampments were assuming a new symbolic place in the imagination of the white middle class. As everyday life became more urbanized, the leisure encampment fulfilled a white, middle-class yearning for a connection to nature and to one another that was becoming an increasingly rare aspect of everyday modern life in the United States. American

Romantic authors like Henry David Thoreau, naturalists like John Muir, and a bevy of health practitioners extolling the moral and physical value of leisure time spent in the rural outdoors, combined with an increasingly consumer-driven white, middle-class desire for adventure, fueled an explosion in popularity of something that came to be known as camping.[23]

Leisure camping established property possession as the dividing line between desirable and undesirable encampments. Drawing inspiration from both military and frontier encampments that enabled the extermination and expulsion of the Indigenous population, white families of means, aided by the expansion of the national and state park systems, were able to redefine the encampment from peri-urban geography of necessity to state-subsidized rural geography of leisure, health, and belonging. The enclosure of public lands for recreational use, which was initiated in Washington by the creation of Mount Rainier National Park in 1899 and expanded throughout Washington State during the first few decades of the twentieth century, not only served to expel Indigenous and informal populations but also redefined Indigenous and other nonpropertied dwellers on public land as foreign interlopers in settler landscapes. To have access to property—a proper home to which to return—was the sine qua non of recreational camping.[24] A proper camping trip is optional, leisurely, and most importantly, temporary. Thus, the settler on camping holiday was able to enact a return to a more natural or primitive environment through a healthy and social ritual of self-reliance, whereas those forced to dwell in informal space by necessity were increasingly viewed with skepticism, fear, and disgust for perceived laziness, antisocial behavior, and disease.

As white settlers increasingly occupied the nation's northwestern frontier, dwelling in urban areas like Seattle, the encampment became a symbolic anachronism that was at once historical residue, nostalgic retreat, and a symbol of ongoing disorder and threat in America's increasing urbanizing landscape. In the first decade of the twentieth century, the normalization of private property as the essential condition of home in the settler city merged a lack of access to property with notions of deviance and pathology to create a new class of Americans called "the homeless." The confluence of factors that created homelessness as we know it today closely paralleled the structure of settler colonialism to which it belonged. The enclosure of land as property displaced and expelled poor and nonwhite individuals who were unable to access it. Their status outside property, as it did for their Indigenous forebears, produced the propertyless as a subject who was at once defined by its difference from a homed norm and its presumed similarity to a specific population that could be recognized as homeless. Through this process, homelessness was born as a category, and the ground was laid for its refusal by the founders of Seattle's Tent City.

Sowing the Seeds of Refusal: Settler Normativity and the Birth of Homelessness

While Shacktown and the early shantytowns that occupied Seattle's southwest were, like Tent City, spaces of sanctuary for their marginalized residents, the specific conditions for Tent City residents' refusal of homelessness were the product of three entwined developments: banishment from urban spaces, quarantine in carceral spaces of care, and the emergence of the camp as a spectacular symbol of government failure. Although these factors have been present in some form in propertied societies for centuries, the specificity of homeless refusal, as expressed by those who created Tent City, derived from unhoused people's displacement from propertied space and their reclamation as homeless subjects in the first decades of the twentieth century.

While people unable to access official titled property were not new, the concept of homelessness was. The term *homeless* was popularized in 1911 with the publication of the book *One Thousand Homeless Men*, written by Alice Solenberger and published by the Russell Sage Foundation. The term covered formerly distinct groups of unhoused people, including itinerant workers, those unable to work due to infirmity or age, and those who refused to work for various reasons. The one thing that united them was their lack of access to private property. With the demarcation of a coherent class of nonpropertied people came efforts to expel them from the settler city. Prior to this time, shantytown dwellers, though vilified and widely considered to be poor, infirm, or itinerant, were not likely to be considered without a home. Moral panic about the growing "tramp problem" that accompanied urbanization of the United States, the formalization of its spaces, and the boom-and-bust cycles of its economy led to increased use of punitive vagrancy statutes, passage of new "tramp laws," and variations on nuisance laws, such as ugly laws or sundown town laws, to facilitate and justify the removal of racialized and unpropertied others through either imprisonment or banishment.[25] These laws, their presuppositions, and the displacements they wrought laid the foundations for the punitive urban environment that inspired both the creation of Tent City as a sanctuary and the conditions for its residents' refusal of homelessness.

The second development that influenced Tent City residents' refusal of homelessness was a response to what resident Howard Tenke referred to as the "dehumanizing" nature of homeless services. As Josephine Ensign chronicles in *Skid Road*, the disciplinary quarantine, pathologization, and dehumanization of those who lacked access to private property went hand in glove with the increasing formalization and commodification of Seattle's housing stock in the late nineteenth and early twentieth centuries.[26] Ensign traces a cyclical path between the spatial dispersal of informal dwelling spaces and the emergence of increasingly complex forms of care in Seattle, including a poorhouse run by nuns near the mouth of the Duwamish River, a makeshift hospital and flophouse on a boat docked on the shore of Puget Sound, and the eventual construction of a public hospital on Yesler Hill. As Ensign's story unfolds, it becomes clear that Seattle's response to homelessness, like settler colonialism itself, was to transform informality and mutual aid to quarantine and pathologization.[27] The result has rendered both public space and the sanctioned spaces of the poor and unhoused decidedly and purposefully unhomelike.

Over the course of the first two decades of the twentieth century, informal housing arrangements like Shacktown slowly gave way to propertied dwellings. At the same time, punitive tramp laws and the disciplinary spaces of the poorhouse and hospital performed a single discursive function in public space: to distinguish the practices and character of the unhoused as deviant and to reaffirm the virtues of now transparent norms of propertied urban order as the singular and monolithic goal for recuperating unhoused residents. In the last decade of the twentieth century, when Tent City founders declared their desire to create a space outside the disciplinary gaze of "religious organizations or social-service agencies," US federal policy came to refer to this relationship through the language of a "continuum of care," based upon the objective of making the unhoused "housing ready."

The third development that served as direct inspiration for the creators of Tent City was the enduring symbolism of Hooverville. The link between access to property and the character and propensities of the poor was already in place by 1932, when the largest homeless encampment in Seattle history began to cascade down Yesler Hill into the waste heaps and infill that Seattleites now refer to as the SoDo neighborhood. Swollen by high unemployment, the eight or so encampments that composed Seattle's racially mixed but mostly male Hooverville were described by University of Washington doctoral student Donald Roy as "conglomerations of grotesque dwellings . . . stuck together in congested disarray like sea-soaked jetsam spewed on the beach."[28] Both spectacle and sanctuary, the camp grew in size and complexity as traditional mechanisms of charitable aid were overwhelmed or abandoned by the residents—people (mostly men) seeking a stable and dignified place to call home.

The shift from Shacktown to Hooverville marked a national development in the symbolic meaning of encampments in the ostensibly settled space of the United States, setting the stage for the spectacular and symbolic claim to public space that would become Tent City. In contrast to the vilification of the personal character and practices of Seattle's earlier Shacktown residents, the name Hooverville was coined in 1933 to call attention to the presidential policies that many felt were responsible for the growing number of unhoused people. This shift in the symbolic meaning of encampments and their residents from personal deviance to structural injustice not only marked a change in the way people thought about poverty in the 1930s but became part of an American semiology of urban encampments.

With the propertied enclosure of urban space, encampments in cities became out of place and unsettling occurrences. Understood by residents and city officials alike as temporary aberrations, the informal dwellings of the poor gained symbolic power as bellwethers of broader American views on poverty that continue to this day.[29] In times of national prosperity, the informal dwelling conjures disorder, decay, and criminality. In times of uncertainty and economic precarity, the settlements of the disenfranchised call attention to economic inequality and social injustice. In both cases, however, the symbolic power of informal dwellings derives not from any inherent physical characteristic but from their violation of a particular normative view of urban life in which the visible presence of poverty has no place in the American city.

In the enclosed settler space of the United States, the unsettling image of the encampment and its unpropertied residents rendered visible the cracks, holes, and fractures in narratives of settler colonial completeness. In its out-of-placeness, the encampment became spectacle. Hoovervilles are remembered even today as a spectacle that conjures images and ideas of extraordinary tragedy, injustice, and inequality. Like the Hoovervilles that preceded it, Tent City drew on this spectacular history to protest a perceived state failure. As original camp member Mark noted, "We want to say, hey, we've got a problem here. We have to erect tents to survive."

In the case of Seattle's Hooverville as with most protest encampments, spectacle soon gave way to settlement. As the spectacle of Hooverville morphed into long-term settlement, it became unsettling. Seattle's Hooverville was the nation's longest-lasting, occupying the city's southern waterfront until 1941.[30] During this time, the settlement developed its own political, safety, and economic structure, as well as a distinct set of cultural norms. Yet, as the emergency of the Great Depression began to wane, the city ramped up the efforts to dismantle the shacks and displace the residents. Beginning in the late 1930s and continuing to the final demolition of the encampments in 1941, Seattle citizens' groups formed a chorus calling for elimination of the settlement.

For some, it seemed that Seattle was dying. In a series of articles and letters that would not be out of place in Seattle today, concerned citizens petitioned the city government for action. Opponents of the encampment decried it as unsightly to the "civic-minded" and framed the residents as "immoral" and "evil," thus creating what historian Dustin Neighly has called a "'discourse of otherness' that positioned Hooverville as expendable and alien to the rest of the city."[31] As urban and peri-urban encampments persisted into the twentieth century, they came to represent, for propertied citizens and governments alike, a departure from normal life and a failure of settler governance. Informal dwelling spaces today can represent, like Seattle's Tent City, a suspension of norms, a spectacle, an escape, an incursion, or a transitory presence on the landscape. However, when a camp becomes permanent—when a camp becomes *home*—it becomes a settlement and therefore a threat to acceptable, normative white settlements and spaces.

Securing the Settler City

As the Great Depression slowly gave way to the war economy, housing gluts and labor shortages reduced the number of those living informally along Seattle's fringe. Then, in February 1942, a new kind of camp emerged. Despite lacking any evidence of internal threat, President Franklin Roosevelt signed Executive Order 9066 authorizing the emergency exclusion from military zones and incarceration of more than 120,000 people, mainly of Japanese ancestry, of whom more than two-thirds were US citizens. Beginning in April 1942, people of Japanese descent were forcibly removed from their homes in the Seattle area, as elsewhere on the West Coast. Seattle's Japanese Americans were transported first to detention in the temporary Puyallup Assembly Center and then to the Minidoka incarceration camp near Twin Falls, Idaho. The incarceration camp marks both a development and a continuation of the encampment in the context of settler colonialism. Like reservations, Indian boarding schools, asylums, poorhouses, and jails, the incarceration camp represents state attempts to manage and eliminate deviant populations through carceral control.[32] In contrast to the "problem" camps created as collective attempts to create homespaces in the context of hardship and marginalization, the incarceration camp produces an American semiology of the camp as a site of state control and quarantine.

By the end of World War II, the regulatory erasure from urban space of encampments, shantytowns, and other informal dwellings gave way to "slum clearance" and "urban renewal," which destroyed and failed to replace viable housing options for those excluded from costly and racist housing markets. In their place, the heteronormative nuclear family—with its spatial cognate, the single-family home—was posited as the proper environment for the development of healthy, rational individuals.[33] In this space of colonial exclusion and erasure, the normative construction of the home as private property cements the discursive decoupling of the unhoused from the affective "home" in the latter half of the twentieth century.

In the settler space of the American city, informal dwellings represent vestiges of a disorderly and lawless past that are destined to, and therefore must, give way to planned, platted, propertied progress. They are rendered illegal, made inadequate. Property-based urban policy and planning render the informal habitations of the poor as temporary spaces of conquest and quarantine that mark the limit and the constitutive outside of the American urban frontier.[34]

It is here that the creation and purpose of the tent city becomes legible. At the edge of settler urban frontier, the visible poor appear as abject victims of structural and personal forces that are themselves exceptional, out of place. The presence of their bodies and their makeshift habitations represents not simply abominations but an existential threat to the ongoing settler colonial project of American capitalist modernity. In this context, the self-provision of nonpropertied housing becomes a spectacular aberration that, for some, calls attention to the injustice of poverty and homelessness in the American city. For others, though, such aberrations signal the incompleteness of propertied norms. In both cases, however, the goal of urban governance is reclamation of a propertied status quo. Against this backdrop, the original inhabitants of Tent City in 1990 sought to disrupt the displacement, erasure, and dehumanization of unhoused people through the spectacular construction of a homeless camp in a highly visible location.

Viewed through the lens of settler colonialism, displacement and erasure become logical and appropriate responses to the poor and their habitations. As

Neil Smith notes and many others have echoed, gentrification efforts, in their attempt to tame the "urban frontier" of racialized poverty and homelessness, can be read as ongoing cartographies of settler colonial displacement, eviction, and quarantine of poor and marginalized spaces and bodies.[35] When the original Tent City was constructed, Seattle was in the early stages of a postindustrial transformation that continues to this day. In the late 1980s and early '90s, Seattle, like many other cities, was beginning to shift from its former economic role as a small industrial and port city to that of a globally connected and technology-driven hub in a new economy. By 1990, *Fortune* magazine had declared, "No city has a better shot at replicating the potent mix of techies, dollars, and drive that made Silicon Valley great."[36] This newfound wealth, combined with Seattle's enduring status as one of the nation's most "livable cities," converged in the 1990s in the entrepreneurial remaking of Seattle as a "spectacular space of upscale consumption and leisure . . . that seamlessly weaves together upscale retail and world-class cultural activities with gleaming office towers and affluent urban residences."[37] Visible poverty has no place here. As both a vestige of a less prosperous past and a stain on its gleamingly affluent future, the poor and their habitations must be removed from the "livable city."

In 1990, however, Seattle's affluent future was far from secure. As Seattle struggled to become a "world-class" city, its efforts were accompanied and aggravated by a growing wealth gap, stagnant wages, and an increasingly unaffordable housing market. A product of broader neoliberal shifts toward banking deregulation and global commodity production, Seattle saw increasing unemployment in industrial sectors that had historically paid a living wage. Further, wages in the new burgeoning service sector failed to keep pace. By the dawn of the 1990s, the stagnation of working-class wages had combined with federal funding cuts to increase the number and visibility of the permanent economic refugees commonly referred to today as "the homeless."

The increasing visibility of Seattle's unhoused population did not sit well with Seattle's "world-class livable city" image. Expressing sentiments remarkably similar to 2019's "Seattle is dying" narrative, many business owners, residents, and city officials in the early 1990s viewed visible poverty as an invasive attack on perceptions of safety, livability, and even the city's viability. By the end of 1990, the downtown core was beginning to feel the effects of a recession that, within a few years, would decimate the city's retail core. Perhaps in an effort to stave off this exodus, Seattle's business elite began to blame slowing retail activity on the presence of the poor. Articles began to appear in the news telling harrowing tales of homeless people causing violence and mayhem that targeted middle-class shoppers and overwhelmed the downtown core.[38] Despite the lack of verisimilitude in these articles, a media push shortly thereafter urged a harsher approach to the disorderliness of the visible homeless. Responding to the outcry, Mark Sidran ran for and was elected as Seattle city attorney on a promise to restore law and order through implementation and intense enforcement of civility laws. These laws aimed to remove the visibly poor and homeless from Seattle's business, retail, and entertainment areas by criminalizing ostensibly private behaviors, such as sleeping, sitting, or lying down in public spaces.[39] In backing Sidran's program to drive the poor from Seattle's newly sanitized downtown, Seattle voters embraced a national trend toward punitive measures that closely echoed the tramp, vagrancy, and ugly laws of the late nineteenth and early twentieth centuries.[40]

Unsettling the Settler City: Tent City and the Spectacle of Refusal

In Seattle's gentrifying space of exclusion and erasure, the first incarnation of Seattle's Tent City was born. Fed up with dwindling housing options and an increasingly hostile urban environment, some unhoused people chose to take matters into their own hands by erecting a self-governed encampment on public land. The brainchild of a small group of unhoused and formerly unhoused individuals referring to themselves collectively as Seattle Housing and Resource Effort (SHARE), the first Tent City was erected in the fall of 1990 just south of downtown in what is now called the SoDo neighborhood. Responding to an urban environment not unlike what is experienced by Seattle's unhoused today, SHARE members created Tent City to stake a claim in the city that had marginalized, mistreated, and banished them from public view.[41]

Like similar encampments that emerged around the same time in places like Portland, Oregon; San Jose, California; and Chicago, the original incarnation of Tent City was established for three primary reasons. First, it served as a pragmatic way to provide shelter and a safe space for Seattle's unhoused community. Second, the self-governed structure provided residents with a level of dignity and autonomy seldom encountered in traditional shelters. Third, the camp functioned as a symbolic gesture to render visible the plight of the homeless in Seattle.[42]

Befitting its symbolic purpose, the initial location of the camp conjured specters of Seattle's long history of informal habitations and the settler colonial desire to eradicate them. The initial location of the somewhat ragged collection of military surplus tents calling itself Tent City was a city-owned vacant lot south of the racial divide of Yesler Street, near the city's largest event venue at the time, the Kingdome. The site was directly adjacent to the site of the Hooverville that had occupied the area in the 1930s and the Shacktown of a decade earlier. It was just a handful of blocks southeast of the informal shantytown that, in the 1840s, was home to Kikisoblu, daughter of the city's namesake, Chief Seattle, and less than a mile from where the area's Indigenous residents located their seasonal encampments prior to white occupation.[43] On the day when a group of homeless activists and their advocates marched to the location and began erecting tents, however, it was a large open lot visible from the local interstate, the sports arena parking lot, and many surrounding streets.

Unlike the dystopian encampment reportage of *Seattle Is Dying*, media response in the winter of 1990–91 was largely positive. During the first two weeks after its opening, Seattle's two major newspapers ran multiple feature-length stories sympathetic to Tent City and its residents. One front-page article opened by noting the ignorance of nearby shoppers and sports fans whose "minds were apparently oblivious, at 12:15 in the afternoon, to the enclave of poverty, homelessness, and pain around them, for their voices were filled with joy and laughter and cheer. But life at Tent City, whether it is noon or night, is never so merry. It is harsh."[44] A year-end article by the *Seattle Times* editorial team compared Seattle's unhoused population to "refugees seeking harbor from a relentless war" and urged readers to "start the New Year with a focus on housing."[45] Finally, attempting to walk the line between business pressure to remove the camp and activists and advocates seeking an expansion of housing options, city officials offered temporary use of an abandoned bus barn as a more habitable and less visible form of relief. Although the bus barn residency was short-lived, this initial publicity was enough to develop the base of political and financial support necessary to sustain and eventually multiply SHARE's shelter resources.

After a short hiatus following the bus barn eviction, the tent city concept was revived by SHARE in 1998. Following a series of "sanitation sweeps" of a large encampment located on a wooded hillside on Seattle's south side that had resulted in the loss of shelter, belongings, and community for dozens of people, SHARE, together with the displaced residents, created Tent City 2 on the northwest side of the city's Beacon Hill. The purpose of the new tent city was threefold: to provide shelter for those displaced by the sweeps, to demonstrate the desire for and effectiveness of self-managed encampments, and to draw public attention once again.

The camp was short-lived, but after an unceremonious bulldozing by the city, Tent City was resurrected on private land donated by a nearby community center.

This incarnation, dubbed Tent City 3, met with immediate resistance from city officials. By this point, the organizing model of self-governed encampments created by Tent City, SHARE, and a newly formed sister organization, Women's Housing, Equality and Enhancement League (WHEEL), was familiar to many in the city. The city government's main point of opposition wasn't the camp itself or its structure but the precedent it might set. As deputy mayor Tom Byers told a *Seattle Times* reporter, "If you tolerate an encampment by well-meaning people who want to police themselves, then there will be similar encampments with people who are shooting heroin every night." Although he claimed that he had met with Tent City 3 residents and felt that they were "well-meaning and principled people," he insisted, despite no demonstrable knowledge, that they were the exception and that "the way to solve this problem is not to adopt a tolerance policy on illegal encampments."[46]

Unsurprisingly, in 2000, Tent City 3 was denied a city-issued camping permit and was once again forced to take down the tents. This time, however, drawing on support from El Centro de la Raza, the community center hosting Tent City 3, the pro bono legal services of attorney Ted Hunter, and the legal privileges of private property, the group appealed the decision in King County Superior Court. There, a judge ruled that tent camps on private land were not de facto illegal. As a result of this decision, the city attorney's office signed a consent decree enabling the tent city to exist in perpetuity by permission of the landowner, provided it changed locations every ninety days in compliance with temporary use statutes that govern nonpermanent structures, was obscured from the street by vegetation or fence, and did not allow children under eighteen.[47] In so doing, Seattle became the first city in the nation to grant permanent legal status to a peer-operated tent encampment, forever changing Seattle's urban landscape.[48]

With the mandate of the consent decree, Tent City 3 became one of a growing number of what have come to be called durable encampments.[49] Banished to the urban periphery, those who lacked access to formal property banded together into increasingly permanent settlements that, unlike many of the short-lived protest camps that emerged on the steps of city halls and in public parks in the 1980s, were notable for their large size and relative permanence. In contrast to other encampments, Tent City 3 is relatively unique in that, while many camps were evicted or co-opted by local governments or shelter providers, Tent City 3, like Portland's Dignity Village, was able to gain legal status to exist in perpetuity. This retained the tent city's structural autonomy, ensuring its visibility and persistence in Seattle's urban landscape.

At the dawn of 2023, Tent City 3 continues its nomadic existence. Moving every sixty to ninety days, mostly among Seattle's gentrified neighborhoods and inner-ring suburbs, it has been in continuous operation for over twenty years. In contrast to Seattle's Shacktown and Hooverville, Tent City 3 has become, in a way, settled. In 1990, when Tent City erected its first tents, it did so upon land that had long been inhabited by those who had been excluded from Seattle's propertied spaces and norms. As with the Indigenous ancestors, shack dwellers, and Hoovervillians who trod before them, their presence is viewed as an outdated, out-of-place aberration to be resolved in the name of settler colonial modernity. Yet, for those who reside there, those spaces are today, as they have always been, primarily a place to call home.

Undoubtedly, the tent city's symbolism has an important political, social, and financial function. Indeed, throughout its existence, the visible example of Tent City has been fundamental for SHARE's ability to gain the political, social, and material support necessary for the continued existence of both the camp and the SHARE/WHEEL organization. However, for its residents past and present, the primary value of Tent City lies in its function as a space in which those deemed homeless can enact structures and subjectivities that reflect their own needs and desires in ways that would be impossible within what I describe in the next chapter as the carceral framework of homeless care. Or, in the words of camp founder Howard Tenke, "We are here because we want to manage our own lives and our own place in which to live." For nearly all Tent City residents, Seattle's carceral geographies of homeless management were felt as unwarranted and dehumanizing. Tent City 3 offered a space where residents felt they could reclaim these losses. It was, and is, a homespace.

Both the need and the desire to create a city of tents arose in direct relation to the settler colonial relationship between property and home. The creation and ongoing practices of homemaking I explore in this book are enacted as a form of refusal. For residents of Tent City 3, it was being deprived of the affective aspects of home, not the physical hardship of tent dwelling, that was most deeply expressed as injustice. While lack of safety and stability and demeaning treatment or structures often keep people away from sanctioned shelter, unhoused people consistently cite security, belonging, and stability as reasons for creating or staying together in encampments.[50] Though some have pointed out that such arrangements are often precarious and fleeting, and can enable or exacerbate conditions for coercion and abuse, for many of those who live in the marginalized spaces often referred to today as tent cities or more simply encampments, the self-provision of dwelling structures and community, no matter how fleeting, represents an attempt to recapture the sense of stability, agency, and belonging of something resembling home.[51]

In this recapture, refusal becomes a possibility to think otherwise. The story of marginalization, displacement, and erasure of informal dwellings and their residents that I have traced in this chapter will be familiar to those who dwell in or pay attention to today's informal dwellings. While these might offer temporary sanctuary, they are soon swept away by the need to cleanse the settler colonial city. Tent City 3, however, persists. Through this persistence, possibilities for thinking home against and beyond normative property relation are negotiated, struggled over, and enacted.

Example of a tent name on a couple's tent, circa 2007. Residents were required to name their tents and post the name prominently. It was not uncommon for campers to personalize their tents or surrounding spaces with decorations. This one had a stuffed bear in overalls affixed to the front of the tent.

2. The Making of Homespace

The most obvious and visible manifestations of homemaking in Tent City 3 are the tents themselves. Like an officially recognized address, a tent in the tent city is a testament to and manifestation of one's presence—a space where you belong that is both yours and an expression of self. But a tent in the tent city is more than simply a residence in a neighborhood—or even a home in one's hometown. The process of homemaking in Tent City 3 asserts a spatial politics of belonging in a world in which the dwellings and possessions of the informally housed are often treated as a blight or trash by local authorities.[1] Tents and the tent city offer residents a space of refusal and reclamation in the settler colonial present.

For most of a person's stay in Tent City 3, their tent is their home.[2] When an individual or couple is assigned a tent space, that person is required to give the tent a name. Ostensibly, tent names have the pragmatic purpose of allowing other residents to locate someone in case of a visitor (or, more often, to attend to some chore). However, these names also serve as markers of ownership and individuality. While there are no fixed rules regarding tent names, residents tend to choose names that reflect some sense of self. Folks frequently choose names that hold some sort of spatial significance, such as Arctic Trap Line, Dixieland, or Gnome Alaska. Sometimes names reference the lack thereof, such as Nowhere, Transient, or Just Passing Through. Others choose names that display a sense of irony or humor, as with the names Tent-mahal, Arkham Asylum, or Tent-atious D. Others simply name their tents after themselves or their nickname.

Tent names are often used as conversation starters and, for many, are deeply personal. My own tent name was the object of much discussion. When I couldn't think of anything, another camper suggested it should have some reference to my position as a researcher "so people know why you're writing stuff down all the time." "Dr. Is In" was floated by someone at a nearby table, but I said I wasn't a doctor yet, so that would be false advertising. "Well, *grad student* just doesn't have that ring," quipped someone else. Finally, the group rallied around the name "the Professor" instead of doctor. Recognizing the utter ridiculousness of the politics of academic titles, I relented. A paper plate, a sharpie, and duct tape were retrieved. I wrote out my new *nom de tent*, and carefully taped it to the tent wall while the group looked on with what felt (to me) like a ceremonial air. This was now how and where I would be known. Like the tradition of naming boats, vacation homes, or even vast estates, the naming of tents functioned as both an assertion of belonging and a projection of self.

The personalization of tent space extends beyond naming. Of mostly equal size and all covered with the obligatory blue tarp, the tents in Tent City 3 appear remarkably homogenous from a distance. Up close, though, things look very different. Many choose to arrange their tent both inside and outside to reflect their own character and sensibility. Some arrange potted plants on the pallet around their tents; others adorn the tent itself with small objects or pictures. Inside, some people use found objects to construct elaborate organizational systems, platform beds, or even small lofts.

Of course, placing potted plants, decorating, or adding a touch of personality are all common domestic practices among housed people. While for some residents these acts of domesticity served simply, as one resident put it, to "make it as much like home as possible," for others, the domestication of their tent space was a conscious act of refusing their homeless status. As longtime resident Dave was fond of telling me whenever the conversation turned to the differential treatment of the homeless, "Our houses are just like theirs; they just happen to not be made of bricks!" Such claims to equality simultaneously reject the concept of homelessness and call attention to the constructed distinction between the dwellings and character of those deemed homeless and their housed neighbors.[3]

Yet, for most unhoused people, such acts of domestic freedom and autonomy are impossible. Despite the common use of *homeless* to describe those without access to sanctioned housing, loss of one's home is neither a simple nor an immediate result of losing access to housing. Rather, what we often call homelessness signifies an ongoing violence of colonial unhoming, of which housing displacement is only the first instance. In the contemporary settler city, the mythology of settler totality is maintained through processes of eviction or carceral management.[4] One may lose access to housing, but the loss of home is an ongoing process of violent excision, expulsion, and erasure. Geographers Douglas Porteous and Sandra E. Smith coined the term *domicide* to capture the violence of home's loss.[5] Building upon this work, Richard Baxter and Katherine Brickell highlight how domicide is not a single act or event, but the result of the "precarious process" of "home unmaking," whereby "components of home are unintentionally or deliberately, temporarily or permanently, divested, damaged

Example of tent interior arrangement, circa 2007. People often added items, such as the blankets and milk crates in this photo, to make their tent feel more homelike.

or even destroyed."[6] Homelessness is not something that just happens to people. It is a collective act of unhoming perpetrated by those who have the power to define home and homelessness, who is deserving of home and what kind, and who can be at home and where.[7]

The production of tents as domestic spaces can be seen as a refusal of both the idea and the subjectivities of homelessness. For nearly everyone I spoke with, it was the deprivation of the affective aspects of home, not the physical hardship of tent dwelling, that was most deeply felt as injustice. Though very few tent city dwellers self-identified as homeless, it wasn't uncommon for conversations about home to be infused with a sense of loss. However, rarely was this loss discussed in relation specifically to housing. Occasionally, people would speak nostalgically of particular homes, hometowns, or even beloved possessions, but far more often, residents spoke of the loss of autonomy, freedom, or what people frequently referred to as their "humanity" that they felt accompanied the loss of an officially sanctioned dwelling. For them, the production of the tent city as homespace was a refusal of this dehumanization and its justification, their

The Making of Homespace 49

homeless status. These acts of refusal occur against and within settler colonial efforts to displace, erase, and quarantine. However, although they occur in opposition to the presuppositions of propertied personhood, these acts take place within the complicated territories of property. In their attempts to produce a homespace where they can reclaim the liberty, autonomy, and privacy denied them in the carceral spaces of homeless care, tent city residents attain these goals through acts of commoning that allow for more inclusive and expansive ideas of home.

In this chapter, I attend to some of the ways residents of Tent City 3 craft a homespace within and against settler norms of propertied exclusion and unhoming. I begin by discussing how homelessness is produced not by a loss of housing but by a series of violent acts of unhoming that render one unable to be at home in the city. I then explore how the space of the tent city enables residents to refuse homelessness and reclaim their humanity. In the final two sections I demonstrate the importance of privacy and security in producing the tent city as a commons.

Unhoming, Propertied Personhood, and the Violence of Becoming Homeless

In the contemporary United States, the unmaking of home that accompanies a loss of formal housing occurs through multiple and overlapping processes at multiple scales. As Jean-Paul Addie and James Fraser note, "Urban settler colonialism is intimately linked with processes of neoliberal urbanism and gentrification that depend on brute force in regulating space, whether through sanctioned state violence, housing evictions, or restrictions placed on public space."[8] However, unhoming seldom happens all at once or in a linear fashion. It marks a displacement of not only a physical space but one's relationship to oneself and others, in what Ananya Roy refers to as a "lived process of loss."[9] For many who are, or have been, unhoused, this lived process can feel like being in a pinball machine. One is shot out, bounces through the available options, and is shot out again to repeat the process until time, money, or connections run out. There might be couches and spare bedrooms with friends and family, cheap motel rooms, brief overnight hookups, a car, or a van parked on a quiet street. Underpasses, parks, doorways, and hidden tents become places of last resort. Each of these displacements takes a chunk out of one's sense of home, leaving one slightly more vulnerable, exposed, and alone.

But the real violence of unhoming begins when these strategies dwindle (or were never an option in the first place), and one enters today's most common sanctioned spaces for those in need of shelter. In their analysis of the settler colonial city, Michael Simpson and David Hugill point out that "settler colonial power depends upon managing the movement of people, permitting some bodies to move freely while constraining the movements of others using carceral logics including not just prisons, policing, and the criminal justice system, but also reserves or reservations, residential schools, social service agencies, borders, citizenship, and the entire nexus of governmental institutions that employ state violence and surveillance."[10] Unhoused individuals encounter that power in the form of the homeless shelter and the service apparatus. Here, unhoused people enter a "continuum of carcerality" premised upon the presumed deviance of those who lack access to sanctioned housing.[11] In these thera-carceral places, one's sense of home is not simply lost but cut away.

Thera-carceral shelter spaces operationalize the discourses of recovery, rehabilitation, and other forms of therapeutic governance through carceral securitization, surveillance, and social control. Consequently, unhoused persons, because of a lack of sanctioned housing, surrender their ability to be active agents in their own lives—to be at home. In the shelter, one's time, space, and actions are seldom under one's own control. Many shelters require residents to be in at a certain time (usually evening) and out at a certain time (usually morning), as if the need for a place to stay magically disappears with the light of day and jobs only happen in daylight hours. Although some shelters do their best to make guests feel at home, this is rare and largely out of the control of the person seeking shelter.

While shelters offer a roof for the night, that often comes at the cost of safety, privacy, agency, and belonging. Shelter availability as well as one's place and surroundings in the shelter are largely out of one's control. Many shelters do not allow personal possessions, and those that do generally require that they be stored in a separate locked location. This renders difficult, if not impossible, even the most meager attempt at personalizing the institutional space one will inhabit for the next nine hours. Different surroundings, noises, smells, comings, and goings and the unpredictability of the environment conspire to make sleep difficult and anxiety high. Where you lay your head and next to whom are no longer under your control. Not only does this add to perceptions of danger and anxiety, but it renders human familiarity, relationships, and mutual care nearly impossible.

Even when the luckiest among the unhoused gain access to one of the rare longer-term shelters, transitional housing units, or residential hotels (SROs), a presumption of homeless deviance perpetuates the process of unhoming. Access to many of these locations is premised upon a lack of "housing readiness." As such, job training, mandatory therapy, and life skills classes are often required for residency.[12] Additionally, many of these longer-term sites closely monitor, limit, or forbid visitors, limit privacy, and tightly regulate or forbid the recreational use of alcohol and other legal substances that many of us enjoy upon arriving home after a long day. Together, presumptions of deviance, pathology, and dependence in longer term, very-low-income housing options offer the appearance of a more homelike space, while continuing to deny residents the ability to make, claim, or be at home.

Outside the shelter, the unhoming continues. On the streets, the unhoused must grapple with near-constant displacements that further erode any ability to be at home in their hometowns. Almost every city in the United States enforces a suite of what have come to be called antihomeless laws.[13] These laws, also referred to as quality of life or civility laws, use park hours and prohibitions on sleeping, sitting, lying, or panhandling in public spaces to keep those without housing on the move. Seattle is no exception. Citywide camping bans and overnight parking enforcement make sleep all but impossible. Citations, banishment orders, or simply invocations to move along systematically prevent attempts at respite, as well as disrupting social networks and inhibiting access to food, restrooms, or other basic needs usually met within the private confines of home.[14]

Often, it is the unhoused person's properly housed neighbors that instigate their displacement from their home neighborhoods. Chris Herring has documented how police response to complaints about unhoused people and their habitations results in the constant churning of the unhoused. This ongoing displacement prevents them from accessing services and jobs and renders them more vulnerable to crime.[15] Such displacements, many have noted, are neither solely punitive nor benevolent but rather are aimed at keeping the unhoused in proper homeless spaces and preventing them from becoming too comfortable in what for most unhoused people is their hometown.[16] For those without housing, the process of unhoming is both ongoing and cumulative, a slow process of many displacements that leave those without housing few places to go, and nowhere where they can be at home.

Undergirding and justifying the violence of home unmaking lies an initial act of political dehumanization that is rendered invisible through the simple equation of homelessness with a lack of proper residence. This too is an excision, an unbecoming, an unhoming from the homeland. Excluded from full protection and participation, deemed unfit to act as active agents in their own lives, the unhoused find themselves vulnerable and excluded—unhomed within their homelands.[17] What is at stake in the process of unhoming, Ananya Roy and others remind us, is a dispossession not just from property or place but from personhood.[18]

In Western liberal political and legal tradition, home and personhood are intricately bound up with the concept of property. Political personhood, or what Hannah Arendt called "the right to have rights," relies on state recognition of humanity's natural capacities for rational autonomy and self-governance.[19] However, such recognition requires not simply a presumption of autonomy and self-governance, but also their demonstration. In this relationship, famously articulated by C. B. Macpherson as the political theory of possessive individualism, the possession, management, and maintenance of legally recognized property function as a necessary precursor for political inclusion.[20] From this relationship emerges a liberal presupposition of propertied personhood in which one's capacity for rational autonomy is performatively embodied through the visible demonstration of property ownership.

The theoretical presupposition of propertied personhood finds its visible manifestation in US policy and jurisprudence through what Roy has aptly termed the "American paradigm of propertied citizenship."[21] In this paradigm, the ideal of propertied personhood is foundational to defining the model citizen and its other. Those displaced from or otherwise alienated from property possession "are therefore rendered marginal in the discourses and practices of citizenship."[22] Unhoused people, because they lack access to private property, are displaced from political personhood as "the alien figure that at once violates and thereby reinforces the norms of citizenship."[23] Through the "lived process of loss" that is domicidal displacement, unhoused individuals are systematically displaced from their homes, hometowns, homelands, and ultimately their humanity.[24]

These acts of unhoming are integral to the settler colonial project. In a country where personhood is predicated on property and property is inextricable from colonial processes of racialized dispossession, anyone without housing becomes, as Roy puts it, "a trespasser in the space of the nation-state."[25] The unhoused person is not simply one who lacks shelter, nor is he or she fully a person in the liberal sense, as a subject who has the ability to freely choose, act, and identify. Rather, the person lacking sanctioned housing exists as *homeless* in a space where difference is made legible by a colonial vocabulary of conquest and supremacy that justifies the removal and carceral management of the colonial other.[26] In the normative universe of settler colonialism, those without housing are transformed into uncivilized, unruly, and not-quite-human interlopers in settler space. They are simultaneously incapable of self-governance and unfit for inclusion within the bounds of home.[27]

The Right to Be Left Alone: Refusing Homelessness and Reclaiming Humanity

Against these unbecomings, Tent City 3 offered a place where residents felt they could refuse both the carcerality of homeless management and the dehumanizing assumptions behind it. This was driven home for me just a few weeks after I arrived at Tent City 3. It was a rainy February afternoon, and two campers, Paul and Rick, who had been helping me settle in but whom I did not know very well, invited me to join them in escaping the soggy confines of the camp for a nearby coffee shop. I was excited just to be invited. Although people had been friendly to me around camp, this was the first time anyone had engaged me in anything other than my duties as a camp member or to question my rationale for being there as a researcher. In hindsight, although Rick, Paul, and I would become friends over the coming months, at the time, I think they just felt sorry for me.

Prior to that moment, I had spent most of my time trying to get to know people and figure out how everything in the camp worked. I could see the sustained attention to creating a homelike space, but I didn't yet understand the context. But now, I was wet, my tent was leaky, and there was not much to do around the camp. Both Paul and Rick had been living in the camp for several months and were definitely better geared up for, and accustomed to, rainy tent life.

Paul, a quiet and reserved Seattleite with long, flowing white hair, had grown up not far from my grandparents' house in West Seattle and had worked in the old Bethlehem Steel plant that now lies dormant near the bridge that connects West Seattle and Seattle proper. Paul tried very hard to appear aloof. I often saw him spend what seemed like hours sitting in camp scratching his long chin, smoking and staring off into the middle distance. But as I got to know him, I found that he was often the first to pitch in to help someone in need and would not hesitate to step in when he felt someone was being cruel or a bully.

Rick, by contrast, never stopped talking. He was large, gruff, and foul-mouthed. He could get very loud while pontificating on any number of subjects, particularly if he had had a bit much to drink or smoke. He could also be quite mean on occasion, yelling at other campers for small infractions of camp rules or just because they got on his nerves. Yet he was almost compulsively generous. Over time, I came to suspect that he collected things just to give them away. In hindsight, it makes complete sense that it was these two that reached out to me. But on that day, I was just excited to be out of the camp in the company of two potential interviewees.

Once we had settled in with our drinks and shed a few layers of clothes, Paul mentioned hearing that, due to the threat of snow, some of the local shelters had opened additional beds. "Are you thinking of going?" I asked, mainly just to make conversation.

Rick threw himself dramatically back in his chair, hands raised like I had just accused him of murder. "No way!" he almost shouted.

"Why not?" I asked innocently.

He sighed heavily as if that was the dumbest question he had ever heard. Nevertheless, he waited for me to get out my recorder before explaining that he had tried many different shelters but concluded that they were just not for him. "Because it's not the kind of person I am," he explained. "I don't like having somebody know when I come and go. That's my business, not theirs. And only being allowed so many visitors or having to check them in ahead of time? That ain't none of nobody's business who comes to visit me. I'm not dealing drugs or anything like that—it's just . . . it's a personal thing and that's rude in my opinion." As Rick told it, shelters were only for people that "couldn't wipe their own asses." For him, and presumably for most others, the strict control of movement and association posed by many shelters was an affront.

Rick, who had bounced among motels, shelters, and the tent city for a couple of years, felt very strongly that the ability to control his and his visitors' coming and going was an important facet of his dignity and sense of self. Paul, who for some time had been nodding along in what I suspect was his best Silent Bob impression, concurred, explaining that the emergency shelters were even worse: "You have to be in at a certain time, out at a certain time. Doesn't even matter if you have to work. Sometimes you get there, and they are already full. I did that circuit for about a week and a half. Then I couldn't take it anymore. I am not a child. I do not need to be told when to take a damn piss." Although he had stayed in shelters during extreme weather, he tried to avoid them at all costs. For Paul as well as for Rick, who also frequented motels when he could afford them and was nodding ever more vigorously as Paul spoke, attempts by shelters to control or monitor their movements were not viewed as beneficial, therapeutic, or even punitive; they were simply rude. For both men, underlying the invocation of rudeness rested a basic assumption that freedom to come and go unhindered and unmonitored and have visitors at their discretion were basic and natural human rights. For them, the everyday carcerality of the shelter was an affront to their basic humanity.

Rick and Paul were far from alone. Far and away the most frequently invoked reason for staying in the tent city was the ability to come and go as one pleased. Outside presuppositions of homeless dependency, such a refusal of the shelter system would seem unremarkable. For most Americans, the natural rights presumption that liberty is necessary for the exercise of one's innate freedom would seem so basic as to simply be common sense. However, liberty, like property, has never been universal but is rather premised upon exclusion and carcerality. In the United States, it has always been the case that the liberty of settlers relied upon the removal and quarantine of Indigenous bodies, the enslavement of Black bodies, and the exclusion of poor bodies. Indeed, the need to constrain and control Indigenous and racialized bodies continues to define contemporary settler urbanism.[28]

In keeping with this logic, there is virtually no place in any US city where someone who lacks access to property can enter and leave at will. For residents like Paul and Rick, the outsize importance of the ability to come and go as they pleased was directly in relation to both its denial and the perceived reason for its denial: that being displaced from their homes rendered them incapable of managing their own lives. Tellingly, every one of the people I interviewed cited the ability to come and go as the single most important reason for staying in the camp rather than in shelters or on the streets.

Although Rick's refusal of shelter was premised on what he felt was "just rude," the refusal of carceral management and the desire to reclaim basic freedoms were frequently a reaction to the productive, rather than simply restrictive, functions of carceral homeless management. For instance, Donna, a woman in her early twenties, had recently come to Seattle from a wealthy island suburb and moved to Tent City 3 with her husband after a short stint at a nearby shelter. This was the first time Donna had been unhoused, and she expressed to me in our first interview how deeply surprised and hurt she felt about how people's perception of them changed after finding out they had lost their apartment. "It's not like I have changed," she told me. "I still make myself presentable, still have the same job, but people treat us like we have a disease or committed some crime!" She was likewise shocked to discover the lack of freedoms granted in the shelter.

When I asked how she was settling in at the camp, Donna spoke at length about the "exhausting" list of rules at her previous shelter. "It was like they didn't have a life, and they didn't want anyone else to have one either," she said exasperatedly. "Here I feel like they actually give you that opportunity. Like you at least don't have to worry about when you are coming and going. You don't have to be out of there at a specific time. If you need to just sit down and take a breath, or if you happen to not get any sleep the night before and you need to catch up on that, that is provided for. Whereas, at other shelters it was like a treadmill—you can't really get ahead."

While Donna equated the ability to come and go with the ability to "take a breath" and "get ahead," Andy was more specific about what these attributes meant in the everyday lives of those who found themselves without housing. Andy, a man in his twenties with dark hair that stood up in a way that, when combined with his black-framed glasses, made him look eerily similar to Waldo in the *Where's Waldo?* books, was, like Donna, a fairly new resident. Before coming to Tent City 3, he had alternated between couch surfing with friends and staying in shelters. When we sat down for an interview at a nearby Chinese restaurant, the first question I asked was simply, "Why Tent City?"

He didn't miss a beat before responding, "That you can come and go as you please." He went on to explain that because he was able to rest, run errands, or just sit and read a book when he felt like it, "I finally feel relaxed enough to actually get some of that stuff done and figure out what I need to do." Both Andy and Donna pointed to how incredibly difficult and time-consuming it can be to negotiate the various carceral regimes of homelessness. For those who have the privilege of property, the things these people point to—coming and going when you please, resting when you are tired, or taking a moment to recharge—are taken-for-granted aspects of everyday life and nearly synonymous with the idea of home. For those who lack access to officially sanctioned dwelling places, these basic necessities are often systematically prohibited by criminalization on the street and in the official systems of care.

Donna's and Andy's comments point to how the processes of unhoming not only deprive those without housing of the stability, autonomy, and security of home but produce the dependent subjects that they presuppose. It is their treatment on the streets and in shelters, not their lack of housing or deviant character, that prevents them from "getting ahead" or "having a life." In this context, the naming and decorating of tents are more than window dressing. The assertion that "our houses are just like theirs" reveals itself as a politics of refusal where people categorized as homeless create spaces that allow them to refuse a carceral politics of containment and spatial management but also the underlying settler notion of propertied personhood.

And yet, the very notion of home presupposes a relational space of not-home, an "away," as Sara Ahmed calls it.[29] Home requires a boundary—indeed, *is* a boundary, both physical and affective, between inside and outside, self and other. Whether that boundary is made of wood and concrete or plastic fencing and tarps, the boundary between home and not-home has an essentiality that for many feels so fundamental as to be almost visceral. For residents of Tent City 3, the essentiality of walls was expressed through the ideas of privacy and security.

Within and Against Property: The Social Production of Privacy and Security

The importance of boundaries and their role in producing homelike feelings of privacy and security was first expressed to me a couple of weeks after my arrival. Manny and I were strolling down a mansion-lined street in Seattle's North Capitol Hill neighborhood. It was cold, and the ubiquitous Seattle drizzle was falling. Manny, a tall, affable guy with long, straight black hair that he kept pulled back in a ponytail, was wearing an old-fashioned yellow rubber raincoat over his typical uniform of flannel shirt, hoody, jeans, and worn work boots. I had spoken to him a few times before but only in passing. I had been trying to arrange an interview with him for a while, but he had a regular construction gig and was seldom around the camp. When I finally had a chance to speak with him after he had been staying at Tent City 3 for about a month, he had agreed to an interview on the condition that we did it while walking. "I think way better when I walk," he told me in a characteristically chuckling voice that made it difficult to tell if he was joking or not. In this case, he was serious. So, as we dodged puddles on the root-raised sidewalk, the rain creating a steady background to our conversation, I asked him about his experiences and thoughts regarding the tent city. After a short pause he began, "Oh, I dunno, it's a lot better than a shelter."

"In what sense?" I asked.

"Well, [in a shelter] everybody's in together, out together, eat together. We all sleep in one room, y'know?" I nodded inside my raincoat hood, and he continued, growing more emphatic, "There is no sense of privacy! Here, you've got your own tent." He laughed as he concluded, "It's even got your name on it!" We walked on a bit in silence, listening to the radio-static sound of rain on our raincoats. After crossing a particularly busy street, I asked if he was serious about the tent name stuff. After a bit of teasing about my own admittedly stodgy tent name, I asked again. Continuing in a more serious tone, he explained, "That's pretty important 'cause it gives you more a feeling of that . . . that you're home, I guess. That you actually got a place to go lay your head at night, and you can keep your stuff there."

Manny's words stuck with me. Later that evening, I jotted a formula in my notebook: "(privacy = tent w/ name on it) + (stable place to lay your head) + (keep your stuff) = home." As I would come to discover, this haphazard formula and its oppositional relation to what many felt were the carceral spaces of shelters were consistently recurring themes in how folks described their relationship to the camp and one another.

In a world in which property and home are synonymous, Manny's association of home with a tent with your name on it, where you can lay your head and keep your stuff appears unremarkable. Philosopher Gaston Bachelard famously invokes a similar set of relations in his formulation of the home points as the physical manifestation of the psychological division between I and non-I. In Bachelard's formulation, it is the bounded space of home that both protects and enables the self to exist. It is the privacy provided by the protective physicality of the home that "shelters daydreaming . . . protects the dreamer . . . and allows one to dream in peace."[30] It is, in effect, the privacy enabled by the home/away boundary that enables humans to be human.

Bachelard's formulation of home as an insulated, protective space echoes the spatial imaginaries of what C. B. Macpherson and Ananya Roy have referred to as "possessive individualism" and "propertied citizenship," respectively. Here, the liberal presupposition of an autonomous rational individual that exists prior to and outside social relations must be reified, enforced, and enabled by the legal fiction of property. In this context, the propertied home constitutes the legal, figurative, and literal barrier between a subject and the outside world. The home as property serves as the physical and legal embodiment of our ability to create boundaries that shield us from outside judgment or interference and allow us to negotiate our own identities and interactions.[31]

These formulations of home and privacy rely, however, on strict divisions between private and public, inside and outside, and self and other. In other words, home for both Bachelard and liberal theorists is a very isolated, lonely, and individualistic place. It is also a space of control and violence. Liberal formulations of the property-privacy-home triad have relied since their inception on racialized, gendered, and colonial ideas of patriarchal control to enact violence against marginalized others in the name of protecting the home, hometown, and homeland. Nicholas Blomley notes, "While we are all inside property only a legally privileged few enjoy the full exclusionary benefits of liberal capitalist settler property, given the differential value attached to particular property arrangements" that occur within and through white supremacy and settler colonialism.[32] Property, borders, and other juridically constructed boundaries serve to constitute a social order that both masks the violence of a private property regime and organizes access for some while denying it to others. The naturalization of juridical property relations makes it possible for most Americans to take for granted the protective relationship among property, privacy, and personhood that defines the modern American homespace. However, for those who lack the wealth and privilege to access the protective yet exclusionary bounds of property, privacy—as the means through which inclusion and exclusion are mediated—becomes the terrain upon which home, nonhome, and unhoming occur.

Yet the terrain of the property-privacy-home nexus is far from fixed. Feminist scholars have long called attention to the ways that foregrounding the negotiated and contested nature of home and the public/private divide highlights the limits of the propertied conception of home and individuality. Unlike Bachelard's freely imagining individual, homemade identities are forged within and against wider social and spatial relations.[33] Home as a bounded realm is not merely a site of exclusion or identity formation but a relational site of production through which center and margin, normal and deviant, and self and other are constructed. Like the legal fiction of private property, propertied notions of privacy both rely upon and produce an ideal of bounded individualism largely at odds with the lived realities of homespace. In the real world, the freedom and autonomy that home-as-property provides is seldom complete. Rather, the boundaries and content of privacy are constantly negotiated in the context of complex relations of power. Even in a private household, unless one lives in complete isolation, privacy is limited. Parents, siblings, partners, housemates, and neighbors all negotiate a shared privacy within which localized and broader social norms are observed, enforced, and contested.

These complex entanglements of the relationship between privacy and possessive property are apparent in the ways residents conceived of privacy in the tent city. A frequent topic of conversation, privacy was discussed in a variety of scales and situations, but two main themes arose repeatedly: privacy was assumed to be necessary, and a lack of privacy was most often attributed to one's homeless status. Outside the tent city, residents are subjected to a world where shelters are chaotic and often harshly disciplinary, and trespassing, loitering, and sidewalk ordinances keep them constantly on the move. There is often literally no space where one can find a moment for private respite, security, or stability of place. In a world where one's possessions are considered trash to be swept up and thrown away, the physical barrier of the camp is a sometimes literal line in the sand between the homespace of the camp and the harsh and demeaning conditions of the outside world.

While most people in the tent city spoke of privacy as a natural right, there was also frequent talk of specific legal privacy rights. One of these was the Fourth Amendment. One of the defining features of the juridical public-private divide in the United States is the enhanced Fourth Amendment protection against unlawful entry, trespassing, and search and seizure that comes with access to private property. By contrast, people without housing often spend their time entirely in public space. As a result, their actions and behaviors are much more subject to carceral surveillance, seizure, and social control.[34] These incursions are deeply felt by those forced by necessity into public space.

For Tent City 3 residents, invoking privacy rights involved controlling and maintaining the boundary of the camp from the incursion of state authorities in the same way private spaces are protected. One story that illustrates the function of the camp border in the creation of homespace was told so frequently that it had reached a sort of legendary status in the camp. The story most often involved a tent city resident accused by a local shopkeeper of selling drugs nearby. The police were summoned, but by the time they arrived the perpetrator had returned to his tent in the tent city. At that point, things got exciting.

On the night of the retelling recounted here, the camp was abuzz with news of a drive-by shooting that had occurred only a few short blocks from the camp. Tent City 3 had recently moved to a locally notorious corner, and camp residents were already attuned to heightened levels of police and criminal activity around the camp. The shooting had set off a flurry of discussions about crime, safety, and fears that camp residents would be targeted by both police and criminals. When I got to the camp, a cluster of people were standing around the camp entrance discussing the day's events and their implications for the camp and its residents. It was an unusually pleasant March evening, and as a police cruiser slowly rolled by on the road adjacent to the camp, Aaron, who was working the EC desk at the time, took the opportunity to regale me once again with the story. Aaron was a hulking man with a shaved head and a booming voice. He had served in the military in both Iraq and Afghanistan and was a stickler for rules and order.

In his typically loud and confident voice, he explained, "Most cops are pretty good about it. They usually come straight to the desk and tell us what they are there for. But"—his voice quickened with enthusiasm—"this one time, they just came marching right in!"

Joe, a friend of Aaron's who was on security at the time, concurred: "Oh yeah ... they just came marching right in—asking people where this guy's tent was. Security had to escort them back to the desk!"

"Did they tell them where the guy was?" I asked, already knowing the answer but eager to hear Aaron's version.

"Nope," he boasted. "Our sign-in list is confidential! We don't have to tell them anything unless they have a warrant!"

"So, what happened?" I asked.

"Nothing, nada," Joe replied.

Before he could say more, Aaron broke in: "They just turned tail and left mumbling something about a warrant!"

The air of exceptionality that surrounds this story and the frequency of its retelling highlight the assumption of privacy in the city and the pride with which this privacy is regarded. In the mythology surrounding the incident, the unauthorized police entry represents a clear violation of what they felt was the private space of the tent city. All versions of the story agree on this particular point.

For the tellers, the story served as a demonstration of how Tent City 3 gave residents an ability to assert their Fourth Amendment rights against unlawful search and seizure, just like housed persons. Yet this assertion of privacy rights rests on a refusal of the propertied basis of privacy. It is also a reclamation of their status as rights-bearing humans as well as their claim to the specific rights of liberty and autonomy that the fourth amendment ostensibly protects. However, the sanctuary offered by informal dwelling is tenuous at best. As emphasized in the previous chapter, the existence of informal spaces and bodies within the American paradigm of propertied citizenship is always precarious.

Despite the pride many tent city residents took in the power of the camp barrier to exempt them from certain kinds of state interference, the reality is more complicated. The consent decree that enables the camp's existence requires that Tent City 3 ultimately grant the powers of inclusion and exclusion to the host property owner. In the story above, if the police really wanted to enter the tent city, it would be up to the property owner—not the camp. Likewise, if a warrant was obtained to search the camp, that warrant would be issued to the property owner, not the camp.

Fortunately, churches and private landowners have been extremely generous in ensuring that the tent city is seldom left without a home. Yet the private property provision of the consent decree, while enabling the existence of the camp, also produces its precarity. On the one hand, the private property mandate releases the city from the care and protection of its unhoused citizens by placing liability with the camp hosts. On the other, it makes the privacy, autonomy, and security of tent city residents dependent on the good faith of the host.

For those who have access to officially sanctioned property, it is easy to take for granted the notion that privacy is enforced not only through solid walls and locked doors but also through the laws and codes that mandate, support, and reinforce them. In the formal realm of property and the rights of ownership, the much-cherished right to privacy provided by the camp fence simply does not exist outside the limited rights granted by the consent decree. Rather, in the realm of the informally housed, rights that some consider human are precarious and contingent. As a small part of a larger encampment located on someone else's private property, there is scant legal privacy or property protection for residents of Tent City 3. Yet both the camp and the tent function as border zones that distinguish the legitimate (property) owner from the interloper and the homed from the homeless. As such, the invocation of private space is, for camp residents, a fundamental act of reclaiming home in the context of its denial.

This reclaiming occurred both within and against the exclusions of private property. Tent City, like many informal habitations, highlights the complex production of the privacy-personhood-homespace triad. In contrast to the rigid distinction between public and private established by propertied conceptions of home, in the realm of the informally housed, the line between public and private is far more fluid and less defined. As Nezar AlSayyad and Ananya Roy argue, the resident of the squatter encampment "is not simply a figure that is either included or excluded, within the gated enclave or outside it; rather, this figure is one that crafts intricate forms of negotiability and rationality."[35] In these spaces, boundaries are neither legal nor physical; rather, they are social products.

Given the idea of crafting negotiability and rationality, I want to return briefly to Manny's formula to explore the social production of privacy in the liminal space of the tent city. In the context of possessive individualism, Manny's association of home with a space of privacy where one can lay one's head and keep one's stuff appears unsurprising. For both Manny and Bachelard, home is primarily defined in terms of one's ability to feel a persistent sense of stability, privacy, and security. Yet, while Bachelard's home is a quiet, lonely space of the individual

The Making of Homespace 63

mind, Manny's, like the tent city itself, is imminently relational and social. Like Manny, most everyone spoke about the security and stability afforded by the private space of the tent as a fundamental aspect of home, especially in relation to its deprivation in shelters and streets. Yet, in contrast to the propertied privacy protection of ownership-based trespass law, privacy in the camp was a highly circumscribed and participatory endeavor.

Production of the Tent Commons

As Nicholas Blomley reminds us, the ownership model of property—where the right to exclude falls to a single entity, be it private or government—is only one way of conceiving of property and its protections. Without the physical and legal protections of private property, privacy in Tent City 3 was maintained through the enactment of shared beliefs and practices that constitute what Manuel Lutz has called "the tent commons."[36] Unlike individualist conceptions of ownership, Lutz notes, the tent commons is produced not only through the appropriation of space but also through commitment to the "power of collective labor to shared reproduction."[37]

If the idea of the commons today sounds naive or archaic, that is not because it doesn't exist but because we choose not to look. Common property—or, more simply, the commons—although often disregarded or denigrated in the ownership model of property, not only persists but is omnipresent.[38] From global squatter encampments to beaches to shared households, we encounter and experience the commons in many facets of our daily life as we negotiate the use and upkeep of shared spaces through interactions with our own housemates or with strangers in public space. If we fail to notice or recognize the commons, we render invisible whole swaths of human settlement and placemaking.

In the tent city, the role and importance of commoning for the production of the camp as homespace is particularly well illustrated through the collective provision of safety and security. Like privacy and the ability to come and go, security for themselves and their belongings was a highly valued aspect of life in Tent City 3. These three things were also deeply interconnected acts of collective commoning. This was certainly true for Donna, who had confided to me that when she first moved in she was constantly terrified of possible assault or theft: "It's just a flimsy-ass tent!" A few weeks later, I met Donna at a coffee shop where she worked as a barista. I asked her if she felt any safer now that she had had a chance to settle in. "Yeah, I do," she told me. "One thing we are really grateful for at Tent City is that we can pretty much leave anything there, and we know it won't be bothered because we haven't heard of *any* instances of theft or we haven't noticed anything disturbed. It just seems to be like a deeply respected code of honor." When I asked her to tell me more about this code of honor, she explained, "I think maybe part of it is because everyone has their own area. And everybody knows how valuable that is to have your own area. I mean we were freaking out [earlier] because we have never had—y'know—it's just a tent but it is *privacy*." In this exchange, Donna expressed the important interrelatedness of privacy, security, and stability. In her comment that it was a deeply respected code of honor, Donna highlighted a fundamental aspect of tent city homespace: that privacy and security are fundamentally collective.

Rick, who earlier decried the lack of autonomy in homeless shelters, spoke to the collective production of Donna's code of honor. When I asked him about issues of safety and security, he explained with an air of nostalgia, "In Alaska, man, you don't have to ask anybody for help—they instinctively—they know. And there is a little bit of that mentality here. If you want your stuff looked after, you need to look after the other guy's stuff too. 'Cause otherwise he ain't gonna look after your stuff. He ain't gonna care."[39] For both Donna and Rick, the private space of the camp and the tent were essential to their feelings of safety and security. Without the property-based protections of legal recognition or physical fortification, the privacy and security of tent city residents was the product of both necessity and tacit agreement.

For Michael the collective provision of security felt like home. Michael was the first person to link the social production of security and privacy with notions of home, although this too would become a common theme in my interviews and experience. When we sat down for an interview, Michael had been in Tent City 3 for just under a month. However, I had known Michael for the better part of ten years. Michael and I had come from the same small town in northern King County and had gone to rival high schools a few years apart. When I was in college, Michael worked in the Capitol Hill neighborhood where I lived, and we ran into each other from time to time and occasionally grabbed a beer together at the restaurant where he worked. Now, as residents of the same tent encampment, despite the awkwardness of interacting as interviewer and interviewee, Michael was as thoughtful, introspective, and talkative as ever.

When we sat down, the first question I asked was simply, "Why stay in the tent city?"

He began by emphatically stating that the tent city was his home. When I pressed him further, he touched on the privacy and freedom afforded by the camp. But as he reflected, he explained that for him, the homelike aspect of the tent city wasn't simply about personal space but also about his relation to others. It was not just that he could come and go as he pleased—or that his stuff would be safe. It was, in his words, because "even though there are people in the tent city that I don't really like or don't really even talk to, when I am outside the tent city I started referring to the tent city as my big dysfunctional family 'cause even though we don't always like each other or even know each other, there does seem to be the sense of helping each other at least in the sense of sharing the same circumstances—we together." He paused here for a moment before returning to the family theme that had been running through our conversations: "Like they say you don't have to like your brother, or your father or your mother, but you have to love them—that's something I like to follow in my daily life, and I think most people in the tent city are kind of the same way."

The more I got to know the camp, its residents and its rhythms, the more apparent the assessments of the relation between privacy and security and the social environment of the camp became. This, I think, was summed up best by Peter, a self-described Buddhist, foodie, and DJ, well known around the camp for his ability to wax poetic on any number of subjects. After he had lived in the camp for about a month, I asked him offhandedly, "So what do you think so far?"

He replied, "What do I think of tent city? I think tent city is an absolute blessing in disguise. And the reason why is because it's a place where people can actually call their home if they choose to. They have a place to live, they have security, they have food, a place where they can store their bags to go on and do their work, and if anything at all it's a little commune where people can actually choose to learn how to live with each other." Peter's connection of the material provision of privacy and security as a part of "choosing to learn how to live together" I believe succinctly summarizes the production of the tent commons. Here the propertied right to exclude is reformulated as a right to participate. The space of no property that defines homelessness becomes not an absence but an opening through which boundaries between inside and outside, us and them, self and other are open to negotiation, contestation, and experimentation.

Through collective practices of homemaking, tent city residents enacted a process of commoning. Through these practices, the liberties, protections, and privacy of home were produced and maintained not through juridical protection of private property but through practices of commoning. These practices both speak back to and render visible alternatives to settler logics of propertied enclosure, expulsion, and quarantine and are thus irreducible to their logics.[40] As Tessa Eidelman and Sara Safransky write in their overview of the commons, commoning practices are not only about producing homespaces but about producing "new social relations, forms of social life, creative encounters, and forms of sharing."[41] In Tent City 3, the practices of commoning enabled the spaces and protections of property not through title but through the shared and negotiated goals, practices, and participation of its inhabitants.

Rather than the strict normative divisions between public and private, ownership and exclusion, inside and outside that form the architecture of settler colonial territoriality, Tent City 3 residents crafted a homespace where the exclusions of propertied personhood could be resisted through collective practice. In contrast to a right to exclude enabled by access to wealth and privilege, the participatory inclusion of the tent commons blurs the boundaries between home and away, us and them, self and other, potentially opening the door, so to speak, to a broader and more expansive conception of home.

The commons, however, like home and the camp itself, is a process. It must be forged, and like the idea of home itself, that takes time. The homemaking practices of the tent city were not simply based on normative or nostalgic visions of home. Rather, residents drew upon culturally produced norms, experiences of exclusion, and the negotiated privacy of informality to inform ideas of home and homemaking in the tent commons. As such, the homespace of the tent city relied on a deeply localized and contextual understanding of home, self, and other.

In the space of the tent commons, the division between public and private is rethought as public and private for whom, and to what end? In Tent City 3 the practices of homemaking elaborated in this chapter were not simply individual efforts but a process of identifying oneself and each other as being both in relation and in common. But these are thin, fragile, and porous borders. Within days of my arrival in the tent city, I was approached by my neighbor who told me in a cautioning tone, "These tent walls are mighty thin. You can't fart without someone hearing. You have to watch what you say. Most people are pretty good [about respecting your privacy], but if you're not careful, pretty soon people will be all up in your business." While this word of caution may have been simply a polite way of complaining about my nightly snoring, the simultaneous affirmation of privacy and its opposite point to the particular sociality of space through which homeness was enabled.

Tents do not have locks, and thin nylon provides little in the way of actual physical privacy. As such, privacy and security in the tent city relied on a shared sense of being together and the surveillance that such arrangements entail. In other words, the ability of campers to conceive of their tents as private space required a tacit negotiation of intervention and nonintervention on the part of all residents. While possibly taken for granted, the coproduction of privacy and surveillance through which homespace was articulated was definitely public knowledge.

As the word of warning from my campmate suggests, the lack of privacy was painfully evident, despite the collective effort and desire to pretend otherwise. Nevertheless, at some level, most residents recognized that there was something necessary and perhaps even desirable about these constant incursions into one another's daily lives. As new residents quickly realize, the lack of privacy that arises from sharing close quarters (and thin walls) and the shared responsibility for the operation of the camp engender a type of disciplinary surveillance in the camp that ultimately serves as the territory upon which the norms of tent city belonging are enacted, negotiated, and contested.

Thinking about residents' attempts to create a homespace in which they refuse the carceral and dehumanizing logic of propertied personhood through practices of commoning enables alternative ways of thinking about property and home. However, the production of the commons likewise requires the production of subjects proper to those spaces.[42] The question then becomes, Who can be at home in Tent City 3 and how?

3. Becoming a Good Camper

Through their refusal of homeless subjectivity, camp residents produced the camp as a commons situated both within and against propertied exclusions. Yet to say that the tent city was a commons does not mean residents had anything in common. In fact, most people living in the camp were strangers most of the time. While domestic relations typically form and evolve over a period of years or decades, people were constantly coming and going from Tent City 3. Most people stayed only a few weeks, and very few stayed more than a year. In addition, the camp itself migrated every few months, resulting in radical changes in both space and population. Thus maintenance of the homespace of the camp required the ongoing production of Tent City subjects, or what I call "good campers."

Being a good camper was about giving, receiving, enabling, and fostering care. In the lexicon of Tent City 3, a person who actively contributed to the well-being of the camp through various volunteer duties or went out of their way to help fellow campers was referred to as a good camper. While not everyone embodied or desired good camper status, the specter of the good camper inhabited all aspects of tent city life. Whether spoken of overtly or not, the good camper functioned as the normative embodiment of desirable camp behavior.

In this chapter, I draw on Audra Simpson's concept of feeling citizenship and Jean-Luc Nancy's formulation of being-in-common to explore the development of a specific form of relational subjectivity of the good camper. Taking this figure as a guide, I focus on how the ethic and practices of care in the camp allow tent city residents to know themselves as unique individuals and as members of a specific population. I begin by elaborating how through their refusal of homeless subjectivities, residents reclaim feelings of autonomy, agency, and belonging in the acts of care that form the basis of the good camper. I then explore how the enactment of care allows people to feel and recognize themselves as not only autonomous agents but as active members of the camp collective. Next I turn to the ways the ethic of care that defines the good camper is fostered, demonstrated, and modeled through participation in camp maintenance and caring activities.

This ethic of care thus comes to underscore the good camper as a performative subject, simultaneously embodying and expanding the boundaries of inclusion through participation in both caring labor and the gift economy of the camp. The production of the good camper as both a caring and collective form of "feeling citizenship" thus allows the boundaries of home and citizenship to be rethought as neither fixed nor exclusionary but rather porous, participatory, and potentially expansive.

Through attention to the production of the good camper, I explore how the social order of the commons is produced and maintained in the space of Tent City 3 through "intercommunity recognition, affection, and care, outside the logic of colonial or imperial rule."[1] In her ethnographic exploration of Mohawk sovereignty in the settler colonial spaces of the United States and Canada, Simpson unpacks these emergent and relational subjectivities through a concept she calls "feeling citizenship." Formed in the complex web of sovereignty and exclusion that constitutes the Mohawk nation, feeling citizenship rejects the colonial hierarchies of state recognition produced and enforced through settler boundary-making. Both within and against these divisions, feeling citizenship is derived from affective feelings of belonging and practices of care in the context of shifting scales of inclusion and exclusion.

The idea of feeling citizenship allows for an interrelated articulation of collective belonging that, like life in Tent City 3, is neither entirely private nor public but instead is negotiated through a structured set of everyday practices. Mirroring the collective practices of privacy in the tent city, the concept of feeling citizenship, in its emphasis on affective notions of home and belonging, renders walls and borders porous, fluid, and expansive. Against the fixed and exclusionary walls of propertied and state citizenship, feeling citizenship creates space for thinking of the "unfolding, undetermined possibilities" of home.[2] Citizenship in this formulation is neither a formal status nor a static identity. Rather, it is an ongoing production of the self-in-relation-to, or what might be called "becoming together," in the sense of a collective subject that is particular but not fixed, bounded, or complete. It is in a perpetual state of relational subject formation that is never finished but always in process, always becoming.[3]

Becoming the Good Camper

I experienced an intentional transformation from person-off-the-street to good camper on my very first day. It was rainy and cold, and as I approached the camp from the bus stop across the street, I was nervous about what I was going to say. It had been a few weeks since the vote that allowed me to become researcher-resident. During that time the population of the tent city had swelled from about thirty to nearly eighty, and I had no idea whether the person on the desk would recognize me. As it turned out, Felix was on the desk. I had met Felix at my introductory meeting a few weeks prior. After a few minutes of small talk in which he chided me for waiting to move in ("Hopin' the weather would get better, weren't ya?"), Felix got down to the business of my intake. This consisted of an oral reading of the ten rules that make up the Tent City Code of Conduct. After reading each one and asking if I understood, he asked me to sign two copies: one he said was for the record and the other mine to keep. Next he took me on a brief tour of the camp. He pointed out the location of communal spaces, including the kitchen and TV room, as well as the porta-potties. As we walked around the camp, he explained that it was divided into sections, large communal tents at the front, private tents around the perimeter, and medium-size "couples' tents" clustered in a group toward the middle. I would start out in the large communal men's tent affectionately referred to as the Hilton (or sometimes the MASH because of its military origins). After I had been there for a while, Felix explained, I would be able to move into one of the small private tents on a space-available basis.

After the tour, we returned to the EC desk. Felix explained that one of the few requirements of tent city life was the performance of "security." He then explained all the duties that had to be performed while I was working my security shift: walking the perimeter, making coffee—there were far too many to absorb. "Don't worry," he said, somewhat forebodingly. "Somebody will always tell you what needs to be done." He next pointed to a clipboard with a week's worth of days divided into four-hour blocks. "You gotta complete your first security shift within twenty-four hours of sign-in," he explained. There were only two slots available—2 a.m. and 6 a.m. I chose the latter. "Great," he said, "now let's find you a spot!"

"Oh, and don't forget," Felix called over his shoulder, "if you miss the security shift or the weekly meeting, you'll be barred from the camp for three days!"

The things I experienced on this first day were not unrelated. On the contrary, in the course of my intake Felix was providing me with the ground rules for becoming a citizen of the tent city. Reading the rules and providing me with a signed copy established that I was an informed resident. Mapping out the layout of the city explained my place in the spatial hierarchy. And requiring attendance and security details ensured that I would perform the actions required for becoming a good camper.

Becoming a Good Camper

As with all aspects of Tent City 3, production of the good camper was also a refusal of homelessness. While new arrivals to the tent city arrived as strangers, they shared with their campmates a shared experience of estrangement and exclusion around which tent city norms were forged. As Sara Ahmed argues in reference to migrants, "The shared experience of not being fully at home . . . presupposes an absence of a shared terrain," yet this absence or lack of home "becomes reinscribed as the precondition of an act of making."[4] The good camper is a subject formed against and within domicidal exclusion.

Against stereotypes of pathology and dependency that constitute the homeless subject, the practices of care and recognitions that produce the tent city citizen foreground the dignity, autonomy, and respect of camp members in the practices of collective self-management of camp space. In contrast to the mainstream shelter system, the camp is run entirely by the residents. In practice, this means that residents are responsible for the day-to-day maintenance of the camp. For many, this aspect of the camp is fundamental to establishing a feeling of belonging in the camp and reclaiming the dignity and humanity denied on the streets. Nick, who had been without housing for several years but had only been in the tent city for a couple of weeks, emphasized that the participatory structure of the camp affected both his personal and collective identity. In reference to the police and shelter workers, he emphasized that "they treat you like you're a little kid, and after a while, you become a little kid—it's really easy to fall into that 'bum' role if that's how everyone treats you. Here, you're responsible for something. If you don't like it, you can work to change it. If you don't do what you say you're gonna do, everyone suffers—yeah, it's a big deal!" Nick would know. Unlike most camp residents, he had been without stable housing all his adult life. Having aged out of foster care into homelessness in northern King County, he had bounced around the shelter system for a couple of years before deciding he would be better off on his own. Nick alternated between living in the Jungle, a large informal encampment on the city's south side, and various squats in vacant houses and apartment buildings. Now almost forty, with slicked-back brown hair and a slight body covered in tattoos, he considered himself an expert on the various lifestyles of "the homeless."

Of all the homeless types identified, he most despised what he called "the bums." According to him, bums weren't born; rather they were created by the "homeless industrial complex." The shelters, soup kitchens, and government offices, he argued, treated people like "such idiots, such utter imbeciles" that eventually they started to believe it. For Nick, self-provision of shelter, whether alone or collectively, "keeps people sane by reminding them that they are human." In his outward disgust for bums, Nick articulates refusal. For him, the space of Tent City 3 recognizes and allows this refusal.

For many campers, participating in the everyday operations of the tent city offered a sense of individual dignity and agency denied them outside the camp. This often came through in campers' interactions with the general public. During camp tours, at neighborhood meetings, and at church- or host-sponsored events, residents often included their in-camp duties in their introductions. Introductions like "Hi, I am John, and I am the camp kitchen coordinator" (or tent master, donations coordinator, etc.) were common refrains. Though camp members seldom reflected on this self-identification, it was frequently noticed by noncampers and camp hosts, who noted with surprise residents' "pride" and "sense of ownership."

For those outside the tent city who see individual labor and ownership as capitalist virtues to be fostered and admired, these traits undoubtedly appeared exceptional in those they considered homeless. Yet, in a world where those without housing were stripped of nearly all agency or responsibility—as clients, consumers, or objects of charity for some, or as garbage, criminals, or blight for others—noting one's camp occupation was a way of putting oneself on an equal footing with others and reclaiming one's dignity and agency. As one tent master explained, "I used to do a lot of set work, building rooms and such. But now I got this record and all these failure-to-appears, nobody will hire me to do shit. Fixing tents and building stuff at least reminds me that I still have skills." This camper's comments point to the particular mechanics of participation in the tent city.

This was care work. Through applying their construction skills, they were able to reclaim the sense of humanity and self-worth they had lost, but this worth was enacted through practices of care—in this case, "fixing tents and building stuff." Unlike waged work, participating in camp maintenance paid no money and offered no individual rewards. Although people spoke of personal dignity and purpose, these terms only had meaning within the collective maintenance of the homespace of the camp. These were not jobs; they were necessities, and the payment was a feeling of usefulness and collective membership in the camp.

The felt linkage between the deprivations brought about by one's homeless status and feelings of collective belonging was driven home one day by Monica, who burst out as we returned to camp after a church-provided meal, "It makes me really just angry." Her anger stemmed not from the meal itself, which was delicious, but from the fact that the volunteers serving the meal seemed to have no interest in getting to know, or even interacting with, their unhoused guests. Monica had come to the tent city a few months earlier after a bad breakup. Raised middle-class in the Chicago area, she likely had little experience with life without access to property. Having been brought up Baptist, however, she did have experience in churches. She had gone to dinner well dressed in blouse, jeans, and leather jacket and was very much looking forward to sharing a meal with what she most likely felt were her people. But unfortunately, they did not feel that way to her. Clearly frustrated by her dinner experience, she explained through welling tears that "all these organizations just want to help, and they're like, we're here for the needy, but you go to churches or whatever, and you feel like you can only talk to other homeless people. You're made to feel like you're an outsider. You're made to feel like you are a lower form of human being." As we walked, we shared a smoke and tried to lighten the mood by doing mock impersonations of the folks we met at dinner. As we got closer to camp, she gestured toward the entrance, and her tone softened. "At least around here, people understand. Sometimes if you feel like you're actually doing something, actually contributing something, it does give you a little bit more energy—it's just that sense of strength in numbers." Like Nick above, the exasperation Monica experienced from being treated as less than human was alleviated not by personal freedom or individualized autonomy but through a sense of "contributing something."

While many indicated that they felt a heightened sense of purpose and personal dignity as a result of performing various camp duties, most foregrounded the importance of these duties in terms of the successful functioning of the camp as a whole. Nick's claim that in the shelter system "they treat you like a little kid" was immediately followed not by claims of personal responsibility but in terms of the collective well-being of the camp insofar as "if you don't do what you say you're gonna do, everyone suffers." Responses such as these were common. Most often these responses were framed in the context of "doing my part" or "being a good camper."

While participation in the self-managed structure of the tent city allowed residents to define themselves as productive and active agents, it also enabled the articulation of autonomy in terms of their relation to the tent city community. Or, in other words, to be a good camper meant to recognize oneself and to be recognized as a citizen of Tent City 3.

Recognizing the Good Camper

Recognition—to recognize oneself and to be recognized as proper to a place—lies at the core of ideas of home, belonging, and citizenship. Yet recognition is a double-edged sword. Recognition can also mean acknowledgment of a subjectivity. In contexts of settler colonialism and racial capitalism, for instance, Indigenous or Black recognition is simultaneously a recognition of one's status as not fully human—not fully citizen and thus subject to the carceral violence of the settler state. At the same time, recognition can also form the basis for a decolonial politics of belonging. In refusing recognition as a dependent pathologized homeless subject, the participatory space of Tent City 3 also opens space for new forms of recognition grounded in practices of care and mutual aid.

One of the primary ways newcomers to the tent city began to recognize or feel part of the production of the camps as homespace was by performing security duty. Of all the duties necessary to the functioning of the camp, security duty is the most ubiquitous and visible. At all times—twenty-four hours a day, seven days a week, 365 days a year—there are two security personnel on duty. Each security shift is four hours long, and the number of "securities" required each week ranges from one to three per person, depending on the population of the camp (at one low point, in which there were only around twenty camp members, five securities were required).

Security duty, performed in teams of two, is not only one of the few requirements that every camp member must perform but also one of the very first tasks one performs upon becoming a tent city resident. It is also one of the most highly valued (both symbolically and pragmatically) aspects of life in Tent City 3. As such, it is a key mechanism through which citizenship is performed and regulated. Camp residents often emphasize that security "makes the camp run." This is quite literally true.

Security duty is also care work. Despite the connotation of the name, there is no resemblance between what, in Tent City 3 parlance, is called security duty and the militarized forms of private property and border protection that the term security guard often evokes. As the name implies, the performance of security is, in a very small way, about literally securing the space of the camp. Security duties include walking both the inside perimeter and around the immediate vicinity of the camp, checking for suspicious activity or rule violations. However, this absorbs on average less than one percent of security time or effort. The largest part of security duty by far involves social reproduction and maintaining the camp as a homelike space. For instance, most security duty shifts are spent picking up trash in the camp and the surrounding neighborhood, making coffee, keeping the kitchen clean, refilling water jugs, checking cleanliness and toilet paper availability in the porta-potties, noting rule violations, helping with donations, performing wake-ups (the practice of knocking on tents to arouse people with early morning appointments), emptying the trash, alerting campers of visitors or phone calls, and many other miscellaneous duties.[5] Not surprisingly, those on security duty are often the busiest members of the camp. When security is needed for any reason, whether it is a shortage of toilet paper or the arrival of a carload of donations, one simply yells out "Security!" as a summons. As a result, the shouted word "Security!" issuing forth from various parts of the camp is as much a part of the auditory landscape of camp life as the morning chirp of birds or jets soaring overhead.

In this sense, security performs the function of maintaining the homespace while also allowing those on security duty to recognize themselves and be recognized or become feeling citizens in the production of collective well-being. In the negotiated commons of the tent city, the enactment of home falls outside the domestic bonds of family and kinship, while being negotiated below the level of the formal state-subject relationship often conjured by the notion of citizenship. Within the blurred boundaries between public and private in the tent city commons, normally private or domestic functions are shared duties performed in public and as such are formative. Here care becomes the essential act of commoning through which the commons is produced, and commoners come to recognize themselves and be recognized as part of a collective.

While many viewed security duty with begrudging acceptance, most acknowledged that the practices of care they performed during their security shift played an integral part in developing feelings of care, affection, and belonging. These sentiments were clearly expressed through the traditionally gendered assumptions of care work in a conversation I had with Michael over coffee at the café adjacent to the camp where many of my interviews took place. Michael, who was nearly 6'2" and sported a mustache that evoked something between Groucho Marx and Mario of the Mario Brothers, was wearing an exceptionally dated pair of nylon shorts and a tank top with a heavy red plaid flannel shirt draped over the top. It was an awful ensemble. "Oh my god," I said, or something like that—I didn't record this part— "I didn't know this was a date, I would have worn something more appropriate!"

"Fuck you!" he cried, feigning offense. "I live in a tent, and it's laundry day."

After talking about old times and sharing gossip, we got down to talking about the tent city. Michael was typically thoughtful and introspective. When I asked him what he thought about security duty, he seemed to have a ready answer. "Security is all about do unto others as you would have them do unto you," he began, stopping just long enough to take a sip of his latte. "It's about making sure there is a sense of cleanliness, order, home—taking the mother role without being the father." I raised my eyebrows at what I thought at the moment was an odd use of gender stereotypes, but he continued unabated. "Security is the mother—making sure there is fresh water, making sure there is coffee made, making sure the kitchen is clean, making sure everyone's needs are met, and if anyone is in trouble, helping them and making sure their needs are met—I think it can help people be more empathetic toward others."

In invoking the feminized stereotype of the mother-as-homemaker, Michael's comment calls attention to both the caring and affective aspects of social reproduction embodied in security duty. At the same time, however, by emphasizing not just the performance of security duty itself but also how the caring acts of security are potentially formative for those who perform them, he illustrates one way that caring acts done while on security duty were an integral part of the process of becoming feeling citizens.

While Michael was the only one who spoke of security duty in explicitly gendered terms, Michael's assessment of the function of security duty was surprisingly widespread. Being both required and essential, the caring aspects of security duties were simultaneously a source of pride, a way of giving back, and a manifestation of responsibility that made them feel as if they were active agents rather than guests at the tent city. On one particularly beautiful spring morning, I was sharing a 5 a.m. security shift with Jim, a forty-something man with weathered skin and bright blue eyes. He was fresh from an Alaska fishing gig but got stranded in Seattle when the contract he had with the fishing company was canceled. It was cold, and we must have looked like old-fashioned hobos in our many mismatched layers, each of us with a cigarette in one hand and a Styrofoam cup of coffee in the other.

While he and I slowly walked the perimeter of the camp, watching the sunrise and talking about Alaska, his kids, and his incredibly complicated and clearly devastating divorce, he told me that morning shifts were his favorite. He explained that he liked watching over the camp while everybody slept: "I love mornings. Walkin' security right now makes me feel like I am part guard dog, part host. Like this whole thing is my hotel, and I am in charge of making sure everyone has a good, safe visit." While the gendered presuppositions of care work were masculinized in this conversation, Jim's assessment echoes Michael's. For him, the caring labor involved in watching the camp, making coffee, filling water tanks, emptying trash, and performing wake-ups created an affective connection between Jim and the camp that evoked a sense of pride and belonging through which he was able to recognize himself as a valued member of the collective.

On another occasion I was walking security with Donna, with whom I had become friends by this time. On this day, she had expressed annoyance with people who complained about having to perform security duty. When I asked her why, she told me, "Because it's their *job*. We don't pay rent here. A few hours a week pitchin' in to help is *really* not much to ask in return for a place to stay." However, after a few moments, she added, "Personally, I like security duty. Most of the time, I totally feel like some kind of hopeless charity case. When I'm on security, I get to kind of like be the one helping for a change, right?" Performing security duties enabled campers to come to know themselves both as individuals and as members of a population in the context of the tent city. While security was, for many, often burdensome and sometimes miserable (especially in wet, cold weather), performing the care work of security duty was a way for residents to exercise a level of agency often denied them and realize themselves not simply as autonomous individuals but as active members of a collective—to become, in effect, feeling citizens.

Performing security duty isn't simply about recognizing oneself as a member of the collective; it also produces a specific form of subjectivity necessary for the functioning of the camp commons as homespace. This is no easy feat. Since its inception, Tent City has prided itself on the fact that it is open to anyone who participates in camp duties and abides by the camp code of conduct. The only time people are turned away is if there is no space available, if they are barred from the camp for violating the code of conduct, or if they are or have children under the age of eighteen. New people arrive nearly every day. They arrive as strangers, but they do not stay that way. Just as the commons comes into existence through acts of commoning, so must the citizens of the tent city become familiar, homely, in common.[6] Over the course of the prior ten years, the camp had developed a vast culture of informal social control and subjectification through which newcomers came to be citizens of the Tent City commons.

Disciplining the Good Camper

As is the case with any social grouping, the making of a good camper occurred through an ongoing process of discipline and social control that demonstrated and demarcated the boundaries of inclusion and exclusion. Security duty was essential to this process. I asked about this when I had a chance to sit down with one of what I had come to consider the camp's elders. Mel had been in the camp for well over a year. An air force veteran in his late sixties, he had a bald head and a short-cropped gray beard that stood out on his dark brown skin. Mel received a monthly check from the Veterans Administration and a small disability payment from a work accident he had sustained a few years prior. He told me it "was enough to survive but not enough to live anyplace worth living." Tent City 3, he said, suited him "just fine as a retirement home." Every month, when Mel received his check, he treated himself to a dinner out and a couple of nights in a motel. As a longtime resident of the camp, he was treated with a good bit of reverence around the camp and was frequently called upon to serve on the camp executive committee and in various other volunteer positions.

As a result, Mel had extensive experience with new campers. Indeed, he was the first camper to take me under his wing and went out of his way to integrate me into camp life. Because of this, although we talked all the time about growing up in the segregated South and our shared love of the outdoors, I was eager to sit down for a formal interview. He agreed but only if we could do it over dinner. So, while we munched on a loaf of sourdough as we waited for our entrees at a local bistro, I asked him about how, as a camp leader of sorts, he integrated new members into the camp. "Well," he began, pausing to wipe his face with a napkin, "the older campers sit back and watch and see how you do on security."

"Because everybody," he explained through a mouthful of warm buttered bread, "has to do securities, and we won't—well, I won't—straight out tell them what to do. More like I'll *suggest*. It allows them to know what's expected of them—and it should happen right away. There shouldn't be no surprise—'Oh well, you didn't tell me this.' You should know right away what's expected of you. As we always state, this is a working camp. Without security, we don't run." As Mel's assessment illustrates, the disciplinary function of security duty was acknowledged and actively utilized by camp residents.

For many, performing security duty provided an obvious opportunity for both learning and mentorship. Indeed, as a researcher (and new member of the camp), I found security duty one of the most fruitful opportunities for understanding how the tent city functioned. At times, I felt that simply donning the bright orange vest with the word "Tent City 3 Security" handwritten across the back was an open invitation for friendly advice and gentle (and sometimes not so gentle) correction.

Through the demarcation of desirable from forbidden behavior, security duty operated as a disciplinary mechanism in producing the relationships and practices that defined tent city citizenship. While there was great leeway in which duties were required while on security, consistently shirking those duties (by sitting, reading, or watching TV) caused the individual, no matter how friendly or outgoing, to be at least treated with suspicion, or in extreme cases shunned or even barred. However, the converse was also true. Even the most introverted or churlish, if they diligently conducted their security duties and heeded more seasoned campers' suggestions, were considered valued members of the camp. As Rick, who by this time had been in the camp almost a year, put it, "[If] you get up, and you do your job like you're supposed to . . . it doesn't matter if you dislike someone or not, you gotta be fair—they are members of the camp." Rick's thoughts were not unique—nor was it just old-timers who viewed security this way.

The utilization of security shifts as a conscious disciplinary mechanism was so widespread that at times the informal policing of people correcting the missteps of security personnel itself became disciplinary. Gossip in the camp was incessant. Perhaps it was the central location of the public areas, often situated between the EC desk and the residential spaces of the camp, but at some point, conversation would turn to those on security and the EC who were responsible for their supervision.

Over cigarettes, coffee, and maybe some donated day-old pastries, campers, usually but not always old-timers, would dissect the work being done (or not) around them. Recalling one of these times, Rick, in his typical loud, gruff, but somehow also endearing way, recalled one of these episodes in a one-on-one interview. While we sipped coffee and before I had even formally started the interview, he jumped right in: "What I don't like about some campers is that they will sit there, and they will let new campers—if they don't like 'em—get in trouble."

Although I already suspected he was telling me this as a way to vent about a fellow longtime camper, I nodded and asked, "Like who?"

He banged both hands on the table and yelled, "Ralph Falcone for one. He *knows* that security is not supposed to be in the TV room watchin' TV, all right?

And I walked in over there, and what is happening? There is Ralph Falcone and like two new security folks—in the TV room sittin' down bumpin' their gums! The first thing I said was 'Ralph, WHAT THE HELL ARE YOU DOIN', MAN?' You have been around this system long enough to know. What are you trying to do? Get them kicked out? Do you not like these people or something?" For Rick, despite his exasperation, his concern was not primarily Ralph's poor behavior but the consequences that behavior might have on the social development of the two new security people. In his mind, like Mel above, Rick felt that one's ability to fit in and, in his words, "be happy campers" was directly correlated to being consistently reminded of the right thing to do.

However, this operated both ways. In my discussions with residents who had been there less than a month, people valued being informed and even gently corrected but bristled and often complained or refused to work with those they felt were too "bossy" or on "power trips." One middle-aged woman I interviewed after she had been in camp about five days explained that during her second security shift, her security partner, who had been in the camp for nearly a year, "sat there and rode my ass the entire time . . . so I was like I'm not even gonna do anything—maybe she'll leave me alone." But her next shift was different "because [my partner] had a good attitude. He was just doing his job, not really expecting anything, and that created the desire in me to help him—and we got a ton done!" Through these ongoing interactions among security personnel and between security and the general population, the bounds of tent city subjectivity and belonging were negotiated and reproduced.

The production of this normative order, however, differs from the hardened boundaries of ownership that divide insider from outsider, us from them, or homeless from homed. Through the slow, constant, ongoing process of homemaking in the tent city, people were able to recognize and be recognized, to become feeling citizens.

In addition to formalized care work, the development of feeling citizenship was also evident in more aesthetic forms of expression in the camp. These took the form of sometimes transitory tent and common area decorations, or intentional arrangements of chairs in the common area to foster conversations, or even occasionally the artful plating of donated food or pastries. Aesthetic touches like these are common within encampments large and small in the United States and globally. As Jessie Speer points out regarding a camp in Fresno, California, encampment dwellers engage in an ongoing struggle to claim and shape domestic space in the context of state intervention and propertied colonialism.[7] Similarly, tent city residents sought through their homemaking practices to reclaim domestic agency and to assert "alternative notions of home grounded in community rather than family, mutual care rather than institutional care."[8]

For instance, one woman had a stuffed moose that she frequently rearranged into different scenarios and situations. When somebody donated a child's tea set to the camp, Moose was at a tea party. Other times, he frolicked with other stuffed animals or held signs with inspirational sayings. At one point he even had his own tiny tent (another donation), aptly named Moose Lodge. When I asked Moose's owner about it, she said that it had originally started as a joke. But when the camp switched locations and gained a large number of new residents, she saw it as a way to make new residents feel at home. "Really," she told me finally, "he is just my way of spreading a little sunshine—remind people not to take things too seriously." Although clearly an expression of its owner's personality and sense of humor, Moose's presence in the camp projected a normative view of mutual care and belonging.

Similarly, Peter, always the philosopher, maintained an elaborate altar outside his tent, composed of objects collected during his travels that expressed his beliefs and his relationship to others. When I asked him about it, he explained, "I have pictures of all these saints that I've put up there. Right when you walk in, you can see all these saints. So, if you take from me, you have all these things looking right at you." But what I initially took to be an explanation of an elaborate guilt-powered antitheft device soon morphed into something much more personal. When I asked about the altar's effectiveness, he shook his head, laughed, and said, "I try to look at it like just, hey man, try to take care of each other, I mean, try. And my three rules is this; if you can't love them, try to understand them. Which is, they're both hard. And if you can't love them or understand them, just try to be kind to them—that's the least thing you can do is be kind. And that's all you can do really. Those are the three greatest things that I believe you can do for anyone. That's why I put that shit right front and center on my doorstep." Like the moose doll, Peter's altar wasn't simply a projection of personal identity but rather an expression of himself and his hopes for his community.

In many ways, Moose and Peter's altar were not unlike yard decorations or a tiny library placed outside a suburban home—a way of inserting one's feelings and desires into a public space, a way to make a city a home. Yet in the context of a transient encampment with an extremely fluid and often stressed-out population, these practices of homemaking reflected a refusal of homelessness and a visible invocation of care and belonging.

Care and the Performance of the Good Camper

Attributes of care and belonging were not simply decorative. In the course of the everyday practices of Tent City 3, residents performatively embodied the collective recognition, care, and belonging that demarcated the good camper through mundane but essential practices of camp maintenance. In addition to security duty, many other volunteer-based positions were necessary to the functioning and maintenance of the camp. These included kitchen coordinator, donations coordinator, bookkeeper, and tent master. In their own ways, the care work performed in these positions was a visible and performative embodiment of the good camper.

Manny summed this up perfectly one day while we were hanging out in the camp's communal area. Manny and I had been discussing how a young couple, who had arrived at the camp shortly after the move to Saint Mark's, were faring. "Broadway rats," Manny had called them with his kidding-but-not-kidding chuckle. He was referring to the young, often liberally tattooed and pierced youth who often panhandled and socialized on the nearby and historically diversity-tolerant avenue nearby. These youths were somewhat notorious for crashing for a few days at the camp when it was in the neighborhood. When the couple arrived, nobody thought they would stick around long.

However, as Manny and I were now discussing, this couple had now been staying for a couple of weeks, and as Manny made a point of noting, one of them had even volunteered for kitchen duty at the last meeting. "Yeah," Manny said when I questioned him about this, "they're more used to people and stuff. They are more comfortable—they know more people. They've become part of the family, I guess." While it may be simple familiarity that for Manny indicates family, this familiarity is a product not of simple proximity but rather of a comfort expressed as the caring practice of cleaning the kitchen. The meaning of family here is specific. One becomes part of the "family" not simply by becoming more familiar but through contributing to the process of homemaking that marks the camp as homespace.

Often but not always filled by people who had been in the camp for a month or more, volunteer positions like kitchen coordinator were chosen by nomination and vote at the end of every camp meeting. When the time came, campers nominated somebody for each position. Sometimes people nominated friends or people they felt had done the work well in the past. More often, though, nominees pulled someone aside before the meeting to ask if that person would be

Becoming a Good Camper 83

willing to nominate them. If the nominee accepted, the camp voted to approve or disapprove. In practice, the vote was a technicality. During the entirety of my stay, I never witnessed a disapproving vote.

Like security duty, these everyday maintenance tasks were integral to the formation and naturalization of the ethic of care that marked the good camper. In my interviews with people who had served in these positions, many cited a desire for a sense of purpose or giving back as a reason for accepting a nomination. In practice, the enactment of these duties seldom appeared entirely personal or altruistic. Instead, this everyday care work also had a performative function. Regardless of intention, the effect of accepting the position and publicly performing these everyday care and maintenance tasks was to continually enact and reenact a normative vision of the good camper.

In some cases, this normative performativity began at the nomination stage. For example, there were a few instances in which people either volunteered or were nominated for a position but, for any number of reasons, were not capable of performing its required duties. Not once during my stay was someone denied. In these cases, other campers would often volunteer as assistant. In fact, sometimes there were as many as four assistants. One such assistant offered the following explanation: "Even folks who are physically or emotionally unable to do the whole job should at least have the chance to take part." In these cases, both the volunteer and the assistants were enacting normative ideals of tent city belonging. As in the performance of security duty, the normative values of autonomy and responsibility were enacted as inseparable from equally normative performances of inclusion and care. In these moments, the boundaries of belonging were reiterated and expanded.

As the example of assistant volunteers illustrates, in the performative arena of tent city citizenship, markers of homeless pathology were reconfigured as assets. Although an internal survey conducted by SHARE in 2006 found that 30 percent of tent city residents reported having a mental illness and roughly 10 percent reported issues with substance abuse, these attributes did not preclude members from active citizenship or service in positions of leadership.

In fact, during my observations and interviews, neither mental illness nor substance abuse seemed much of a hindrance in terms of either participation or social standing. As one resident put it, "Yeah, there are people with all sorts of problems 'round here. It's like the land of broken toys—makes us unique!" Occasionally, this uniqueness combined with collective governance manifested itself in interesting ways. For instance, those with amphetamine habits often volunteered or were elected to perform detailed or repetitive tasks, like sweeping the camp or scouring the coffee pots, because of their incredibly high prowess in these areas. Likewise, those with bipolar disorder often made highly motivated and effective public speakers during manic spells. As these examples illustrate, neither homelessness nor mental illness nor substance abuse necessarily precluded active citizenship or self-governance. Rather, the presence of these attributes served to reinscribe and expand these categories in ways that were responsive to the needs of both the individual and the group.

The performance of camp maintenance likewise served a spectacular function that was not lost on those who volunteered. As one resident told me in response to my asking why she seemed to volunteer so often, "I stood up again 'cause I am sick and tired of people who don't volunteer. If you are not a part of the solution, you are part of the problem! I wanted to show these people what it means to be a productive member of this community." Others made a spectacle of the act itself, loudly proclaiming things like "Looks like Alfred left a mess in the microwave again!" while cleaning the kitchen tent. Occasionally, competition and arguments erupted over who was the most communitarian in the performance of service tasks. Donations coordinators, whose job it was to categorize, store, and distribute donated goods, often publicly accused those who had performed the duty in the past of favoritism or hoarding. Likewise, tent masters who were charged with repair and maintenance of the tents often declared that unlike other tent masters, they would perform repairs in the order they received the requests rather than prioritizing friends. Through such spectacles, residents, both in performing an act and in calling attention to that act, managed the tent city trifecta of foregrounding their own autonomy, their caring labor, and the normative boundaries of tent city citizenship.

An ethic of care is enacted through mandatory participation in security duty, the election of people for volunteer duties, and the informal labor of assistants to those positions. As simultaneously personal, communitarian, and spectacular, these volunteer activities—cleaning the kitchen, fixing the tents, restocking the toilet paper, and so on—highlight the performative aspects of tent city citizenship. These caring practices constitute at once the subject, the subject's relation to the community, and the conditions through which the performances of tent city citizenship are reproduced. Through their repetition, the everyday maintenance activities of the camp function as a sort of ritualized production that both illustrate and naturalize the participatory norms of being a good camper.

The Good Camper *as* Becoming

In the production, enactment, and recognition of the figure of the good camper as a performative subjectivity of care and collective inclusion, the refusal of homelessness became something more. It became a "re-envisioning of and re-embodiment" of citizenship and home formed within and against the logic of coloniality.[9] The result was a form of participatory belonging in the tent city that was manifested through acts of care and inclusion captured in Jean-Luc Nancy's concept of "being-in-common." Nancy uses this concept to elaborate an idea of community that is neither preexisting nor exclusionary but imagines a togetherness where the boundaries of both self and community are relational and open.[10]

Though often unspoken or perhaps taken for granted, these combined ideas of an emergent and fluid sense of belonging manifested through an ethic and practice of care underpinned much of what residents considered the homelike aspects of the tent city. Although built upon the space of the camp and expressed through the tents themselves, care and caring were similarly fundamental to the production of the homespace of the tent city.

In the camp, care practices were frequently enacted through the distribution of resources. Many necessities in Tent City were provided. The tents were donated, as were coolers, desks, tables, the coffee maker, and the microwave. Some food was also donated. Community and church groups, as well as individuals, often brought meals to the tent city. People donated foodstuffs. There were nearly always day-old pastries and some canned food in the kitchen. But donations were spotty and unpredictable, and arranged meals did not always fit people's schedules. Thus one of the more common practices was the sharing of food.

It was not uncommon for residents to pool food resources to provide for more than themselves or to combine SNAP allotments to capitalize on bulk discounts. These acts of food sharing were a very small part of the ongoing practices of care and mutual aid that allowed camp residents to enact and reclaim a sense of home and belonging. I had a chance to discuss this at length with Brian and Tanya. Both in their late twenties, the couple had migrated to Seattle from Los Angeles the previous November. Lured by a job offer that turned out to be fraudulent, the couple found themselves in the tent city. Both were deeply dedicated to giving back to the camp, because, as they humbly put it, "we get bored easily."

On one particularly sunny day in May, Eric, my tent neighbor at the time, and I accompanied the couple to the nearest food bank. We had carefully calibrated our lists so that we each focused on certain items of need in the camp. When we returned, our scrounged wheeled luggage carrier was completely loaded, and Tanya's backpack was so full it pressed against her large Afro, giving her a mushroomy look. This was my first trip on the tent city wagon train to the food bank. But it was neither the first nor the last for camp residents. Although group trips to the food bank were not a regular occurrence, they were part of a practiced culture of care and gift. After we returned from our trip and put away our bounty in the coolers and milk crates that lined the sides of the kitchen tent, I sat down with Brian and Tanya to speak with them about the practice.

They were one of those couples who were so ridiculously into one another that it was hard to tell where one started and the other began. They also teased each other relentlessly and had a habit of finishing one another's sentences. Tanya, who was tall and strongly built with hair that made her appear even larger, was well known for preparing huge meals cobbled together from donated goods, so I began our conversation there. "It all started in Skyway," Brian began before Tanya interjected, "People were saying they hated each other. It was bad." It had been January. The weather was cold, and the camp was located in a remote part of the city.

Brian, who was even taller than Tanya, had twinkling blue eyes, straight black hair, and an eager, expressive face that must have made him an awful poker player. He continued, "A couple of days when we were over at Skyway, we didn't even have any food." Tanya then explained that when the food began to run dangerously low, she went to the kitchen coordinator to ask if she could scrounge the supply bin. In it she found some old military rations and created enough of a haphazard version of sloppy joes to feed the whole camp. Later, she was able to create some spaghetti with donated ramen noodles and scrounged tomato sauce. After some reticence on the part of the other campers, she soon became known as the unofficial cook of that location. These wintertime meals were somewhat of a legend among campers who lived at the Skyway camp that slushy winter. While nobody thought the food was good, many credited Tanya with not only feeding the camp but providing the morale boost necessary to get them through and keep the camp running.

They were, however, quick to remind me that Tanya's actions weren't unique or even uncommon. When the camp moved to the much more centrally located (and wealthy) Saint Mark's Cathedral, there was a dramatic uptick in donated meals, and the church hosted dinner once a week. The duo felt that there was less need to cook but the camp lacked the snacks and staples necessary to fill in the gaps. They recruited a couple of friends and started what they called "the wagon train." When I asked if they ever felt taken for granted or overburdened, both vehemently shook their heads.

"No way," Brian said, still shaking his head. "There's always somebody pitching in—you just gotta keep an eye out—"

Tanya broke in, "It's not always in food . . . it's whether someone needs something or help with their tent. They help them out in that way. You know, it's just capable people helping each other."

Brian again spoke up. "You get a real sense of family that way . . . yeah."

While Brian's point about a sense of family echoes Michael's association of family with mutual care, Tanya's reference to capable people helping is a reminder that the particular contours of home in the tent city always occur in relation to the presupposition of dependence and pathology that justifies the unhoming practices that occur in more formalized spaces of care.

Brian and Tanya's comments did not come as a surprise. In fact, they echoed much of my experience dwelling in Tent City 3. When I returned from the hospital to find a homemade footrest and an array of pain medications in my tent, while the footrest was a surprise, the painkillers were not. Over the time I spent living in the tent city, residents proved themselves to be both extremely generous and knowledgeable when it came to nearly every kind of medication. This was prior to public acknowledgment of a link between prescription opiates and addiction, and hospitals and free clinics often preferred to dispense pills rather than provide more costly care. Hence medications of varying types were always in plentiful supply.

Ray, a former opioid user who had been prescribed a bevy of drugs as a result of an AIDS diagnosis and who would be classified by the government as chronically homeless, made a point of putting aside a little of his own medication each month and pressing his doctor for samples to help treat other tent city residents. Ray was thin and wiry but well muscled. He had long hair and a receding hairline. His small eyes and sharp, narrow nose gave him a comic-book bad-guy sort of look that I am sure he enjoyed but which belied his soft, mellow demeanor. When asked why he shared his meds, I expected him to say something about making extra cash. Instead, he said he never charges for nonrecreational meds. Instead, he told me, "We all try to work together—keep each other well and keep each other happy. We have to. [If] somebody needs something, I give it to 'em. I got stuff for tummy ache, Prilosec, or whatever. I got allergy medication. I got antibiotics—best antibiotics money can buy. Twelve hundred dollars a month is what it costs the county, or whoever's paying for it, y'know what I mean?" When I inquired about how he knows which medications to give out, he shrugged and laughed. "We learn all that on the streets. We are all livin' on the streets, and we pretty much know what's gonna work for someone else, and you usually know who's got it. It's like, oh, he has somethin', or he's had that, he can help you out, that will work good for ya 'cause I had it and I took it. Everybody's different, that's true, but most of the time it works."

While Ray was often the go-to guy for meds, many residents I spoke to displayed an amazing amount of medical knowledge, not just about types of medication but also in terms of dosing, counterindications, and allergy awareness. Many were aware of other campers who had been prescribed similar medications as themselves, and borrowing or lending was common. This was particularly prevalent with antibiotics and asthma and diabetes medications.

In acute cases where people in the camp encountered more severe physical or mental issues, a sort of ad hoc nursing care team would tend to the person until he or she was stabilized or a more suitable living situation was identified. This mostly involved checking in on people who were not well, helping people make or keep appointments, running errands, or connecting the individual to the proper healthcare or service agency. For those who had been recently discharged from the hospital, food was often prepared for them, and a volunteer, likely a neighbor, was designated to check in on them at regular intervals. While this form of healthcare is far from perfect, it highlights the ways tent city residents are able to care for themselves and one another and the importance of these practices to tent city residents in terms of enacting ethics of care and belonging.

Apart from medical needs, the tent city was the site of a thriving gift economy. This mostly took the form of small comforts and conveniences. Most basic material needs, like clothing, tents, blankets, and for the most part, food, were kept fairly well stocked through donations and distributed mostly according to need by the donations coordinator. Nevertheless, informal gifting or exchange of goods, money, and labor was constant. While not everyone participated in the camp economy, it was an important contributor to feelings of home, care, and belonging.

Often one's introduction to this economy happened immediately upon arrival. Every incoming resident was given donated blankets or a sleeping bag. But other campers often introduced themselves to the new resident and offered items that they felt might be helpful. For many new arrivals, this came as a surprise. This was the case with James. James was a very young-looking guy with close-cropped hair and a stained blue puffy coat who wandered into the camp looking hungry and exhausted a few days after we had moved to the Central District location across from Cherry Hill Baptist Church. A few days after James's arrival, I introduced myself, told him I was a researcher, and asked him how he was getting along. He told me that when he arrived, he honestly didn't know what to expect. He had recently been released from the King County jail downtown and wandered up to Tent City 3 "on a random tip." He had been skeptical of spending his first night in a big tent full of strangers, but his neighbor in the MASH tent surprised him. "Gosh," he told me. "I didn't have any blankets the first night, and what he do? He gave me a blanket and two pillows. Then, after laundry day, when he saw that I didn't get my blankets back, he gave me his big blanket. I didn't ask him—I came back after serving my security shift, and they were there. He didn't say, 'This is what I did,' but I knew it was him."

What came as a surprise on the first day quickly became a regular occurrence in James's life in the tent city. A few weeks later, when I asked him if he had experienced any more actions like that of his neighbor, he responded, "I've seen people give things there that maybe they couldn't afford to give. Like I have seen people say, 'Here, have a sandwich. Look, you take the sandwich, I'll have the salad. You look more hungry than I am.' I have seen that happen. Things like that happen all the time around here."

Although it may be a stretch to say that such acts of sharing happened all the time, the generosity and the ubiquity of accounts like James's reflected my own experience as well as the experience of those I interviewed. Indeed, nearly two-thirds of those I interviewed described good tent city citizenship as inseparable from practices of mutual aid—or, as Donna more simply put it, "People care for me and help me out, and I care for other people and help them out—like a pay-it-forward thing. We just all have each other's backs."

Mel, who had been in the camp for a long time and was well known for his generosity, had a more philosophical approach. In response to my asking why he gave so much away, he replied, "Cause it will come back eventually." When I asked him what he meant by that, he continued, "Oh, somebody needs a sleeping bag. Oh well, I got an extra one. If somebody needs some blankets . . . I guess so. I have given stuff away, and people say, 'Oh, I'll give it back,' and I say, 'No, give it to someone who needs it. I don't loan stuff. I give it, because that way there is no interruption in the friendship. And you'll see. It's contagious. The next thing you know you'll hear someone who you had given a flashlight to just last week, and he'll be givin' it to someone else." Although Mel began his discussion of gifting with an invocation of reciprocity—it will come back—his explanation echoed Donna's pay-it-forward comment. For both, the core function of gifting was not the gift but the perpetuation of the practice.

As Mel and Donna suggested, gifting often served as much a social as a pragmatic function. This was certainly my experience. After about a week in the tent city, I was lamenting to Mel that many of the more established residents seemed reticent to talk in my presence. The next day, he showed up at my tent with an apple pie. When I protested that I could not possibly eat a whole pie, he scolded, "It's not for you. Bring this out to the table tonight. They'll talk to you then. They just wanna know you're one of 'em." I did, and they did. In this case, sharing the pie was not merely friendly but a performance of belonging.

Participation in the gift economy, the sharing and provision of food and medicine, enable Tent City 3 residents to resist their exclusion and pathologization and re-create a homespace based on practices of care and inclusion. The peer-run structure and the practices of self-management in the tent city shape and enable a process of becoming together that creates a feeling citizenship where belonging occurs through ongoing processes of care, recognition, and reaffirmation. Tent City 3 is not simply a collection of individuals with a shared need for shelter but rather a deeply interconnected community where individuality and agency are expressed and understood in relation to the camp and its residents.

These localized expressions of feeling citizenship stand in stark opposition to the exclusionary logic of norm and deviance that drives contemporary policy and private sector approaches to homelessness. Although this localized form of citizenship occurs against a backdrop that I earlier referred to as propertied citizenship, tent city residents strive to reclaim their sense of dignity and autonomy through practices of care and inclusion.

Yet, while suggesting a more fluid and open form of belonging than the hardened boundaries for property and state, the practices, surveillance, and social control through which the good camper was produced were felt by some to be exclusionary. Although no one in the camp expressed these views, I spoke informally during my time in the tent city with some individuals who had refused to stay in the camp or left shortly after arrival because they found these processes of subjectification to be overly burdensome, socially manipulated, or in one case, "cultish." These cases point to a broader critique of the idea of commons and commoning based on the idea that the act of boundary-making is always exclusionary to some extent, and as such is not outside broader social structures of inclusion and exclusion.[11]

Visualizing the collectivization of Tent City 3 residents through the lens of feeling citizenship enables a way of envisioning the boundaries of home and citizenship as neither fixed nor exclusionary but rather porous, participatory, and potentially expansive. The peer-run structure and the practices of self-management and care in the tent city shape and enable a process of becoming together that creates a form of feeling citizenship where insiders are produced through practices of inclusion and caring labor in the everyday social reproduction of the camp.

Observed over time, in the context of a fluid population and a changing social context, these homemaking practices were more than relational; they were productive. Judith Butler notes that while it is ritualized performance that makes possible the production of the "natural" subject, the indeterminability of each iteration opens space for the possibility of contestation, experimentation, and change.[12] Each performance of commoning, care, and collectivity in the tent city not only occurs in reference to past norms, iterations, and practices but is also a product of the specific personal, social, spatial, and temporal context in which it occurs. When someone volunteers to assist someone who is otherwise unable to perform a given set of duties, cares for someone in a time of need, or shares what little they have, the boundaries of tent city citizenship are simultaneously reenacted *and* expanded in ways that are highly malleable and responsive to the needs of an extremely fluid and diverse population.

In the course of defining themselves in relation to the domicidal production of homelessness, residents also lay the groundwork for something new: the production of new forms of caring, commoning, and collectivity. These efforts are not unique to the tent city but speak to the fragile and partial nature of settler colonial geographies of exclusion. To use the language of Michelle Daigle and Margaret Marietta Ramírez in their explanation of decolonial geographies, by "interweaving spatial practices of resistance, refusal and liberation," residents of Tent City 3 through their homemaking practices become one node in a "constellation in formation" of "historical and always emerging relationships across decolonial struggles [that] transcend colonial boundaries."[13]

The ability of the camp to function as a collective homespace relies on the production of specific forms of subjectivity and belonging that are intentional, temporal, and ongoing. In this sense, the ability of the tent city to provide homey feelings of autonomy, security, and belonging is not a product of simple existence nor of the particular people who inhabit the space. Rather, the homespace of the tent city is largely a product of time, of persistence, of an ongoing effort to produce homelike spaces of collective belonging.

4. Seeing Like a Tent City

In their refusal of homeless subjectivity, Tent City 3 residents produced homespaces and subjectivities based on commoning, care, and collectivity. However, it was through camp governance that these norms persisted. To say this persistence was improbable is an understatement. Not only does the camp relocate every thirty to sixty days, but the residents, propelled by various needs and circumstances, are likewise in constant flux. It is rare for a camper to remain for longer than a few months. Nevertheless, Tent City 3 has persisted. At the time of my stay, the camp had been in continuous operation for six years. In 2023 that number stands at twenty-three. And the camp is still in operation, continuing its peripatetic existence across Seattle's gentrified landscapes. It has outlasted seven mayors and four presidents. This temporal persistence is a luxury not often afforded to the informal habitations of the poor in the United States.

In this chapter, I explore how the norms, subjectivities, and spaces of the camp are sustained and negotiated through practices of collective self-government. I explore how, as both a home and a city space in which the boundaries between public and private are porous and fluid, the camp's collective self-governance produces a localized form of informal "governmentality."[1] This localized governmentality was forged within and against presuppositions of homeless deviance and difference but became something more. Governance in the tent city was an ever evolving system of contextual negotiation that occurred through and within intimate, embodied, and contextual relationships. These practices were exercised through the collective management of the camp, the selection and operations of the camp executive committee and the creation, application, and enforcement of camp rules. When taken together, the governmental practices of Tent City 3 refuse colonial hierarchies and modernist monocultures of knowledge through an anticolonial art of governance based on contextual fluidity and negotiability.

Governance Within and Against a Colonial Property Regime

From the first iteration of the tent city to today, collective governance and self-management have been the motivating principal for all SHARE/WHEEL spaces. In Tent City 3, as in all other SHARE/WHEEL shelters and tent cities, governance revolves around weekly meetings in which rules are made, community activities and outreach are planned, grievances are aired, and duties are assigned.

The self-governing structure of the tent city is not unique. All informal dwelling arrangements develop some form of decision-making, resource allocation, and ground rules. As anyone who has ever had roommates can attest, these basic governing structures are essential to shared homespaces. All informal communities, from a pair of tents on the sidewalk to large sprawling slums or favelas, rely on some form of self-governance to manage the needs of residents in the absence of, or dispossession from, formal state infrastructure and legal protections. Many larger encampments in the United States, such as Portland's Dignity Village, LA's short-lived Griffith Park and Veterans Row encampments, Oakland's Wood Street Village, and Seattle's Nickelsville encampments, like Tent City 3, foreground their self-governing structures both internally and in media communications. In doing so, these camps' very existence flies in the face of common stereotypes of homeless pathology and dependency that serve to both justify state intervention and deny the autonomy of homeless individuals. Self-governance is homeless refusal writ large.

Set both against and within the broader context of urban governance, self-governance in the tent city at first blush looks and feels remarkably like a microcosm of the formal urban structure that it inhabits. For instance, the administrative heart of the camp, the executive committee desk, serves as a sort of border guard and, as my own intake experience illustrated, immigration and naturalization center. Yet it also serves as a city hall where executive decisions and functions of the camp are carried out. The space in the city is clearly divided according to familiar American Euclidean zoning principles. The space is organized into administrative, public, residential, and what would be in a typical American city the commercial entertainment spaces, embodied in Tent City 3 by the TV tent and the kitchen. Like most cities, this layout is meant to foster the well-being and social reproduction of the camp. Also, like any US city, the governance of the space is democratic. Not only are people elected to various operational and maintenance duties, but the democratic governance of the camp extends to both its executive and urban planning functions.

While in many ways the space of the camp resembles the formal American city, the manner, methods, goals, and outcomes of Tent City 3 governance vary dramatically from the settler colonial context in which it resides. In a possessive property regime such as the United States, urban governance manifests as the arrangement and management of urban space to foster property-based and market-driven well-being.[2] This form of propertied government is founded upon the tripartite assumption that land can and should be divided into distinct parcels organized based on specific uses, and that these uses can be predetermined and maintained indefinitely. Fixed notions of who can be where (property), what can be done where (land use), and who can do what where (nuisance) form the backbone of this rationalization of space. In each case, the purpose of governance is to fix a particular kind of order and foster particular ways of understanding oneself in relation to urban spaces.[3]

The practices of controlling and managing urban spaces serve to establish and normalize settler presence by displacing, erasing, and confining racialized individuals. In the propertied space of US cities, Black, Brown, Indigenous, and poor bodies have been and continue to be displaced and quarantined through the use of city-wielded tools such as exclusionary property laws, nuisance laws, and land use violations.[4] Thus the production and management of urban space in settler societies give physical form to the division of humanity into distinct groups in a hierarchal order of propertied white supremacy.[5]

These enactments of settler colonial urbanism draw upon and abet broader modern Western forms of knowledge production and statecraft. Drawing on biblical notions of man's patriarchal dominance over the earth and its inhabitants, as well as Enlightenment ideas of the universal truth of Western knowledge and experience, a modern art of governance emerged that Michel Foucault argues operates through the state's ability to prolong and enhance the lives of the governed.[6] James Scott's seminal work *Seeing Like a State* illustrates how, within this form of state reason, the state functions as a sort of master optimizer of human and natural resources.[7] In this framework the state governs at a distance—it "sees" only in the abstract, through the production of statistical and scientific knowledge that serves to naturalize Western prerogatives of property, ownership, and governance, while rendering invisible Indigenous and other forms of knowledge and place making.[8] These "God's eye" visions function, in the space of white supremacy and settler colonialism, to consolidate the power of Eurocentric experts and expert knowledge to marginalize and quarantine bodies according to race, class, gender, sexuality, and of course, property lines.

Persistent spaces of informal dwelling unsettle the legitimacy of Western knowledge production and statecraft. Urban informality, by its very existence, renders visible the limits of property, planning, and law as instruments of statecraft. It also illuminates the possibilities for thinking governance otherwise.[9] Informal governance, or governance in the global spaces of informality, operates on a very different register. Informality, as Christian Haid and Hanna Hilbrandt note, is "a governmental practice of flexibility" that calls attention to "discretion in decision-making processes—especially in the everyday."[10] In contrast to a modernist rationality of governance in which individual needs and desires become comprehensible through expert or juridical divisions between norm and deviance, the informal governance of Tent City 3 functions through contextual variability, flexibility, and experimentation.

As a twenty-three-year-old self-governed encampment that serves as a collective home to up to one hundred individuals, the very structure and existence of the tent city disrupts stereotypes of irrationality or dependency that the normative construct of property defines as homelessness.[11] As homeless individuals living in a temporary encampment, as pathologized objects of state and civil society intervention and carceral management, and also as US citizens under the formal jurisdiction of Seattle, Washington, residents of the tent city live as what Leonard Feldman called in *Citizens without Shelter* an "inclusive exclusion."[12] Drawing on the work of Giorgio Agamben, Feldman argues that people without access to formal housing in the United States dwell literally and metaphorically both inside and outside multiple formal and informal regimes of governance. In these liminal spaces, the unhoused residents of Tent City 3 grapple with the democratic promise of liberal ideals of democracy in the context of their own exclusion from such ideals. Seattle's Tent City 3, he argues, in its persistent presence on Seattle's urban landscape, makes "space for citizenship."[13] By enabling a space within which residents can refuse and resist exclusion, Feldman argues, Tent City 3 establishes a place where those rendered irrational and dependent by their homeless status can speak and act as rational actors in the management of their own lives.[14] This manifests in the collective self-governance of the camp.

In an interview, camp coordinator Michelle Marchand explains how feelings of exclusion inspired the self-governed structure of the tent city. Michelle, whose matter-of-fact demeanor belies a deep commitment and care for her work and those she works with, had been the camp coordinator for Tent City 3 for three years when we sat down for our conversation. Prior to that she had been part of the formation of and an organizer for the Women's Housing Equality and

Enhancement League (WHEEL), which joined SHARE as its sister organization in 1993. I met her for lunch at FareStart, a nonprofit café run by people experiencing poverty in Seattle's Belltown neighborhood. Over sandwiches, I asked her to explain why she thought self-governance was an important part of the Tent City model. Putting down her sandwich, she took off her large plastic-framed glasses, tiredly wiped her eyes with the back of her hand, and brushed back her long brown hair before explaining in a voice that suggested I was not the first to ask this question: "Well, I mean first, I think it's a fundamental human belief in individual powers and gifts and rights and responsibilities." She paused, took a sip of her coffee, and continued. "I think that was the groundwork. Things work better, though, when people get to choose for themselves. When SHARE started, I guess there was a lot of talk in the traditional social service world about how it would never work because people are so fragile, and they have no self-interest in making a structure like that work."

"Well," she said, cracking a smile and letting out a small laugh, "they do actually, as it turns out. It's having a good, dignified place to stay, and it's having a voice, and a vote. I mean those are pretty strong self-interests." In Michelle's view, skepticism about the viability of a peer-run homeless shelter arises from an assumption among legislatures, service providers, and the general public that homeless people are incapable of knowing or articulating their own self-interest. By foregrounding the agency of homeless individuals in the traditionally liberal language of self-interest and democracy, Michelle illustrates both the referential and oppositional character of the tent city. By emphasizing the importance of having a "voice and a vote" in the tent city, she instrumentalizes democratic values of equality and participation, while at the same time shifting the language of citizenship from formal inclusion as a state subject to the informal space of Tent City, where residents are envisaged as active agents in the production of collective belonging.

In practice, I found the most visible expression of the structure outlined by Michelle to be the camp's weekly meetings. Generally held in the evening to allow those who work during the day to attend, the weekly meeting is where rules are made, community activities and outreach are planned, grievances are aired, and duties are assigned. In these meetings, every activity, policy, and strategy change is subject to discussion and vote. The meetings are also the time when the camp coordinator presents news related to homelessness in Seattle and updates on the ongoing activities of SHARE/WHEEL and the tent city.

Michelle, the camp coordinator at the time, was one of the few paid employees of SHARE/WHEEL. She did not live in the camp, and her role in the meetings was to provide information, secure bus tickets, note rule changes, manage the camp's ad hoc committees, and make announcements pertaining to the camp's relationship with the SHARE/WHEEL network and the outside community. As Michelle put it, her job was to be "a sort of housekeeping person." As a nonresident of the camp, she was not allowed to put forward motions or vote in camp decisions. However, it was not uncommon for her to provide and advocate for her opinion on a given topic or to detail potential benefits or consequences of a given camp proposal. Michelle was also responsible for providing printed copies of the meeting agenda and supplementary materials. While time was set aside during the meeting for people to air grievances and call for motions, people were encouraged to contact Michelle prior to the meeting to have their issue put on the agenda.

In meetings, after agendas were distributed, the first item was the appointment of a meeting chair by nomination and vote. During my stay, the chair was most often chosen for their ability to allow everyone to have their say while keeping the meeting moving and on track. Brevity was key, as few people wanted to sit through many hours of meeting. The chair's duties consisted of reading the meeting agenda as prepared by the camp coordinator, facilitating discussion and voting on each point, and announcing the outcome of various votes. Meetings generally ranged between forty-five minutes and two hours, sometimes longer. After choosing a chair, the meeting began with introductions. Next, the chair presented the latest news regarding the camp's relationship with the current host. Issues often involved logistics, such as dumpster pick-up, as well as discussions and votes about host-provided amenities, such as movie nights, shower provision, and meals. After immediate camp business, time was allotted for problems and solutions. At this point campers were invited to discuss any proposals, grievances, and proposed rule changes. This was done through a loose interpretation of Robert's Rules. After initial discussion, people were free to put forward any motions for planned solutions. The motion was then seconded, discussed (often the most time-consuming part of the meeting), and then put to a vote. A simple majority carried the motion. This process was referred to colloquially as a motion being "MSP'd" (moved, seconded, and passed) and was the procedure for all proposed activities and rule changes.

To be clear, governance of the tent city was messy. Like all forms of government, it was susceptible to corruption, power grabs, petty infighting, missteps, and at times, a slide toward tyranny. Yet there was an underlying logic, an art of governance, or governmentality, that produced and enabled the persistence of practices of homemaking and citizenship characteristic of the tent city.

The practice of collective self-governance—its messiness, fluidity, and negotiability—was particularly on display one May afternoon. The weather had been unusually warm and dry. The vacant lot where the camp was located had been covered in grass when the camp moved there a month earlier, but by May all that remained were a few patches of weeds in a sea of dusty dirt. Fine dirt covered nearly everything, and some folks already seemed a bit on edge as we gathered for our weekly Wednesday all-camp meeting. We gathered under a large maple tree in the common area near the entrance to the camp. People grabbed drinks, snacks, and smokes, and settled in. Most of the meeting proceeded normally, announcements and plans were made, and elections were decided. But when it came to the open discussion part of the meeting, things began to unravel.

For weeks the issue of rule enforcement had been simmering. When the camp had moved from Saint Mark's Cathedral to a lot at 22nd and Cherry across from our host, Cherry Hill Baptist Church, there was a large population turnover, resulting in a camp largely composed of people who had been there longer than a month and those who were brand new. Neither group was familiar with the other, and both were skeptical of each other. Most importantly, there was no one in the middle to mediate or relate their experience of becoming a good camper. Over the course of the previous month, the new campers had begun to take a more confident and active role in camp life. Recently, there had been grumbling, petty arguments, and outright accusations of executive committee overreach, vindictive punishments, and favoritism. These charges, mostly leveled by the recent arrivals against more established camp members, finally came to a head on this dusty, hot Wednesday afternoon during a generally routine discussion on enforcement of cleaning duties that anyone who has ever lived with others will recognize.

The discussion started as a conversation about a perceived lack of cleanliness both around the tents and in common areas. A motion was put forward about requiring extra cleaning duties for anyone caught leaving dirty dishes or empty containers in the common areas. This prompted the question of how that rule would be enforced. Would it just be he said/she said? This devolved into a short but heated argument over the appropriateness of some rules and the enforcement of others.

In theory, Tent City 3 is governed according to a brief code of conduct issued to every camper upon arrival and posted at all times at the executive committee desk. The wording of this code of conduct is as follows:

TENT CITY CODE OF CONDUCT

We, the people of SHARE/WHEEL, in order to keep a more harmonious community, ask that you observe the following code of conduct.

The tent city is a drug and alcohol free zone. Those caught drinking or using drugs will be asked to leave. Sobriety is required.

No weapons are allowed. Knives over 3½ inches must be checked in. Any violence will not be tolerated. Please attempt to resolve any conflict in a creative and peaceful manner.

Degrading ethnic, racial, sexist or homophobic remarks are not acceptable.

No physical punishment, verbal abuse, or intimidation will be tolerated.

We are a community. Please respect the rights and privacy of your fellow citizens.

No men in the women's tents. No women in the men's tents. No loitering or disturbing the neighbors. No trespassing.

Attendance of at least one of the several community meetings throughout the week is required. Days and times will be posted so that you may work it into your schedule.

Although this code of conduct lays out a general set of expectations, prohibitions, and responsibilities, its enforcement and application in the day-to-day operation of the camp was far more complex.

Since, other than the relatively brief code of conduct, few rules were actually written down, and even fewer were accessible in the camp, some new campers felt they were at a distinct disadvantage in terms of determining or refuting charges of acceptable and unacceptable behavior. Alex, a young-looking person with freckles and a mop of blond hair who had been in the camp for about three weeks, summed up the issue: "Why don't we put this information out there for people, so they know what's goin' on?" After another twenty minutes of arguments, marked by accusations of laziness, power grabbing, and favoritism, a motion was proposed that all rules, not just the code of conduct, be written down, stored in an accessible location, and clearly made available to all incoming campers. While sentiments like Alex's formed the basis for debates in favor of the motion, more seasoned campers argued that not only would this be a logistical nightmare, since many of the rules only existed in the collective memory of the camp, but that it would take away the discretion to consider mitigating factors. In the end, largely owing to the recent influx of new residents, this motion passed. However, in the weeks and months that followed, few of the motion's provisions ever came to fruition and those that did were abandoned in a matter of weeks.

To an outside observer, such proceedings and their outcomes might look disorderly or even chaotic. However, in the tent city, such moments were normal, ongoing, and I argue, necessary.

Tent City Governmentality

As my stay in the tent city progressed, I came to realize that the tensions and conflicts embodied in such meetings occurred with striking regularity. Each time there was a seasonal or location-induced turnover of residents, the incoming population would once again raise issues of power, representation, and participation. However, as new campers became closely integrated with others in the tent city and more familiar with its norms of governance and citizenship, these issues subsided—until they arose once again.

Through struggles over duties, power, and representation, Tent City 3 residents were articulating a localized governmentality that was simultaneously within and against colonial structures of exclusion. Drawing on Foucault's concept of governmentality in his analysis of slum dwellers' movements in India, Arjun Appadurai coins the phrase *governmentality from below* to describe the diverse ways self-knowledge and representation occur among informal settlement dwellers. While I eschew Appadurai's use of "from below" and its presupposed solidarities of the impoverished and powerless against the wealthy and powerful, the concept is helpful for understanding how the collective governance in informal dwellings resists colonial knowledge production and opens space for thinking of governance in more expansive terms. Governmentality from below, he argues, is a "kind of counter governmentality" that, in opposition to liberal or colonial forms of governance, is "animated by the social relations of shared poverty, by the excitement of active participation in the politics of knowledge, and by its own openness to correction through other forms of intimate knowledge and spontaneous everyday politics."[15] Governmentality from this perspective doesn't occur from below, but rather within and against.

In Tent City 3, countergovernmentality manifested itself in opposition to what Thalia Anthony calls a "settler colonial governmentality of dispossession, displacement and detention."[16] Through the practices of modern statecraft, Anthony explains, settler colonial states produce Indigenous, racialized, and unpropertied people as the constitutive outside of white settler norms of propertied inclusion, subjecting them to its carceral control and recuperation. By demanding transparency in rules and punishments, new campers articulated a right not only to inclusion but to the meaningful participation and equality denied them outside the space of the camp. Through discussions over power and representation, residents articulated a politics of belonging in the context of their exclusion from the spaces and structures of settler rule. Additionally, the ongoing and negotiated nature of these discussions in the context of a seasonally nomadic encampment with an ever-changing population reveals an ongoing process of governmental knowledge production.

Over time, practices of self-governance in the tent city enable space not only for the inclusion and participation of excluded subjectivities but for their relational production. While the collective self-governance of the tent city did allow voices to be heard and decision-making to be democratically shared, there was something more at stake than Feldman's assertion that the self-governed encampment was a place where opinions mattered and actions were effective. Close attention to the topics, struggles, and outcomes of camp meetings reveals a process where opinions and actions do not emanate from autonomous rational actors but are negotiated and ongoing articulations of selves *in relation to* one another, the camp population, and the space of Tent City itself.

These relational subjectivities, like every aspect of the tent city, were constructed and negotiated in the context of homeless refusal. Indeed, refusal, like issues of power and representation, was a common topic of discussion and debate in meetings. One such debate revolved around tours of the tent city. Tours occurred with some regularity. Often, they involved church, school, or community groups looking to support or learn about Tent City 3 and its residents. On this particular day, the discussion was about allowing a group of local middle school students to visit, tour, and share lunch with the camp. In the meeting some expressed a sentiment that tours helped to, as one camper put it, raise "people's awareness up about homelessness." This camper felt strongly that "we *all* need to do something about it. Not just people out there with money, but the homeless people as well, by letting people in but not allowing people to look down on you." These remarks were met with mixed results. Some nodded approvingly. Others argued that allowing tour groups into the camp reaffirmed the marginality of the homeless. The discussion became animated and increasingly tense.

In one particularly heated exchange, a camp member stood up and shouted, "What is this—a zoo?!" In a conversation afterward, I asked him what he meant by this statement. He replied, "Have you ever been to the zoo? [We're] like monkeys—*oooh*, look, there's homeless people, and you're standing there brushing your teeth or whatever and a bunch of schoolchildren just look at you. It reminds you that you feel less than—y'know what I mean?"

Dave, who had long, straight, dirty-blond hair and wire-framed glasses that gave him a professorial air, came and sat next to us at one of the communal tables near the kitchen. After listening and nodding intently for a few minutes, he chimed in. Using what I had come to think of as his wise voice, Dave echoed many commonly expressed ideas about the value of privacy, equality, and home in thinking about the function of the tent city. Leaning forward on his elbows, he said, "I mean, how many times have you had people walk into your apartment and take a tour?" He took off his hat and waved it around while mock-declaring, "Hey, let's take a tour of X townhouse today—I want to see how middle class folks live!" He put his hat down and looked at me directly before continuing, "I mean, they can see it from the outside, but hey, this is our home, and we should feel comfortable in our home—without people walking around."

Dave, who had lived in the camp longer than anyone could remember and who became visibly upset whenever someone implied that those without housing were somehow less than their housed counterparts, was clearly incensed, but his words here are illustrative. Some felt that heightened visibility and bringing awareness constituted proper expressions of care and tent city citizenship, but this conflicted with ideals of privacy and claims of equivalence. Here conflicting ideas about visibility and being good citizens express both tensions and commonalities in ideas of home and citizenship. The meetings, and the conversations that preceded and followed meetings, offered a space where these issues could be explored and discussed in the context of both individual and collective ideals of self, space, and belonging. In the end, the tour was allowed with the caveat that they would give two weeks' notice before their arrival so that those who were uncomfortable could arrange to be away.

Exchanges like this, in which items of small importance became venues for discussion of broader issues of home and homelessness, were a common feature of camp meetings. Through such discussion residents articulated and negotiated the function of the camp as well as their relationship to outsiders and to one another. In another illustrative case, a motion was put forward suggesting that camp residents should be allowed to skip their security shift to attend city council meetings relevant to homeless policy. The camper putting forward the motion argued that since the city council was currently discussing issues directly pertinent to tent city residents, attendance at the meetings should count as working on behalf of the camp. Some disagreed. They charged that city politics was a separate issue from camp duties. The purpose of security shifts, they argued, was to directly contribute to the maintenance and well-being of the camp. Others said that they didn't identify with the issue of homelessness and that participation in political meetings was a personal choice and had nothing to do with the camp. The issue was decided with a compromise: political participation could count as community service but would not count toward the security requirement. Through debates like these, meetings were an occasion for people to negotiate, debate, resist, and articulate ideas of self, home, and belonging within and against property based exclusion.

Governance of Contextual Fluidity

The localized governmentality that emerges from these interactions occurs not simply within and against but in excess of fixed monocultures of governmental knowledge produced by and within a settler regime of propertied normativity. The governmentality produced in Tent City 3 was always in a state of becoming. Not only were tent city populations, locations, and context in constant flux, but rules could be made or rescinded at any time by majority vote. In this sense the self-enumeration and participation in governmentality in Tent City 3 was not simply relational or oppositional but expansive.

In contrast to property-based regimes of law, governance, and planning, the project of governmentality at Tent City 3 was not to fix subjects in place according to their relationship to private property; rather, it was to enable camp practices of care, commoning, and collectivity to be maintained over time despite a constantly changing population and location. It was a governmentality of contextual negotiability. The manifestation of this informal and localized governmentality can be partially glimpsed in the work of the move master. The move master was the urban planner in the governmental apparatus of Tent City 3.

As the name indicates, this person was charged with coordinating and organizing the move, overseeing moving day operations, and most importantly, planning, mapping, and organizing the layout of the new site. This consisted of determining the best spatial arrangement of the camp in regard to particularities of the locale and population. In addition to deciding who lived next to whom in the personal tents, the tent master was responsible for the placement of communal tents, the shape and size of public areas, and the orientation of the tent city in respect to the surrounding neighborhood. In this sense, the move master could shape not only the interactions between individuals and groups but also, to a large extent, the totality of interactions in the tent city as a whole. Many of the discussions that occurred in camp meetings had begun long before. In general, people tended to discuss issues first with their immediate neighbors before bringing them to the attention of the general population. The shape and tenor of these discussions were not necessarily random but rather a product of where, how, and with whom people interacted in the camp. These decisions were made by the move master.

Like all other administrative and maintenance positions in the camp, the move master was chosen by nomination and vote. This job was not taken lightly and was generally undertaken by someone who had lived in the camp through at least two moves. Although such experience was not a requirement, this was the only volunteer position in the tent city where those nominated were regularly voted down. The seriousness this job was accorded underscores both the massive difficulty of dismantling, packing, moving, unpacking, and reassembling what essentially amounted to a small city and the daunting responsibility for creating and ordering its spaces.

Despite or possibly because of this power, there was an almost ritualistic set of consultations between the move master and old-timers, in which information about site specifics and past arrangements were exchanged with those who had lived in that site on a prior occasion. While failure of the move master to heed such advice often resulted in friction, the main issue seemed to be whether the appropriate people were consulted. Deference to old-timers was also a factor in the residential organization of the camp, as the move master often allowed old-timers their choice of tent locations. Rick, who had served as move master a few times in the past, expressed this deference in relation to Mel, the oldest person in the camp at that time. Rick explained that "everybody dogs old Mel, and they bitch because I give him first pick of where he wants to stay y'know—and I do that because he's the eldest person there and he knows what has worked in the past and I think he has earned that right—regardless of if I like the man or not." The end result of this preferential treatment was a loose spatial hierarchy through which those who had been in the camp the longest were clustered in the most desirable spots, followed by those the move master considered the best campers. Lastly, there were those with whom the move master was unacquainted or indifferent. The camp's arrangement to a large extent shaped both the nature and frequency of interactions. For instance, those who were farther from the most desirable location might interact with old-timers and more "model" tent city citizens only in common areas.

In addition to the siting and location of personal tents, the location of communal tents and the overall layout of the camp in relation to the surrounding neighborhood were also contested and debated. Although there was no particular constant to where in the camp communal tents would be located, there were occasionally heated discussions about where they should be. Since mostly only the newest members of the camp lived in the communal tent, its placement was key to ensuring feelings of peace and security in the camp. Some argued that communal tents should be located close to the EC desk and communal areas for closer surveillance of the yet undisciplined bodies; others felt that this large concentration of potentially noisy bodies should be located as far as possible from those sleeping in private tents. A similar set of debates often arose regarding the tent city's arrangement in reference to the surrounding neighborhood.[17] When the neighborhood was perceived as safe, for instance, the primary debates revolved around issues of accessibility for both campers and visitors. However, when the neighborhood was perceived as unsafe, the debates revolved around issues of resident safety and the ability of the EC desk to serve as a lookout point and guard station against perceived outside threats.

These debates reveal the imbrications of the governmentality of Tent City 3 within issues of security, privacy, and surveillance. However, in contrast to contemporary propertied discourses of urban planning where technocratic appeals to highest and best use "inherit and spatialize the racialized property regime," the actions of the move master and the production of camp space were socially embedded processes of negotiation and contestation.[18] In an article titled "What Is Planning without Property?" Heather Dorries argues that such practices of "grounded normativity" unsettle property-based planning's role in reproducing settler colonial exclusion and lay the groundwork for collectively creating what Brenna Bhandar has called "the conditions for turning away from property as we know it."[19] Dorries draws on Indigenous conceptions of the "relationship of land, body and community" to illustrate "a land-based system of reciprocal relations and obligations that are the basis for Indigenous life and for anticolonial and anticapitalist struggle."[20]

Planning in the tent city, operating both within and against preordained visions of propertied personhood and prosperity, was the negotiated outcome of historical practices, societal norms, communal necessities, and physical constraints. Within this complex discursive array, space itself becomes the terrain upon which ideas of inclusion, security, and surveillance are contested, reenacted, and reworked. From these ideas emerges a distinct form of contextual place-based normativity in which the modernist norms of property-based planning are displaced and reformulated to meet the dynamic needs and desires of tent city residents.

Rule Enforcement, Contextual Negotiability, and the Management of Infinite Difference

While the move master plays an important role in the physical manifestation of governmentality in Tent City 3, in the day-to-day life of the camp, management and enforcement of the fluid boundaries of belonging were the purview of the camp's executive committee, or EC as it was commonly known. Although meetings allowed for an exchange of views and the formation of policies and actions that reflected the concerns and desires of the camp population, the everyday enforcement and fulfillment of these policies fell to the camp's executive committee. Thus, understanding the function and operation of the EC, its makeup, and its power is key to grasping both the persistence and the contextual flexibility of Tent City governmentality.

Like all official positions at Tent City 3, members of the executive committee were elected by nomination and vote of the camp population. At the end of each meeting, camp residents voted for five executive committee members and two alternates. The only eligibility requirement for EC duty was that a candidate must have lived consecutively in the tent city for thirty days. A potential EC candidate, once nominated, could either accept or decline the nomination. If the person accepted the nomination, a vote was then held. Over the time Tent City 3 had been in existence, a system of term limits had evolved from trial and error. As of 2012, a person was allowed to serve a maximum of two two-week terms without being reconfirmed. After two terms, however, a new nomination and vote were required for a person to maintain their spot on the EC. Although a revote was required every four weeks, there was no formal limit on the amount of time one might serve on the EC. During my time at Tent City 3, it was technically possible for an individual to serve indefinitely provided he or she was renominated and received enough votes.

While in practice this never happened, during the course of my observations a core group of experienced individuals continually rotated in and out of EC duty. However, it was fairly rare that these individuals all served at the same time. Partly through coordination and partly by serendipity, there were typically three or four experienced ECs and a couple of newer, less experienced folks. Again, as with all tent city duties, the ins and outs of EC duty were learned through mentorship, trial, error, and correction. Whether by intention or accident (and sometimes a little of both), the mixture of more and less experienced ECs (and the mentorship of the latter by the former) meant that in general the tent city was able to maintain a competent and experienced administration despite high population turnover and frequent conflict, while still allowing for an influx of new executive committee members.

Executive committee duty was not for everyone. EC duty was the most rigorous, time-consuming and powerful position in the camp. ECs were required to commit to at least twenty hours a week. However, in my observations, the position often took much more time, as it was necessary to have an EC on duty twenty-four hours a day, seven days a week. The executive committee was responsible for staffing the front desk, supervising security people, making sure sign-up sheets for various tasks were filled, assigning "bars" (temporary or permanent banishment orders), mediating disputes, performing intakes, greeting visitors, and countless other duties. For this and many other possible reasons, only a small number of campers ever served as EC members, meaning that at any given time, a small proportion of the camp populace had substantial power and influence over the day-to-day management of the camp.

For the most part, ECs were elected based on experience, time in the camp, and perceived fairness. There was no formal campaigning. However, occasionally someone who wanted the position would ask a friend to nominate them. Throughout my stay in the camp, a revolving cadre of about ten to fifteen individuals generally filled EC positions. Occasionally somebody new would be elected, with sometimes good, sometimes less than good results. Often, in times of crisis or difficulty for the camp, old-timers who generally eschewed the burden of EC duty would step up and serve for one or two terms to get the camp back in order. Most often, this occurred either shortly after a move or when there was a large turnover of camp residents.

Perhaps not surprisingly, there was a dangerous side to this inevitable concentration of power. Although nothing like this occurred during my stay, and such incidents appear rare overall, camp residents in the years both prior to my stay and since have told me stories of EC members who seized and consolidated power to their own ends. In one of these conversations, I spoke to a former resident who recalled that "when we were at Church by the Side of the Road, things were crazy! Some of the people who were ECs were taking advantage of the position to basically run their own little drug empire."

"Seriously?" I asked.

Nodding, he continued, "They were pretty blatant over there. They didn't care. One time when I was on security, I had one guy offer me money to keep my mouth shut, and I was like 'Just don't involve me in any of this.'"

"Wow, that's crazy," I said, hoping he would tell me more.

Instead he simply said, "Yeah. That was how a lot of that crowd was running. But it's gotten a lot better."

In stories eerily reminiscent of fascist regimes in the United States and abroad, campers both during and after my formal stay in Tent City 3 recounted stories of EC members who courted the camp with a combination of promises, threats, and patronage, only to use the camp as a personal fiefdom. In a couple of cases, SHARE stepped in to remove a problematic executive committee and hold new elections. Luckily, such uprisings have historically been relatively rare and brief, as the constant turnover of the population, combined with the presence of seasoned campers and occasional stern directives from the SHARE camp coordinator, not only kept these episodes brief but resulted in an evolution of camp policies, such as term limits and democratic accountability, to keep these tendencies in check.

At stake in these struggles over power and accountability was homespace itself. In the precarious space inhabited by the tent city, a failure of self-governance, in the form of violent despotism or charges of crime or violence, could easily lead to banishment by the host or revocation of the consent decree by the city. On a day-to-day basis, the burden for maintaining these relationships, as well as general order in the camp, fell on the EC. As the only members of camp who could officially mete out punishment, ECs were saddled with the most responsibility and the most power.

The most extreme form of this power was temporary or permanent banishment. Banishment, known internally as a "bar," could range from one day to permanent expulsion. During my stay, the bar was one of only two forms of official sanction in the tent city (the assignment of extra security duty was the second).

Anyone who received a bar was required to leave the camp immediately. If the bar was less than a week, they were allowed to keep their personal tent or their space in the MASH tent, with all their belongings intact. If the bar was longer or if they did not return after their bar, their belongings were "bagged and tagged": put into garbage bags and stored for thirty days, or longer if arrangements had been made to that end.

Bars were given for rule infractions as well as failure to perform accepted or assigned duties. Bar procedure began with the write-up. Anyone in camp could write up another camp member for an infraction of the Tent City Code of Conduct. The write-up form was then submitted to the EC on duty. Depending on the seriousness of the infraction, the EC on duty would investigate further, assign disciplinary action, or if the discipline was to be more severe than a three-day bar, confer with other ECs. Anything longer than a three-day bar required two EC signatures. Lastly, the bar went to the camp coordinator for final approval. Bars were taken very seriously. Indeed, some camp old-timers refused to serve as ECs for this reason. As Mel, the oldest of the old-timers, put it, "I just can't be responsible for putting another homeless person on the street."

Though outsize, the EC's power to bar someone was not absolute. Although the executive committee had discretion over who would receive a bar and for how long, it was possible for barred campers to contest a bar if they felt it was unfair or unjust. Those who disagreed with a bar or felt the bar was too severe were able to contest their sentence at weekly bar committee meetings. These meetings occurred as part of the weekly "power lunch," in which members from all the SHARE shelters met to discuss issues of particular import.[21] In particularly egregious cases of executive committee overreach, other residents might urge the defendant to appeal the bar or even write statements of support. In response to an appeal, the bar committee, composed of volunteers from other SHARE shelters, would review the written statements from the EC and a written statement from the defendant. If there was any question about the validity of the bar or its severity, the bar committee would send the issue back to the camp to be decided at the next camp meeting. During the meeting, testimony and evidence would be presented by the EC who issued the bar and the person who received it. After testimony had been heard, the barred individual was asked to leave the camp while the issue was debated by camp residents, who then voted on whether to uphold or overturn the bar.

Although extreme, bars were integral to the specific governmentality of Tent City 3. While bars were officially given only in response to violations of the code of conduct, unofficially they served a disciplinary and normalizing purpose. For instance, while specific bars were indicated for each infraction, there was vast discretionary leeway in determining what actions counted as an infraction and whether an infraction had indeed been committed. The result was that those considered to be good campers often escaped with a warning, or light or no punishment, while those who were selfish, disruptive, or lazy were often barred for insignificant infractions under sometimes extremely liberal interpretations of the code of conduct. To my initial surprise, almost everyone I spoke to supported this use of temporary banishment to, as one camper put it, "keep out the riffraff." Although there was some protest over the fairness of some bars, and some campers felt the bar was occasionally used capriciously or to settle personal beefs, the idea that it should exist and be used was nearly universal. My surprise at what appeared to be a general acceptance of a seemingly arbitrary use of the bar arose from countless stories that residents told me of the hurt and trauma caused by past exclusion and banishment from the camp.

Almost everyone who passed through the camp described the pain and anguish of being kicked out of houses, evicted from shelters, and harassed or banished by cops or business owners on the streets. As time passed, however, I came to realize that within the space of the tent city, banishment was seen as a necessary, albeit imperfect, component of maintaining the camp as a homespace and, in a profound irony, maintaining an ethic of care and inclusion in the context of a constantly changing population. Thus, within the camp, although many campers shared my discomfort with the use of the bar, the preservation and persistence of the camp as a homespace motivated their support for its selective and slippery use.

Bars were and are a contentious feature of the governmentality of the tent city. In many ways they seem to mirror propertied logics of exclusion. However, they can also be understood as part of both the refusal of these logics and the production of more fluid and contextual ways of knowing and being in relation to one another. To illustrate these ideas more fully, I turn to the less drastic but more ubiquitous practices of rule creation and application in the tent city.

Although new campers occasionally demanded greater transparency in the rules and their application, these sentiments often diminished as time passed. Whereas transparency in rules and sanctions allows for a clear understanding of rules and punishment that is helpful in navigating new or foreign environments, the vicissitudes of life seldom conform to static boundaries between permissible and forbidden. Maintaining the camp as inclusive homespace in the face of the unknowability of future events meant that the governmental rationality of the tent city, grounded in practices of collective inclusion, was enacted through a sometimes maddening contextual relativity. While residents sometimes found this relativity difficult to manage, most accepted or even embraced the camp's administrative ability to maintain an ethos of caring and collectivity, while being flexible to ever-changing conditions and situations.

The counterintuitive value of the relativity of rule enforcement came through clearly in a conversation I had with George, a sporadically employed construction worker who had been in the camp just over a month. George had a ring of red hair around his bald head that connected to a short, cropped beard and an expressive face that gave him a comic appearance despite his serious demeanor. When I asked what he thought about the uneven application of the rules, he screwed up his face in mock contemplation and said, "I think that technically I should think it's terrible, I should think it's a horrible thing because everyone should be treated absolutely fairly. The rules are the rules and technically it's only fair to enforce them uniformly." After that he paused, perhaps gauging whether he should tell me more or not.

"But?" I prompted.

After a moment, he continued, "Well, on the other hand, no one is ever going to be perfect regardless of who they are. *But* if they maintain a peace in the camp, if you can come in and not have to worry about yelling and screaming and everything, which by God stresses me out, well then?" He shrugged in what I took to mean a let-bygones-be-bygones way. "*But* if there's people crazy, yelling and screaming and violent or abusive, violence and all that stuff. . . ." He trailed off once again, this time brushing off his arms to suggest that he was willing to be rid of them.

At this point, though, he hesitated for a moment, took a drag off his cigarette, and continued in a new, matter-of-fact tone. "Look, I've noticed that people who are annoying, they"—referring to the ECs—"almost find something to do to them even though a different person did the same thing yesterday. . . ." He shook his head and made a small gesture reminiscent of the safe sign in baseball. "That's pretty clear. It happens, I think, any place you go. I mean if it's a tent city or if it's a country club, that's going to happen, and I think it's fine. For all our peace and safety." While George was clearly conflicted, thinking uneven application of the rules "should" be terrible, it was ultimately acceptable for the maintenance of the camp homespace.

Although uneven application of rules and punishments was, for the most part, an accepted and even desirable mechanism for maintaining the norms of tent city citizenship and homespace, this was not a perfect system. Although various checks and balances were developed over the years, there was still ample opportunity to misuse the bar. On occasion, I witnessed bars being issued for what clearly seemed to be personal reasons. Like their brethren in formal executive branches of government, there was often a temptation to favor friends and distance enemies. However, this practice was actively discouraged by camp social norms.

Perhaps more illustrative of the operation of Tent City governmentality than the flexible application of the rules was the rules themselves. While there was a fair amount of leeway in the application of the rules, the rules themselves were somewhat of a mystery. While the Tent City Code of Coduct clearly laid out a series of broad commandments that served as the backbone of tent city governance, the application of these rules, or what actions actually constituted violations of these rules, was open to very wide, often hotly debated, interpretation.

Rules were often made, rescinded, and modified during camp meetings. While these rules were recorded in the camp ledger, old ledgers were often lost, and new people were not versed in many of the minor rules. This, combined with the generally high turnover, meant that for the most part the rules resided in the collective memory of those who had been in the camp for a long time. The result was a sort of oral legal culture where long discussions were had about which rules had been passed, which rescinded, and so on. In addition, because of the wide leeway in interpreting the code of conduct, there was often a heavy reliance on remembered precedent. Again, knowledge of past applications of the rules resided with people who had been in the camp a long time. Thus application of the code of conduct and suitable punishment were also the subject of long and heated discussions in which old-timers held disproportionate power and influence.

While on the surface this arrangement might appear both highly unorganized and inegalitarian, in practice just the opposite was the case. As Rick, who served frequently in EC positions, explained, "Rules are rules, but rules are made to be . . . bent—not broken. There's leeway y'know—if a guy's a good camper and he goes out and ties one on one night and he hasn't dranken in six months, well, why shouldn't there be a little leeway—as long as he goes to bed, and doesn't make an ass of himself." Like the accommodation of individual needs and capacities for the exercise of care work, here the application of the rules also takes in local culture and context.

Indeed, although much was made of the importance of rules and punishment in the everyday life of the camp, the mere existence of a rule, or the perception of a rule, and its corresponding punishment seemed to have little relationship to its enforcement. Rather, rules and punishments in the tent city were largely wielded as a mechanism for enabling and sustaining norms of camp citizenship and homespace. Because most of the rules only existed in the collective memory of the campers, rules and their application could be highly contextualized to meet the situation at hand. Rather than a system of formal rules and punishments, the tent city managed to enact a system that was highly responsive to the individual timing, situation, and character of the offender in question.

The importance of this contextual fluidity to both the refusal of homelessness and the practices of care, commoning, and collectivity that enabled camp homespace was highlighted in a number of interviews with newer as well as longtime campers. James, an Irish expat with curly black hair and bright green eyes who had recently finished his first stint as an executive committee member, pointed to the preservation of both diversity and collectivity as a reason for selectively applying the rules. James and I were in a nearby pub where some of the campers often went to play pool and have a few beers. On one of these nights, after losing our round at the pool table, we retired to a table on the other side of the bar. It was near the door, and we could hear the hissing of car tires on the rain as we talked about James's thoughts about life in Tent City 3. When I asked about rules and their application, he became unexpectedly animated. "They're homeless for fucking Christ's sakes, there's mental problems over there."

He paused and lowered his voice, perhaps in recognition that we were with a group of other campers. He continued, "We can't expect everyone to act like everyone else. We all have different attitudes and different ways we act, and we should allow that, but we should all say, okay, now you gotta do your two security shifts, your outside social commitment, keep your area clean and clean up after yourself, and that should be for everybody across the board. But other than that, if somebody wants to just sit there and stare into space and not talk to anybody, they should be able to do that without being considered antisocial or being considered a problem. Maybe that's just who they are, or maybe they just need that right now." For James, flexible application of the rules was inseparable from the preservation of homespace. For him, home was about being able to be oneself. What was important in that context was an ethic of care, commoning, and collectivity that would allow even people with mental problems to be at home.

A few weeks later I interviewed Mary, who highlighted the stakes of what James had told me. Mary, who had entered the camp a few days prior with a partner who was now attempting to quit methamphetamines cold turkey in her tent, used her personal story to illustrate why leeway in rule enforcement was necessary to the collective functioning of the tent city as homespace. Mary was exhausted, and her partner had become sick and incredibly irritable. To give Mary a break, I invited her over to the café for a drink. Speaking through her long, green-dyed bangs, she explained how contextual application of the rules enabled her and her partner to stay in the camp while struggling with the vagaries of homeless life outside the camp. She stressed that the ECs "need to know when to enforce the rules and when to see if there is valid reasons—like you are trying to create your life outside of this place and that's why they slipped up a little—and be willing to let some things go, y'know. We saw that when Amy didn't come home that night because she was apprehended, and so she didn't show up for her security. I was in tears. By the time she was let out the next day, I already had packed our stuff. But the EC on duty just said, 'I am not going to write this up—it never happened.' That cost him, the camp, nothing, but it may have literally saved our lives. All we really need is just a place to be, and thank God the camp is giving that to us right now." James's and Mary's responses highlight the idea that although the seemingly opaque system of rules and punishments was often a source of anxiety and contestation for new campers, it also reflected a governmentality of care and an inclusive acceptance of difference.

The contextual negotiability of camp rule enforcement is grounded in the unknowability of future events and circumstances. This unknowability, along with the lack of predictability that goes with it, is precisely what modern property-based governance seeks to eliminate. In a series of lectures titled *Security, Territory, Population*, Michel Foucault draws on the example of town planning to illustrate the historical development of modern liberal governmentality. As medieval feudalism gave way to a commodity-based economy, city walls were replaced with urban planning and legal regulations of urban movement and flows. For Foucault, the role of urban governance in a governmentality of propertied modernity is to construct spaces and state structures that secure the well-being of the population in perpetuity through propertied movement, dwelling and exchange. Ensuring this perpetual security, however, requires the banishment, surveillance, and elimination of ideas and bodies that might challenge or threaten the hegemony of property-based prosperity.[22] In the settler city, trespass, nuisance, and land use regulation ensure the security and predictability of property-based well-being through the expulsion, displacement, and carceral management of property's others.[23]

By contrast, governance in the context of the tent city served to reward and reinforce the collective commoning of homespace. In this arrangement, one's good deeds and good citizenship could be rewarded by a lightened sanction or wide leeway in enforcement of the rules. At the same time, this system allowed itself to be highly adaptable to the difficulties faced by homeless individuals. Rules, for instance, were often more lenient near the end of the month, when people lacked money and were trying to make ends meet, or in cases where mental, situational, or physical difficulties were a factor in the transgression.

Through everyday practices of collective self-governance and administrative management, tent city norms were constantly undergoing revision and reinterpretation. Because of this, they remained open to continual modification and change. In this way, one can view the norms of tent city citizenship as both persistent and fluid. Insofar as application of the rules was based on precedent, governance was self-referential. However, as these rules were not written down but rather passed along orally and informally, their exact content was in a constant state of reflection and modification. Yet the tent city and the particular art of governance that maintained and enabled its spaces and subjects persisted. It is this persistence, both its continuity and malleability, that forms the basis for a governmentality of the tent city.

Through infinite movements, iterations, and populations, tent city norms are constantly undergoing construction and reconstruction. However, like Tent City 3 itself, the governing structure, practice, and rationality, while not fixed, persist. They persist in individual and collective memory, in their repetition, and in the practices and duties that make the tent city function. By rewarding those who embodied and enacted tent city norms, contextual application of the rules served to harmonize and perpetuate those norms.

In this chapter I have illustrated how the self-governed structure and operation of the tent city reveals a localized form of governmentality that enabled and maintained tent city norms of home and citizenship in the context of a mobile camp with a constantly changing population. This form of informal governance operated both within and against the racialized and exclusionary governmental logics that underpin settler colonial geographies of displacement and carceral recuperation.

The rationality of settler colonialism—grounded fixed hierarchies of propertied whiteness—manages the population through a racial and spatial logic of purity, deviance, and exclusion. By contrast, the practices of self-governance in the tent city emanate from a governmental rationality that is, by necessity, highly fluid, contextual, and responsive to the needs and desires of an infinitely shifting population. Through this informal governmentality, Tent City 3 residents enact ways of being together and at home beyond monocultures of settler colonial knowledge.

5. Community, Recognition, and Encroachment

Through its ongoing persistence on the Seattle landscape, Tent City 3 has enabled a space where its residents forge a homespace within and against normative boundaries of home and homelessness. For many of Seattle's housed residents, however, Tent City 3 is now a normalized, perhaps even ordinary, feature in Seattle and the surrounding area. The persistence and normalization of Tent City 3 raises an interesting case for thinking about how those deemed homeless contest and negotiate their social marginalization. The normalization, legalization, and expansion of self-governed homeless encampments suggests a level of political inclusion and acceptance of tent city residents as equal citizens. However, these developments occur within an existing structure that relies upon and justifies the erasure, expulsion, and dehumanization of the unhoused to normalize a settler property regime.

In this chapter, I focus on the interactions among the camp, its host organizations, donors, neighbors, and the greater community. I begin by highlighting how, despite normalization of Tent City 3 that suggests an acceptance or even embrace of the camp as a space of collective homemaking, the wider settler colonial context of propertied hierarchies, exclusions, and erasures persists. I then turn to the interactions between camp members and their neighbors, which are shaped and constrained by colonial hierarchies of possessive property. Although the camp relied on donations of private property for its material existence, residents refused to be recognized as homeless subjects. In their refusal, residents crafted, within interactions with camp neighbors and hosts, an alternative form of self-recognition based on dignity, autonomy, and collective self-governance. I illustrate how interactions between residents and their hosts evidence a dialectic of recognition and refusal that both reenacts and contests colonial hierarchies of propertied personhood. In navigating the terrain of these interactions, I investigate the boundaries and potentials of conceptualizing Tent City 3 as an insurgent space of expansive belonging.

Propertied Personhood and the Limits of Inclusion

The persistence and normalization of Tent City 3 in many ways resembles what Asef Bayat has called "the quiet encroachment of the ordinary." Bayat uses *quiet encroachment* to refer to "the discreet and prolonged ways in which the poor struggle to survive and to better their lives by quietly impinging on the propertied and powerful, and on society at large."[1] These encroachments, Bayat argues, when viewed across time and space, constitute social "nonmovements" through which the daily practices of marginalized urban bodies trigger social change. Viewed from a distance, Bayat's characterization of social nonmovements seems applicable to the tent city. By creating a homespace within and against a settler property regime, Tent City 3 has forged a path of normalization that for many Seattleites rendered the camp and its residents, in many ways, ordinary.

However, the potential for overcoming the social, physical, and political exclusion of unhoused people is complicated by the property-driven settler colonial project we call the United States. In *Life as Politics*, Bayat focuses on the collective actions of marginalized groups in the Middle East. He views what he calls "social change" primarily through a macro lens. For him, the power of "non-movements" is their ability to "contest many fundamental aspects of the state prerogatives, including the meaning of order, control of public space, of public and private goods, and the relevance of modernity."[2] Yet, he argues, such concessions are difficult in "advanced industrialized countries," where "infringement of private property, and encroachment on the state domains are considered serious offenses."[3] Property lines, it seems, cannot be crossed.

Indeed, within the colonial logic of property, one's position in relation to property determines one's relation to political inclusion. Ananya Roy reminds us that the ability to claim homespace within an ownership model of property relies upon an "expectative property right." However, the claim to such a right, Roy argues, relies on a politics of recognition, an Arendtian right to have rights that is systematically denied those without access to formal housing in the United States.[4] Residents of Tent City 3 wholly refuse this exclusion. Within the homespace of the camp, residents' collective acts of refusal are enacted through the production of a space in which residents reclaim their right to have rights through shared practices of care, commoning, and collectivity *within* the space of the Tent City.

In the bounded space of the camp, acts of refusal and reclaiming occur both within and against the propertied terrain of the settler colonial city. In enacting these refusals and reclamations, Tent City residents are attempting not to craft a utopia but rather to assert themselves as equals in a world in which their exclusion is predicated on their recognition as *homeless subjects*. The space of Tent City 3 allows them to refuse this subjectivity and assert their own equality.

Community Credits and Why They Suck

The presumption of equality that produced the spaces and subjects of Tent City 3 were not always reflected in the spaces the camp inhabited. Integral to the normalization of Tent City 3 has been its constant perambulation of the city's residential neighborhoods. These movements, however, were not predestined. Rather, in its periodic nomadism, Tent City 3 continually seeks a new host. The original consent decree stipulated that it could be sited only on private land and only for a maximum of ninety days. In practice, this means that much time and effort is devoted to securing and maintaining relationships with new and ongoing host organizations that are willing to let the tent city utilize a portion of their property for a given amount of time. In the course of these interactions, the notion of community emerged as the terrain upon which issues of refusal, recognition, and belonging were negotiated.

In this framework, community became the geographical as well as ideological terrain upon which ideas of inside and outside occurred. In media and public discussions about homelessness, community is often invoked as a bounded realm to which unhoused people do not belong, or conversely, the word is used to constitute those who lack access to formal housing as a coherent entity: the homeless community. Yet camp residents also invoked the concept of community to articulate ideas of inclusion, recognition, and belonging among themselves, their hosts, and the neighborhood in which they resided. For both tent city residents and those who speak of the "homeless," the notion of community functions as a mechanism through which normative subjectivities and spatial imaginaries are consolidated and differentiated.[5] In this way, community can be seen as the outer boundary of "feeling citizenship." While feeling citizenship articulates an idea of belonging and home that is participatory, affective, and potentially expansive, community marks the frontier of these affective inclusions.

In the relation among the camp, its hosts, and its housed neighbors, the contours of the affective frontier are rendered visible through the performance of "community credits." Other than security, the only time commitment required of tent city residents during my stay was the completion of one community credit every two weeks. One of the newer requirements of tent city, community credits came about as an incentive to involve camp members, who may be in the camp only for a few weeks, in securing future locations for the camp, as well as political advocacy, general outreach, and public relations. Generally, the camp coordinator would compile a list of activities and locations where SHARE felt tent city presence was needed or where it had been requested. This list was then posted at the EC desk, where camp residents could sign up for a given activity. Additionally, campers could receive community credits for doing "litter busters": one hour of picking up trash in the neighborhood surrounding the tent city. Through these activities, the performance of community credit was the primary way that camp residents became visible *as tent city residents* to potential hosts and housed neighbors.

The performance of community credits also served a pragmatic function that was in keeping with the camp's ethos of being self-governed and self-managed. The reason for community credits, according to SHARE staffer and camp coordinator Michelle Marchand, is simple: "Because that work needs to get done and, y'know, the campers gotta do it." In many ways, community credits seemed to be an unproblematic expression of the good camper. By participating in activities that helped secure the space of the camp and the well-being of its residents, community credits seem to fit neatly within the practices of care, collectivity, and commoning that enable the production of the camp as homespace. In the camp, however, it wasn't that simple.

Despite obvious benefits to the camp as a whole, community credits were a contentious point for many camp residents. The general attitude of campers toward community credits was well summed up by Martin, a young man with short, cropped hair and a nervous optimism that was both infectious and a little off-putting. When, over donated bagels, I asked him about his thoughts on community credits, he said matter-of-factly, "I think they suck, personally." Martin's views were common. People's reasons for not liking community credits varied. Some resented being "the token homeless" person at city council or other political meetings, but typically campers pointed to the practice of conducting outreach to future host sites.

During my stay in 2006, the work of securing and maintaining relationships with camp hosts was, for the most part, done by camp residents under the auspices of receiving community credits. This work was by far the most contentious aspect of community credits. Residents' dislike of this kind of outreach was particularly acute when the potential host was a religious organization. The vast majority of Tent City 3's hosts were churches, synagogues, and other religious organizations. Although in some rare circumstances community centers, universities, or private owners have allowed the tent city to set up on their property, during my stay and in the years immediately before and after, religious spaces were a mainstay. In many ways, this relationship seems like a natural fit. Not only are religious organizations often privileged with a surplus of real estate, but they are also exempted from some land use restrictions by sanctuary law in Washington State. Additionally, the charitable imperative to minister to the poor is often a fundamental component of their beliefs. These sentiments have worked to the tent city's advantage over the years. Indeed, Tent City 3 has come to rely upon religious organizations not just for real estate but also for material and political support.

Churches and religious organizations have been extremely generous in terms of volunteer time and material resources, such as donating supplies and preparing and serving meals, in addition to providing space. Sometimes, though, provision of these services, when done in a spirit of charity, distanced the residents from the host community. Dan neatly summed up this distancing. Dan, who had been living in Tent City 3 for about the same amount of time as I had, worked the graveyard shift at a construction site, a job he described in a typically tongue-in-cheek way as, "I keep the homeless out." We were both at a Wednesday evening camp meeting when, upon hearing the announcement of a local church's desire to serve dinner to tent city residents, Dan commented to me that "everyone wants to bring us food or have us come to their church to serve us food—but have you noticed nobody ever wants to eat *with* us?"

Dan's offhand comment got me thinking. Up to that point, I hadn't thought much about community credits. At the time, I was so focused on people's feelings about the camp, each other, and how Tent City 3 functioned that I simply assumed, as Michelle noted, that it was just work that had to be done. After this brief encounter with Dan, however, I incorporated questions about community credits into my interviews. I also attended every community credit opportunity that came along. As I delved farther into the issue, Dan's comments began to appear as yet another form of refusal.

Homelessness, Misrecognition, and Refusal

By complaining that "nobody ever wants to eat with us," Dan both highlights and questions his and other campers' relationship to those providing services.

Whereas the generous aid and support provided by religious and charitable communities are very much needed and often welcomed by campers, the relationships they invoke often reify feelings of marginality and dependency. By contrast, Dan views himself as an equal—someone worth eating *with* rather than simply an object of assistance.

The tension between the reality of having to rely upon benefactors for their very existence and the internal imperatives of dignity and collective autonomy arose often in relation to residents' feelings about community credits. Although there were other opportunities to gain community credit, the bulk of credits took the form of attending services and social events at one of the approved churches. These churches and synagogues had either hosted the tent city in the past or expressed interest in hosting it in the future. The point of these interactions was, for the most part, to make the tent city and its residents visible presences to past and potential hosts. While many accepted these duties as a necessary component of camp life, they also frequently mentioned that these interactions made them feel uncomfortable.

At issue were the discursive boundaries of community and the politics of recognition. When I had a chance to interview Dan, I asked how he felt about that church dinner and community credits. He didn't mince words: "I *am* homeless, and I don't like it one bit—and I don't much like churches either." He went on, "To make me go to church *and* basically tell everyone I am homeless? Well, that just adds insult to injury." As I began to query residents more on their feelings about community credits, I found Dan's feelings to be widespread. People felt like they were at best interlopers in communities to which they did not belong. In addition, they suggested that their interactions with church congregations often reinforced social hierarchies in ways they found belittling and dehumanizing.

In general, residents were already uncomfortable with being outsiders in host spaces. However, this discomfort became galling in the context of a property-based hierarchy. Both these themes came through when I asked Manny, over lunch one day, about his thoughts on community credits. "What do I think of 'em?" he asked through a mouthful of burger. "Actually, they don't make a lot of sense really. 'Cause when you go to the church, you just go. You don't know anybody or anything. If you're not a church-going person, then there seems like there is no need for you to go." As a non-church-going person, Manny explained that not only did he feel like an outsider in the church community, but his attendance there made him feel like a "poser." These feelings of not belonging were exacerbated when Manny's reasons for being there became known to the congregation. When I asked if he introduced himself as being from the tent city, he answered, "Well, I mean, I guess some people probably just know you're from tent city. But yeah, I guess I do do that. I wait 'til everybody is gone and then go up to the guy [the minister/priest/rabbi]—I don't want to be up in front of a bunch of people and say, 'Oh, I'm from Tent City!' Then it's like, 'Oh, look at the poor homeless guy!'" Like Manny, many others found these interactions to be awkward and ultimately belittling.

Despite the feelings of discomfort, residents were acutely aware of their positionality in relation to both Tent City 3's need to secure a space and their need to perform a certain kind of abjection. An awareness of the positionality was poignantly described by a camper named Sam, who had been living in the camp for just over a year. Sam worked full time and, although I had seen him at meetings and sometimes around the camp, we didn't really know each other. However, one Wednesday Sam and I found ourselves together at the same community credit activity: a barbecue hosted by a local church and longtime Tent City 3 patron. After the barbecue, I sat down with Sam for a beer at a nearby pub. When I asked what he thought about our experience and community credits in general, he said he thought community credits were like a marketing plan: "We go in, we obviously don't belong there—have never been there. Then we are like, 'Hey, I'm from the tent city!' And they look at you with that pity look that people get. And then you're done! It's a Sally Struthers commercial, except instead of starving African babies, it's us poor homeless folk. I hate it." Indeed, the more community credit opportunities I attended, the more my experience began to mirror what I was hearing from camp residents.

Partly out of curiosity, and partly because I too was annoyed by the benevolent condescension I often encountered from well-meaning volunteers, I occasionally introduced myself at various church socials or events held for camp residents as a researcher, or sometimes just a curious guest, as opposed to a tent city resident. The difference in treatment was astonishing, although not surprising. When people saw me as a tent city resident, they were first curious about my "story"— how I became homeless. Then, they would ask if tent city folks were keeping warm and dry. Finally, they would inquire as to what they could do for the tent city and me. They generally made a point of telling me to take as much of the cookies and coffee as I wanted. When I introduced myself as a researcher living in the tent city, people quickly lost interest. On more than one occasion, when people found out that I was not *really* homeless, they simply turned their backs and walked away.

When I told guests that I was a curious neighbor, the conversation was different still. In these cases, conversation revolved around questions about my spouse, family, and job—questions that *never* arose when people thought I was homeless. This was true even though much of the literature used in Tent City 3 outreach emphasizes that most tent city residents have at least some, if not all, of these attributes. This differential treatment was in no way limited to churches. These differences occurred with striking regularity and similarity wherever I happened to find myself in conversation—in city hall, at activist or community events, anywhere where the presence of tent city residents was known or expected.

Tellingly, this code switching, made possible by my own presentation as a white cisgender man, was not related to changes in dress, diction, or any other typical marker of class hierarchy. I dressed and acted the same in all situations. The only difference in these interactions was my own claimed positionality in relation to my housing status. Here, differences between norm and deviance, deserving and undeserving, were arbitrary, performative, and—much to the frustration of tent city residents—completely necessary for garnering the material resources necessary for Tent City's continued existence.

Leonard Feldman, in *Citizens without Shelter,* directly speaks to these frustrations and their imbrication in the context of colonial recognition. Unhoused people, Feldman argues, "deprived of basic and essential goods and subject to economic marginalization, also face misrecognition through stigmatization and invisibility." He exemplifies this through the use of the word *address*. He writes, "To have an address means to have a place of residence, and to be addressed, means to be spoken to, recognized as a human subject in dialogue." To be homeless, he argues, "means to be addressless in both senses."[6] For residents of the tent city, this was literally true. To be recognized as worthy of the use of a host's physical address, they had to be recognized *as homeless*. Further, as use of the word *address* implies, this misrecognition and its necessity occurred directly in relation to private property.

Misrecognition, in this sense, is not a simple accident of mistaken identity but a colonial recognition that constructs those outside the normative bounds of propertied personhood as abject others.[7] Hosts possess private property, and Tent City 3 needs access to property. Yet it is the absence of access to private property that renders Tent City 3 residents homeless and thus worthy of aid. In this sense, the benevolent care shown by tent city hosts and potential hosts echoes the carceral process of unhoming. In the spaces of shelters and the justification for antihomeless laws, the recognition of people as homeless justifies intervention in the form of banishment, quarantine, or benevolent care. In these cases, the provision of a "domestic space for the performance of such life sustaining bodily functions as sleeping, eating or defecating" is contingent on the unhoused accepting and embodying their role as subjugated other to the colonial normativity of propertied personhood.[8]

Relationships of property-based benevolent dominance and subordination are fundamental to the persistence of the settler project. The settler colonial space of Seattle was made possible through the violent expulsion of Indigenous and racialized bodies. The settler project was reinforced and reproduced through the imposition of a property regime that transformed land into territory that can be owned, which in turn produced homelessness and normalized the settler. Yet, as Glen Coulthard, drawing on the work of Frantz Fanon, illustrates, the stability and persistence of a colonial regime relies not in the last instance on conquest or quarantine but rather on "its capacity to transform the colonized population into the *subject* of imperial rule."[9] If colonized subjects refuse to internalize their own subordinate status, the colonizer exists only as invader or external threat. Thus, the continued illusion of totality in the settler city depends on the colonial other's recognition and acceptance of the naturalness and rightness of their own otherness.

In the realm of homelessness, this transformation requires the production of academic, political, and cultural knowledge that posits and reifies the homeless subject as one in need of carceral correction and recuperation, as well as the unhoused person's embodiment of that subjectivity. In the case of Tent City 3's relation to potential host sites, the ability of tent city residents to performatively embody their homeless subjectivity was necessary to affirm and reproduce the rightness of hierarchical property relations. Residents of Tent City 3, however, refused this subjectification.

This refusal was both conscious and intentional. Camp residents were absolutely cognizant of their own discursive positionality. Just as they were conscious of the stereotypical lenses through which outsiders viewed them, they were likewise adept at adopting, drawing upon, and performing those stereotypes for strategic ends. However, for many this performative destitution did not sit well, even when it accurately reflected their situation. An exact counterpoint to the way that spaces, subjects, and belonging were maintained within the camp, the sort of performative homelessness necessary to procure camp spaces and resources ran counter to what they felt they were doing in the camp. Thus, they refused. Refusal, in this context, did not involve rejecting interactions with the housed community or potential benefactors. Rather, in the course of Tent City 3 residents' interactions with potential hosts, neighbors, and the broader community, the refusal to perform their homeless subjectivity enacted an alternative politics of recognition where residents sought to reframe and reclaim recognition in their own image.[10]

Crafting an Alternative Politics of Recognition

An alternative politics of recognition, like the colonial subjectification it seeks to replace, took place on the contested terrain of community. On occasions when campers felt a heightened sense of difference, or like they were being defined by their homeless status, they tended to speak of community in largely ideological terms, as in the "congregation," "church folks," or more broadly, "those who wanna help out." However, when they were able to participate in ways that made them feel like they were on more equal footing with those around them, people tended to invoke community in geographic terms, as "the neighborhood" or "the city," referring specifically to community as a particular space in which they were included as an integral part. While in the first case, tent city residents felt like needy outsiders in a community to which they did not belong, framing the community in geographic terms allowed residents to see themselves as equal insiders.

These invocations of community hinged on proximity in more ways than one. The way community was perceived as a relation of social and spatial proximity was nicely summed up by Peter one sunny afternoon. Peter and I had bonded over our love of food—especially, talking about food—and were relaxing and sharing a joint in a park across the street from the camp. From where we sat, we could barely see the blue-tarped tops of the tents. We had been discussing the possibility of planning a camp barbecue and had gone beyond menu planning to the logistics of feeding such a large group. During this conversation, Peter used the word *community* a number of times in reference to the camp. Finally, I asked what he thought made the camp a community. At once, he sat back, chuckled, and got the sly smile that I knew meant he was going to wax poetic. I scrambled for my recorder and got it started just as he let out a big exhale and began:

> It makes it a community because you've got a bunch of people from all walks of life, different ethnicity, experience, and background, that come, and basically, they come together in need of help. For the shelter, food, support, and believe it or not, maybe some people come together because they're

lonely and they want to be around people. Maybe subconsciously they're not thinking about that, or consciously, but subconsciously they probably are lonely, and they just need someone else just to feel like they're a part of something. You know, 'cause you think about people who are drug addicts and alcoholics, whatever, every now and then they get so low that they need a human touch. They need to feel that they're part of something, right? And they might just go, "Well, at least I'll be around somebody, whether I interact with them or socialize with them on whatever level, at least I'm around people rather than being way back in the alley or in the woods alone and depressed and—you know." And I think tent city provides that.

While others offered far more concise answers to the question of why they thought of the camp as a community, Peter's answer resonates within all of them.

For Donna, the camp's community existed simply because there were people in the common areas. "It took me a while to recognize it because I had been burned so badly by the last two places," she told me, referring to shelters where she had stayed prior to arriving in the tent city. "So it took me a while to, like, come out of my shell a little bit, but once I did, I found that there are people out there who are, like, fun and would, so far, let me be me."

For Paul, it wasn't just that there were people present but their shared experience of exclusion. As he put it, "It's a bunch of people with a lot in common—I mean we all are homeless—so we don't need to look down on each other or act a certain way or, y'know, civilized, I guess—we can just be ourselves." Community, as Peter, Donna, and Paul describe it here, sounds a lot like home. Community, rather than being a shared set of beliefs, rests upon ideas of being together in shared experience and circumstances as equals, or as Paul puts it, "We can just be ourselves."

The relation between how campers conceived of community and the attributes they sought to create in the homespace of the tent city came through in their conceptions of ideal community credits. One of the questions I asked in my discussions about community credits was, What would be your ideal community credit? Responses to this question varied. While some talked of community credits in terms of the tent city itself, as in "I think community credit should be about helping one another," most referred to their relationships with immediate neighbors. When I asked one particularly outspoken camper, he shouted, "Litter busters," referring to the practice of picking up trash around the neighborhood. "That should be community credit 'cause it helps the community!" Other residents expressed similar opinions. "I don't know why we can't get community credits for helping out the neighbors around here," one longtime camper complained. "Many of them are elderly, and y'know—that's our community *out there*," he emphasized, making a sweeping gesture toward the neighborhood adjacent to the tent city. Still others conceived of the community as the city as a whole. As one resident told me, "We should be able to get credit for going to city council meetings! We are citizens here—it's our responsibility to do what we can to make Seattle a better place!"

Though responses varied, they all evoked a notion of homespace. In these cases, however, residents envisioned not only the camp but the neighborhood and the entire city as potential and desirable spaces of inclusion and participatory belonging. In contrast to practices of unhoming, these notions of ideal community credits sought to expand the spaces in which they could enact their practices of care, commoning, and collectivity, as equals with their homed counterparts. Overwhelmingly, residents discussed their desired interactions with the community in terms of an ability to interact as equals outside the space of the tent city. Camp Coordinator Marchand explains that this is a common desire, not just among tent city residents but for the homeless in general. "Homelessness is hard," she began. "It's hard physically, it's hard emotionally, and it's isolating." She continued:

> Even at Tent City 3 it's isolating. Even in a community of one hundred people, you don't always just want your peers to talk to. You want people in different circumstances. Another analogy is sort of why so many homeless people go to the library—it's not just a place to get off the street, it's not even just the books. What is so great about the library is it's not a ghetto of poor people and homeless people. It's mixed, it's diverse. You don't feel ashamed, you don't feel . . . homeless. It's a humanizing force more than anything else and it brings folks out of the isolation and ghettoization of homelessness and specifically Tent City. It's like, let's talk about books, let's talk about this stupid TV show we all watched last night, let's not have those separations just based on our class or our living situation absolutely. That's just so important—it really is.

While other people voiced these ideas in terms of "being able to be real" or "just being able to have a regular chat, like over dinner," the feelings expressed by Marchand ran as a common thread through nearly all my interviews.

While some simply considered community credits as the price of admission to

Tent City 3—or, as one resident put it, "Everyone has to sing for their supper in some way"—others actively sought to engage with the outside world but on their own terms. Indeed, as my conversations about community credits progressed, what became clear was how different types of community credit reflected differing conceptions of the relationship between the tent city and the community in which it was temporarily located.

As people explained why they disliked community credits, a pattern emerged in which, although they hated some aspects of community credits, they deeply valued others. Shortly after claiming emphatically that community credits "suck," Martin went on to explain, "I do think it's good to interact. I just don't like the sideshow effect. But I think homeless people need to get out there and talk *with* folks—just regular talk—and not let them look down on you." What appeared at first as a condemnation of community credits emerges as a refusal not of community credits, per se, but of the exclusionary logic they sometimes embodied and enabled.

Most of the interactions for which residents received community credits primarily functioned as public relations. Although these necessary interactions were much disliked, nearly all residents agreed that having a stake in the future of the camp, being involved in the community outside the tent city, and calling attention to homelessness were important. Where residents disagreed was in their ideas about how and under what circumstances these goals should be accomplished. Many residents, particularly the more extroverted and outgoing folks, relished opportunities to make connections and share their diverse expertise. Although most community credits related to maintaining positive relations with potential host sites, community credits could also be assigned for speaking engagements, camp tours, school visits, or occasionally for helping with organized neighborhood cleanups or social events such as barbecues or ice cream socials. In contrast to outreach activities with potential hosts, these events rarely focused on what these groups could do for the homeless. Rather, the main imperative of these meetings, at least in the mind of the campers who participated, was to break down stereotypes and highlight commonalities between tent city residents and their formally housed neighbors.

In general, the campers I spoke with enjoyed these events. After one of these, in which some camp residents sat on a panel to discuss homelessness, one woman confided in me that she had really "had fun." Normally very quiet and reserved around camp, she spoke often and animatedly on the panel. When I asked her why she enjoyed it, she told me that rather than feeling like a "charity case or an outcast," it was an opportunity to share her knowledge and "give back" to the community and show that "we are no different from anyone else—we just don't have houses." In these meetings, and in many of the interactions between the camp and its neighbors, demonstrating that "we are no different than anyone else" was an intentional reframing of recognition—this time on their own terms.

For both the SHARE collective and Tent City 3 residents, the refusal to be recognized as homeless and all it insinuated was part of a broader and more fundamental effort at self-determination. Even in its outreach to potential host organizations, the SHARE organization and camp residents themselves attempted to resist homeless stereotypes and foreground collective values of dignity, inclusion, and autonomy in their outreach and negotiations. Material sent by SHARE to potential hosts and the surrounding communities in advance of the camp's arrival clearly emphasize as a point of pride the self-governed nature of the camp as well as the honesty and responsibility with which they conduct their operations. For instance, a flyer sent to a recent host neighborhood emphasizes that "our greatest strength is a reputation for being responsible in our operations." This is a low bar. For me, as a participant observer, these claims always felt both cringey and debasing. However, in the context of perceptions of homeless irrationality, these were powerful and, for many housed neighbors, surprising.

Whether conscious or not, foregrounding honesty and responsibility served as a sort of trojan horse for contesting the boundaries of homeless exclusion. For example, in the mandatory community meetings held in the host community prior to the tent city's arrival, residents, including myself, often emphasized their roles and duties in the camp, as well as their skills and occupations outside the camp. These explanations served a dual purpose. On one hand, residents and the SHARE organization wanted to show that they would be good neighbors and that a self-managed homeless encampment was neither a threat nor a sign of neighborhood decay. Mostly, however, participants in these meetings would simply, as one of my tent neighbors told me, "try to get across the idea that we are just normal people." However, the tent city's desire to foreground these values did not always sit well with housed neighbors and members of host organizations who were used to the embedded social hierarchies of wealth and poverty.

Refusal can be unsettling. For some tent city hosts and those who sometimes unwittingly or unwillingly found themselves tent city neighbors, assertions of collective autonomy, responsibility, and normality were not well received. In the five meetings I attended and in some of the media reports of those events, people suggested that the failure of residents to perform homelessness was at best ungrateful and, at worst, impossible. These opinions are well captured in an article published in 2004, titled "Tent City Residents Are Homeless on Their Own Terms." *Seattle Post-Intelligencer* reporter Claudia Rowe writes about how Tent City 3's spinoff camp, Tent City 4, sparked controversy by rejecting short-term shelter offers and asserting their own terms when accepting help. At a community meeting between camp members and their prospective neighbors near a church on Seattle's east side, residents expressed discomfort with the group's desire to stipulate the conditions of their residency. One woman is quoted as saying, "They kind of make the decisions, and that's not always comfortable." Particularly at issue, Rowe notes, was the group's refusal to accept shelter beds. Rowe quotes one attendee: "Obviously, they don't want our help—they just want a place to squat and people to make dinner for them. . . . They don't even think of themselves as homeless. This is a lifestyle for them."[11] This quote indicates something deeper than mere ingratitude. In emphasizing the fact that, at least in this person's mind, the residents of Tent City "don't even think of themselves as homeless" indicates how residents' assertions of collective autonomy unsettle and, in many ways, undermine tropes of informally housed people's abject dependency.

In some cases, the notion that unhoused people might refuse to perform proper homeless subjectivity has led to the SHARE organization being accused of taking advantage of the helpless and pathological homeless. Critics have on occasion argued that the tent city is not, in fact, a collective of self-governing individuals but rather a small group of political zealots leading a group of gullible homeless half-wits around by the nose. In one article a tent city critic is quoted as saying, "It's a complete fraud. . . . It doesn't help people; in fact, it holds the homeless hostage for political purposes."[12] In another article, a resident who lived near one of SHARE's tent cities suggested, "I believe SHARE exists to help homeless people. . . . But part of their mission includes a political element that may or may not best serve the people in Tent City. Maybe it does in the long run, but in the short run, I think they get played as pawns."[13] While it is true that over the years I have encountered a handful of former tent city residents who felt that SHARE leadership was heavy handed and undemocratic in the pursuit of its political goals, the relationship between being "played as pawns" and SHARE's political stance is structural rather than personal. At the core of these examples, as well as dozens of others voiced by SHARE/WHEEL's critics, lies the assumption that those who lack access to formal housing, if their views do not conform to middle-class homed conceptions of homelessness, must either be unworthy of care or victims of coercion or control. The notion that unhoused people might refuse to be grateful or accepting of whatever was on offer was, for some, unsettling.

In her seminal essay "Can the Subaltern Speak?," Gayatri Spivak illustrates how colonial categorizations of otherness constrain the possibilities of subjugated voices for being heard or understood outside the paradigm of colonial meaning-making—or "worlding" in Spivak's words.[14] The "homeless" residents of Tent City 3 are caught in an analogous predicament. In a world in which exclusion from spaces of private property justifies political and social exclusion, SHARE has an existential need to advocate for the right to self-determination for the unhoused. Yet they are forced to do that work on a terrain that presumes the pathology and deviance of the very people who are doing the advocating. This occasionally has the effect of placing camp residents in the precarious and sometimes unwanted position of political activists simply because they do not look or act homeless enough or, as the commentator above put it, "don't even think of themselves as homeless." Ironically, claims of self-governance and collective responsibility made by encampment residents, when understood through the lens of homeless dependence and pathology, serve to reify and reinforce social divisions and hierarchies. In other words, if they do not self-recognize as dependent and pathological, they must be being "played as pawns" or "held hostage for political purposes." As the object of knowledge defined by and through its difference from a homed norm, the homeless subject, like Gayatri Spivak's postcolonial subaltern, cannot speak.

Encroachment

Seeking public visibility to call attention to the issue of homelessness has always been a fundamental part of SHARE/WHEEL's work and mission. However, this aspect of SHARE's work held little interest for most of those living in Tent City 3. Though there were always a few people present in camp who felt it was important to engage in political issues pertaining to homelessness, this was by and large a minority position. For most people living in the tent city, acceptance wasn't about political recognition or about normalization of the camps. Rather, I found that my campmates sought to extend the same values of dignity and respect that shaped the homespace of Tent City 3 to their relations with neighbors and the communities with which they interacted. As was the case within the space of the tent city, this community-building was also homemaking—an attempt to be at home in their hometown. As in the tent city, this too was a process—a process not just of acceptance or toleration but of interaction, exchange, and self-determined recognition: a quiet encroachment of the ordinary.

Although assertions of collective self-governance by Tent City 3 residents were occasionally met with a repetition of normative divisions between homed and homeless, such occasions nonetheless enabled tent city residents to assert themselves as equals. Under a presumption of equality, tent city residents challenged the boundaries of community, belonging, and inclusion, not through collective action or appeals for state recognition but through one-on-one interactions.

Through their interactions with housed neighbors, refusal and the demand for an alternative politics of recognition morphed into a possibility of thinking differently. The desire to interact as equals with those outside the camp was very much an extension of the desire for dignity, inclusion, and mutual care that formed the basis of homespace in the tent city. These interactions between campers and their neighbors proved transformative for their formally housed neighbors as well.

When I spoke with housed residents who had engaged with Tent City 3, many mentioned transformation. Gary, a college student who had attended the panel discussion mentioned earlier, described the experience as "exploding all my myths about homeless people." In another case, one fifth grader from a local elementary school who had participated in a tour and lunch with Tent City 3 residents confided somewhat disappointedly to his mother and me that "I didn't know homeless people were so normal." A similar chord was struck by a junior high school teacher who was quoted in a *Seattle Post-Intelligencer* article as saying, "I am surrounded here by homeless people whom, if I met them on the street, I would look at with bias and prejudice. I would be afraid. Yet here in this church hall . . . they seem nothing but kind people."[15] Exchanges like these occurred with striking regularity. It seemed like everywhere the camp went, there were housed folks who were genuinely shocked by the realization that people without houses could be normal, kind people.

These interactions occurred not just in structured settings but also through everyday encounters in public space. While chatting with an elderly woman at a bus stop near the tent city one day, it came up in conversation that I was conducting research there. Without prompting or knowing exactly what it was that I was researching, she immediately recounted an incident: "One of the guys from the tent city came by the other day and offered to help me with my yardwork. We were talking, and he told me that part of the reason he was living in the tent city was that he was helping his ex-wife pay for his son's college tuition! Can you believe that? I wish I had that kind of strength!" While I do not know if this particular story is true, it was not uncommon for residents to have significant financial and familial responsibilities. Yet, as this woman's apparent surprise suggests, the physical and discursive walls between formally and informally housed people are high. People are seldom aware, or at least fail to consider, that many of those who are homeless are not only employed but have a variety of financial responsibilities. In my experience, housed people were consistently surprised that informally housed people have lives, interests, and desires that they are interested in expressing. These realizations, while small, would likely not have occurred in these instances without residents' refusal to embody homelessness. In everyday one-on-one interactions with housed neighbors, their refusal opened a possibility for expanding the boundaries of community.

While most encounters outside the tent city occurred with schoolchildren, college students, neighbors, church members, or community groups, one particularly powerful example illustrates how these small interactions can powerfully challenge the norms of propertied exclusion. Shortly after my departure in the summer of 2006, the tent city invited the mayor and members of the city council of the nearby city of Tukwila to come and spend a weekend. They accepted the invitation. A week later the mayor published his reflections on the experience in an editorial in a local paper. Mayor Steven Mullet recounted:

> Council members and city staff accepted their invitation and found honest, hardworking people—people whose jobs didn't currently afford them quite the income to stay in more permanent housing. People who were no different than you and me, people who just want to be productive citizens, who need just a little more time to amass their resources so that they can move on.... We learned that all our pre-perceptions, prejudices and preconceived notions were all wrong. None of the worries that we had as citizens had come to fruition. We learned how fragile our circumstances are and that one major life event can change a person's living conditions overnight. Most of all we re-learned some of the values we learned in kindergarten—that all of us contribute something to the quality of life in our community.[16]

This excerpt poignantly expresses how small, intimate exchanges unsettle the boundaries of propertied exclusion. Through these interactions, assumptions about who is included and who is excluded were challenged and negotiated. In these moments housed and unhomed alike were forced to challenge their own ideas about self and other in ways that were small but meaningful. In enabling the reframing of unhoused people from their constitutively produced positionality as deviant and dependent others to normative propertied personhood—to simply "normal"—residents of the tent city were rendered ordinary. With each move to a new neighborhood, community meeting, panel discussion, tour, and shared meal, Tent City became more ordinary, more normalized. Further, from the persistence and normalization of Tent City 3 and its residents, there emerged another possibility of contesting the hegemony of propertied exclusion—an encroachment of the ordinary.

Even though the colonial necessity to expel and erase nonpropertied others creates and relies on the enactment of a hierarchy of property-based subjectivities, Tent City residents refuse these hierarchies in their relations with potential hosts, neighbors, and the greater community. In doing so they engage in a politics of self-determination and alternative recognition. By demanding to participate as equals in their interactions with camp neighbors, residents sometimes successfully expand the bounds of community and home, not through symbolic exposure but through meaningful one-on-one exchanges. While struggles over the proper physical and social place of home and homelessness are voiced in Seattle's courthouse, city hall, and the pages of its newspapers, they are also made over meals and conversations in churches, schools, and community centers. While the former are certainly important, this chapter illustrates how through small but meaningful interactions, new subjectivities, spaces, and perhaps conceptions of belonging beyond property may arise. In a 1999 reflection on her essay "Can the Subaltern Speak?" Gayatri Spivak poses a question: "How does one win the attention of the subaltern without coercion or crisis?" Her answer is "mind changing on both sides." She explains that "the necessary collective efforts are to change laws, relations of production, systems of education, and health care. But without the mind changing of one-on-one responsible contact, nothing will stick."[17] This mind-changing contact in Seattle is made possible by the specificity of Tent City 3. Through its sustained presence on Seattle's landscape and ongoing interactions with camp residents on their own terms, Tent City 3 embodies a slow encroachment of the ordinary in which those without property might be considered at home in their dwelling's neighborhoods and hometowns.

6. Home beyond Property

Ten years after I left Tent City 3, Seattle passed an ordinance that effectively legalized self-managed encampments. When I first heard the news, I was struck with a mix of emotions. The ordinance was, after all, born from structural failure. As with the original incarnation of Tent City, Seattle's decision to legalize encampments was once again a response to increased media attention, lack of housing resources, and the growing presence of visible poverty. However, I also felt that in the proliferation and normalization of self-governed spaces for the unhoused, there might be a possibility of contesting the hegemony of propertied exclusion. Perhaps, I thought, the normalized persistence of Tent City 3 and the continued, ongoing, and sometimes mind-changing interactions with hosts and neighbors might multiply with the proliferation of new sanctioned encampments—and become an encroachment.

Yet the presence of the visibly poor and their dwellings continues to be an unsettling presence in the settler city. Here we reach the limits of such encroachments. In the last instance, it was only through the persistence and normalization enabled by limited legal recognition that residents of Tent City 3 were able to craft spaces, subjectivities, and governance within and against the colonial logics of possessive property. It was only from the stability of Tent City 3 that residents were able to contest colonial hierarchies and engage in a politics of self-recognition. It was only by reclaiming and enacting home in the normalized context of Tent City 3 that residents could be recognized as members of the broader community. This inclusion did not extend to other nonnormalized homespaces of cars, unsanctioned camps, or streets, which increasingly served as homes of last resort for those displaced in the rapidly gentrifying space of Seattle after the 2008 recession. While the sanctioning of self-governed encampments in some ways expanded the possibilities for being at home, it also hardened the boundaries between acceptable and deviant homespaces and bodies. In this context, my hopefulness is tempered by the realization that the legalization of self-governed encampments that occurred in 2015 must also be seen as part of a broader settler strategy of erasure and containment that continued to intensify up to and through the COVID-19 pandemic.

In this chapter, I discuss the legalization of homeless encampments in Seattle and describe how the sanctioning of these spaces by state authorities represents a tool for managing marginality that reinscribes settler norms of propertied personhood and the deviant homeless subject. Sanctioning encampments offered some potential for expanding unhoused individuals' living space. Yet it also marked a period of increasingly coercive state control and containment of unhoused people in response to a growing crisis caused by the increased numbers and visibility of the informally housed and their habitations. This movement toward coercive containment was further reinforced by the approach to unsheltered people during the COVID-19 crisis. Possibilities for radical transformation in the provision of shelter emerged but were subsumed by the carceral care approach to housing that marks so many state interventions. In conclusion, I consider how the practices of care, commoning, and collectivity enacted by Tent City 3 residents might allow us to foreground home as a process of inclusion and belonging rather than a site of exclusion, erasure, and epistemic violence. Here, I ask that we consider home beyond property, and how this might be the basis for imagining a future where everyone can be at home.

The Homeless Crisis and the Sanctioned Encampment

Homelessness in Seattle had changed since I left the city in 2006. In 2005, King County, in which Seattle is located, released a plan to end homelessness in ten years. The plan argued that homelessness had become normalized, and it was time to ensure that there was an appropriate, affordable roof over the bed of everyone living in King County.[1] Ten years later, though, homelessness had not ended. Not only was there not a roof over everyone's head, but the number of people without access to housing had increased by a dramatic 42 percent.[2] Even more dramatic was the number of *unsheltered* individuals in King County, which doubled between 2005 and 2015.

This increase in unsheltered individuals was the result of several factors. Since 2009, rising housing costs and largely stagnant wages had pushed many more King County residents into precarious housing conditions.[3] At the same time, policy changes at the federal, state, and local levels shifted funding away from simple shelter and toward transitional housing, resulting in emergency shelters becoming increasingly scarce and selective, particularly for single adults.[4] As a result of these trends, the number of people turning to tents and encampments for shelter and safety increased dramatically.[5] In 2015, passage of the ordinance sanctioning encampments took place amid a dramatic rise in the number of people living on the streets.

The growth in the number of unsheltered people and the visibility of their habitations was exacerbated by a tremendous building boom in Seattle and other cities across the American West. In the wake of the post-2008 recession, Seattle, like many other West Coast cities, experienced a period of prosperity largely driven by tech and real estate that remade the urban landscape. During this time, the last vestiges of Seattle's industrial and export-driven past gave way to glitzy new corporate headquarters, high-end condominium complexes, and the restaurants, boutiques, and service infrastructure that cater to an affluent population. Funded mainly by multinational investment capital and following planning trends in high-density, infill development, much recent urban growth has occurred in the very areas of the city that historically served as a refuge for the city's informally housed.

These changes came at a tremendous cost to Seattle's poorest residents. Not only have rising rents and housing prices and the scarcity of low-income options pushed more people into housing precarity, but the private redevelopment of Seattle's marginal spaces, warehouse districts, and former public housing projects have made those who lack access to formal shelter both more prevalent and more visible. This boom in new construction, combined with an increasingly visible displaced and unsheltered population, made encampments an increasingly contentious fixture on the urban landscape.[6]

To address this growing crisis, then mayor Mike McGinn convened an advisory board composed of local homeless care providers and advocates to examine the possibility of allowing self-governed sanctioned encampments on public land. The panel recommended allowing the camps, suggesting that the ninety-day limit imposed on SHARE be lifted to allow for more stability. From these recommendations, the city council adopted ordinance 123729 in 2011. This ordinance effectively allowed encampments to stay in perpetuity on church-owned property. Citing the successful history of religious organizations hosting encampments—of which Tent City 3 is the only example—this new ordinance replaced the consent decree under which Tent City 3 operated. Not only did this ordinance allow for unlimited stays, but it added the ability to cook and to include children in the camp—two of the most hated prohibitions in Tent City 3 during my stay. In addition, it enabled the creation of Camp Unity. Formed by former members

Home beyond Property

of Tent City 3, Camp Unity is a self-managed camp very similar in structure to Tent City 3 and hosted by churches in the North Seattle area. Unlike Tent City 3, though, Camp Unity operates as its own 501(c)(3) nonprofit. Camp members each pay a dollar per month for camp maintenance. While these benefits expand the possibilities for people without access to formal housing, the passage of ordinance 123729 did little to stem the growth of unsheltered homelessness and the presence of visibly homeless persons, and thus unsanctioned encampments continued to increase in Seattle.

In the years immediately after passage of the 2010 ordinance, housing affordability continued to decrease for Seattleites, and the number of unsheltered people grew by 21 percent between 2010 and 2014.[7] Increasingly, Seattleites' attention focused on the growing number of unsanctioned encampments in Seattle's public spaces. Between 2013 and 2015, the number of articles expressing concern about encampments doubled.[8] As the numbers of unsheltered people continued to swell and the cost of housing in the gentrified city continued to increase, people sheltered wherever they could find it. Often grouped together for safety and community, the habitations of the unhoused by 2015 had become, for many Seattleites, an unsettling presence. In the face of this intensifying crisis, Mayor Ed Murray convened another task force to address the issue of the growing unsheltered population.

Once again, the task force, citing Seattle's long history with SHARE and its more overtly political spinoff, Nickelsville, recommended expanding sanctioned encampments. This time, the now left-leaning Seattle City Council agreed, and Seattle Ordinance 124747, also known as the Transitional Encampments Ordinance (TEO), was signed into existence on January 4, 2015. In substance, the bill allowed for the creation on city land of three encampments of up to one hundred people each, two operated by the Nickelsville organization and one operated by SHARE but financially managed by the Low-Income Housing Institute (LIHI).

Tent City 3's normalized ordinariness was fundamental to Seattle's decision to legalize self-governed encampments. As of 2023, twenty-three years of experience with a large, semiformal, self-governed encampment has led to nine sanctioned villages on public land within city limits. These villages are now operated entirely by LIHI and consist of a mix of tiny houses and tents throughout the city. There are also an additional three sanctioned camps, including Tent City 3, in the greater Seattle area and two on Seattle's east side operating on private, mostly church-owned, property. Although each site functions according to its own rules, all rely in some way on the Tent City 3 model of self-governance and management.

Though this might be seen as a win for encampment residents and their advocates, it is also part of a broader settler strategy of erasure and containment. At first blush, the legalization and proliferation of self-managed encampments and tiny-house villages seemed to be in keeping with what I call the "encroachment of the ordinary." The proliferation of these relatively autonomous encampments and villages can potentially enable spaces where residents like those in Tent City 3 might reclaim a sense of dignity, autonomy, and respect, creating a sense of home within and against propertied exclusions. Further, the proliferation of camps, particularly as new, non-SHARE encampments and tiny-house villages are created, gives informally housed people in Seattle a more diverse set of governance styles and priorities, likely making it easier for people to find a space in which they feel at home. Most important, enabling and increasing the visibility of self-managed encampments in Seattle's public spaces has potentially laid the groundwork for disrupting the boundary between propertied and propertyless. While it is tempting to view the legalization and proliferation of self-managed encampments as an unprecedented win for unhoused refugees from an increasingly exclusionary housing market, the realities of poverty management in the postgentrification city paint a more complicated picture.

Camps and Containment

Although transformative possibilities persist, formalization reflects the priorities of the state. In the settler colonial context, this means eviction, erasure, and quarantine of those who unsettle settler norms. In 1990, Tent City emerged as both a political statement and a space of collective self-determination. By contrast, the encampments that emerged after passage of the 2015 ordinance were, to many Seattleites as well as public officials, begrudgingly accepted forms of containment and recuperation.[9] In the face of growing housing displacement, inadequate shelter, and increasing public complaint, the legalization of encampments was envisioned as a stopgap measure to enable the city to move informal encampment dwellers into more predictable and controllable locations. In contrast to the tent city, the state's goal for sanctioned encampments was not to resist or change the settler logic of propertied exclusion and recuperation but to reinforce it.

In the United States, the informal dwellings of the poor represent the frontiers of settler space. Within the mythology of settler progress, informal spaces become temporary, exceptional places that may be briefly tolerated but must ultimately give way to propertied spaces and normativities. This logic is embodied in Seattle's ordinance legalizing encampments. It begins by acknowledging the ongoing growth of unsheltered homelessness in Seattle and refers to the current situation as a "crisis that requires the response of not just government, but by our entire community."[10] While the language of emergency echoes SHARE founders' calls for recognition, the goal could not be more different. Farther down in the preamble, it states that "the City's focus on solutions for people who are homeless should be a roof overhead and services to connect individuals with a pathway toward long-term housing. However, the current capacity of our housing and homeless services continuum cannot meet the needs of all those who are homeless and, as an alternative, tent encampments can offer a sense of safety and community while seeking longer term housing options."[11] Although the reference to "safety and community" echoes the words of Tent City 3 residents, the emphasis on services and the inability to meet needs is telling. In 1990, the original Tent City was the product of a group of unhoused residents and their supporters staking a claim to the city that had marginalized, mistreated, and banished them from public view. By 2015, lacking both the affordable housing and the shelter space to contain Seattle's exploding number of visibly homeless people, the sanctioned encampment had become a cost-effective way to reduce the visibility of the homeless and their habitations while also formally managing their presence in the city.

The city's rebranding of encampments as transitional points to the dual nature of sanctioned encampments in the normative logic of property-based homes. In a trenchant analysis of sanctioned encampments, sociologist Chris Herring demonstrates how sanctioned encampments are "shaped by urban policies and serve varied and even contradictory roles."[12] Sanctioned encampments like Tent City 3 can be a place where residents create a sense of home outside the disciplinary and carceral apparatuses of homeless management. At the same time, they serve as "tools of containing homeless populations." Thus, while the legalization of Tent City 3 in 2000 and the sanctioned encampment ordinance of 2015 differ in intent, Herring argues that they are both "tools and targets in the management of marginality."[13] In the case of Seattle, sanctioning encampments was another tool in state management of marginality, reinforcing the boundaries of normative propertied personhood.

City officials and encampment advocates, for their part, touted the legalization and expansion of sanctioned encampments as a way to remove unsanctioned camps and their inhabitants from city streets and parks.[14] These efforts had already been increasing. In 2013, there were 131 encampment displacements, 351 in 2014, and 527 by November 2015.[15] In spite of state displacement, both the number of unsheltered people and media attention to unsanctioned encampments continued to grow.

The management of marginality itself seemed to be in crisis. In response, Mayor Murray declared a "homeless state of emergency" on November 2, 2015.[16] The declaration allotted an extra $7.3 million in one-time funds to increase the number of available shelter beds and coordinate efforts to move people from unsanctioned dwellings into sanctioned shelter spaces. In the context of Seattle's "homeless emergency," sanctioned encampments became another tool for maintaining settler norms. Whereas the informal habitations of the poor mark the frontier of civilized modernity, the state-sanctioned or formalized version of the encampment serves to both "civilize" those spaces and shore up the borders of propertied normativity. As a transitional site, the encampment also brightens the line between propertied norms of home and deviant others.

Those who reside in these spaces can be seen not as threatening or unsettling to norms of propertied persons but merely in transition to these norms. They are propertied-persons-in-becoming. Like the reservation, the Indian boarding school, the poorhouse, and the segregated ghettos that preceded them, sanctioned encampments serve to fix their inhabitants both physically and socially in the colonial hierarchy while simultaneously reaffirming settler norms and hierarchies as normal, natural, and inevitable.

The spatial fix provided by sanctioning encampment likewise creates its deviant other, the unsanctioned encampment. By 2016, Seattle, along with many other West Coast cities, experienced tremendous growth in people lacking any kind of officially sanctioned shelter.[17] Even though the overall number of unhoused individuals remained relatively stable between 2009 and 2017, the number of people residing outside, on the street, or in tents, cars, or other spaces "unfit for human habitation" had increased by almost 70 percent. Thus, while Seattle was allowing some sanctioned encampments, it was also witnessing a rise in unsanctioned encampments that increasingly unsettled propertied norms.

The solution to the unsettling unsanctioned encampment was, as it has been since Seattle's incorporation, removal and displacement. Rather than expand legal recognition and protection to all habitations of the unhoused, the city chose to sweep them away. "Sweeps"—the demolition and removal of unsanctioned encampments—have long been an issue in Seattle, and encampment sweeps tripled between 2013 and 2016.[18] Then, in January 2016, only a few months after Seattle declared homelessness a state of emergency, the high-profile murder of a resident occurred in a large, notorious unsanctioned encampment called the Jungle.

After the shooting, public outcry about the visible presence of poverty reached a fever pitch. News articles about unsanctioned encampments jumped from 53 in 2013 to a whopping 233 in 2016. The tone of these articles was overwhelmingly dire. Stories of rampant drug use, attempted rape, and general danger, disorder, and criminality flooded the news. In October 2016, the Jungle was swept and bulldozed while protestors held signs saying, "Housing is a human right" and chanted, "Stop the sweeps."[19] But the sweeps didn't stop. Nor did the conditions that displaced people from housing, and visible poverty continued to grow. The specter of the unsanctioned encampment as a space of danger and criminality became the spatial marker of deviance that justified intensified policing and carceral management of the inhabitants.

Erasure of visibly poor and unhoused bodies from urban space performs a dual purification of Seattle's postgentrification landscape. Legal scholar Sara Rankin has described these efforts to cleanse public space of visible poverty as the "transcarceration of homelessness."[20] *Transcarceration*, Rankin explains, refers to "campaigns that confine unsheltered people through means such as involuntary commitment into psychiatric facilities or compulsory segregation into authorized zones or camps."[21] Indeed, this has been the stated purpose of Seattle's encampment sweeps since the practice was formalized in 2017.[22] Forced removal of the dwellings of the unhoused aesthetically cleanses the urban landscape and restores a proper normative urban order.[23] At the same time, the cleansing of visible poverty from urban space is accompanied by a state-driven ordering of another sort: the reclamation and replacement of poor bodies into acceptable spaces of poverty management.

Despite the city's ongoing efforts to remove encampments and move people into sanctioned spaces of care, most people, like the residents of Tent City 3 that I interviewed in 2006, refuse these offers of what they view as carceral care.[24] These refusals, while not unlike those practiced by tent city residents, have been met with a corresponding strategy of encampment sweeps, displacements, and evictions.[25] The sanctioning of encampments created a tautology of property, whereby those without property were either properly contained in sanctioned spaces or improperly inhabiting the city and thus unruly and deviant embodiments of the danger presented by dwelling outside the boundaries of private property.

The city's growing tolerance for sanctioned camps has gone hand in hand with an increase in punitive homeless ordinances, heightened policing, and traumatic, damaging, and costly sweeps. Unhoused residents can accept carceral care or they will be displaced and evicted from city streets. Further, since 2017, access to new sanctioned encampments has been available only via referral. Echoing historical practices of the disciplinary management of the unhomed as both out of place and pathological, the sanctioned encampment is another, albeit less dehumanizing, node in the complex of carceral homeless management that maintains settler norms of propertied personhood and its others. Although the sanctioning of self-governed encampments may disrupt some norms of propertied personhood, the existence of such encampments allows the city to reframe those who are unwilling or unable to access these or other sanctioned spaces as intransigent or "service-resistant" deviants and criminals. In these instances, and for those so labeled, violent and punitive measures are justified in the name of health, safety, and the preservation of urban order.

Order here refers to the recuperation of unhoused bodies and their habitations into settler norms of propertied ownership. None of these efforts addresses the root cause of homelessness. Homelessness is a property problem. In a world in which property, as a state-created and state-enforced right of exclusion, is the necessary yet finite prerequisite for the ability to be at home, homelessness is a product of state-manufactured scarcity. The ability of everyone to be at home calls for a commoning of property that Nicholas Blomley has referred to as "a right to not be excluded."[26] But such a right has never been part of any strategy to end homelessness in the United States. Rather, ending homelessness in this country is not about making everyone at home but only determining who can and cannot be at home in the space of the settler colonial nation-state.

The sanctioning of encampments, while potentially enabling an expansion of spaces of homeless refusal and new productions of home, also creates new territories of confinement and displacement. This once again is a settler colonial story. Within the logic of settler colonial erasure, displacement does not revolve around simply eviction or quarantine but rather concerns the recuperation of nonconforming bodies and spaces to settler norms of propertied personhood.[27] In this case, the sanctioned encampment, following in the well-trod footsteps of the reservation, the prison, and the internment camp, functions as a containment strategy aimed at purifying property-based urban space in times of urban crisis and moral panic.

Crisis, Containment, and COVID-19

In the spring of 2020, the drive to contain the unhoused was quickly overshadowed by the need to contain a much greater threat: COVID-19. During the first few tentative weeks of the pandemic, Seattle and many other cities imposed commercial lockdowns and implored their housed residents to stay indoors while disregarding the lives of people warehoused in congregate shelters. Despite an announcement to the contrary, Seattle also continued the devastating practice of evicting encampment dwellers and destroying their shelters and possessions.[28] These first weeks were a devastating but not surprising response to people already considered alien, invasive, and ultimately expendable.

As with the declaration of homeless emergency still in effect, the declaration of a COVID emergency gave city government broad new powers. These powers included the ability to permanently acquire hotel rooms as housing for the unhoused and decommodify them as spaces of home rather than ownership. These powers went largely unused. Rather, as Ananya Roy notes, "these legal statements linger as a haunting, gesturing at the possible interruption of established relationships between state power and property rights."[29] When they did respond to the dangerous conditions in the streets and shelters, instead of challenging regimes of propertied privilege and exclusion, cities like Seattle overwhelmingly chose to use emergency funds to expand temporary shelter space. This reaffirmed access to owned property as the singular response to those displaced by this very model.

These expansions intensified the already carceral management of the unhoused. In Seattle, the bulk of the COVID response to homelessness was to expand the network of carceral care to accommodate more social distancing. The city added a number of congregate shelter beds while decreasing the density of those already in existence. In addition, the county response included temporarily leasing hotel rooms in surrounding cities. While temporary hotel spaces were, for the most part, welcomed by unhoused people, in many cases residents were denied room keys, subjected to random curfews, or denied the ability to have guests or use some hotel amenities. These shelters continued practices of limiting resident movement, visitors, and ability to leave and return, echoing processes of unhoming that have led many to avoid these types of spaces.

For those lucky few who received housing vouchers or access to permanent supportive housing, such achievements, while better than having no sanctioned space in which to exist, serve also to reproduce the settler logic of propertied personhood.[30] These spaces quarantine the poor out of sight in marginal and precarious housing situations that render them vulnerable once again to displacement. At the same time, acceptance of housing vouchers or other homeless housing assistance cements, as the term *supportive housing* suggests, the marginalization of the poor and acceptance of their dependent status.

For those who refused these spaces, respite was brief. After initially continuing to sweep and displace people dwelling in public spaces, the city, following federal Centers for Disease Control (CDC) guidelines, broadly turned to a shelter-in-place philosophy that included reducing sweeps and providing portable bathrooms and sanitation facilities to those living in informal encampments. However, by summer of 2020 public outcry regarding encampments had once more increased. By fall, Seattle was again engaged in an emergency offensive to eliminate informal dwellings and coax or coerce their residents into sanctioned spaces of containment.

As the pandemic dragged into its second year, Seattle, like many other cities throughout the western United States, faced the daunting task of enticing tourists and remote workers back to vacant offices and a struggling service sector, while wrestling with how to best address the disorderly spectacle of unsheltered homelessness. By that time, although both city and county had achieved a net gain in temporary and permanent shelter spaces, many more emergency spaces were being closed or phased out, pushing more people outside.

On the streets, sweeps and forced evictions from encampments had once again ramped up to pre-pandemic levels. In August 2021, the *Seattle Times* reported that "the tolerance by housed neighbors and business owners for homeless people remaining in place is over. After pulling back from almost all encampment removals in 2020, Seattle has now conducted at least 33 since March."[31] This uptick in city demolitions of the dwellings of the unhoused suggests a return to the pre-pandemic norm of costly, traumatic, and ongoing forced displacement of the city's unhoused residents.

Despite an overall increase in the number of sanctioned spaces available, there continue to be more unsheltered people than there are sanctioned residential spaces, and the spaces that do exist continue to be carceral and dehumanizing.[32] As a result of ongoing sweeps, often in response to housed neighbors' complaints, people are being pushed, swept, and coerced into ever more marginal spaces. The stakes of propertied exclusions, evictions, and erasures are high. In 2020, an unprecedented 184 unhoused people lost their lives. In 2021, that number rose to 221. Twenty-eight of those died from COVID-19.[33] In 2022, there were 310.[34] All of them were victims of the violence we call homelessness.

This is but a small part of the cost of the dispossession of property. As a tool of settler colonial conquest, erasure, and quarantine, the creation and maintenance of land as something that can be owned has always been an act of state violence.[35] Violent removals, evictions, and carceral containment, as well as the violence of dehumanization, cultural erasure, and physical death, are not side effects. They are esssential functions of land enclosure as possessive property. Homelessness is not a lack of property but rather a product of a propertied right to exclude, displace, and dispossess. Trapped in the settler colonial cartographies of property, spatial multiplicity and possibility are reduced to sameness/difference, oppression/opposition, or inside/outside. Within the ownership model of the propertied home there seems to be little alternative to building more walls, hardening boundaries, and policing the interstices in the hope that the spaces and bodies of the poor will disappear. Yet they do not disappear. Despite all efforts to the contrary, spaces of containment—the prison, the reservation, the camp—have always and continue to be rich sites of resistance and creativity that continue to point to something beyond the settler colonial project.

The Settler Colonial City in Crisis?

The intensified carcerality witnessed during the COVID-19 pandemic masks a more complex encroachment. Prior to the pandemic, as 2017 gave way to 2018, and then 2019, gentrification of Seattle's downtown continued unabated, housing prices continued to soar, and the number of unsheltered people on Seattle's streets continued to grow, bringing moral panic surrounding the visible habitations of the poor. This panic reached its apex with the airing of *Seattle Is Dying* in 2019. The imagery and narrative of *Seattle Is Dying* gave voice to public anxiety about the presence of visible poverty in the gentrified city. In this space, the habitations of the poor represented not simply disorder but an existential threat to the settler colonial city.

How are we to make sense of the tent city in this context? How can we understand acts of homeless refusal and efforts to reclaim home and humanity through practices of care, commoning, and collectivity? Most importantly, what are we to make of the proliferation and expansion of those spaces in the context of colonial modernity? By rendering visible the coloniality of the relationship among home, property, and personhood, it becomes possible to view Seattle's efforts to evict, displace, and contain those who lack access to formal housing as not a victory of order over chaos, as *Seattle Is Dying* suggests, but an ongoing struggle between competing yet unequal ideas of who can be at home, where, and how.

In the context of the struggle to define the spaces and subjects of home, the phrase "Seattle is dying" can be seen in another light. Perhaps it is not the city itself but its colonial foundations and presuppositions that are in crisis. From this perspective, intensified elimination of informal encampments and increasing state control over sanctioned spaces do not mark a recovery of order from the chaos of poverty. Rather, they suggest a heightened battle in the struggle to maintain settler hegemony. This calls attention to the incomplete nature of the settler project and suggests the possibility of contestation.

Exclusionary property relations establish and maintain the settler state, yet they also produce the very homelessness that then must be contained through state coercion and violence. Since the formation of Tent City in 1990, efforts to contain the displaced have been ongoing and increasingly expansive. Seattle in the 2010s is exemplary. While the gentrification of the post-2008 era was wildly successful in terms of wealth, investment, and low unemployment, the cost of housing has continued to rise, and along with it the number of those who lack access to private property.

If we judge the success of homeless policy in the United States by its ability to reduce the number of homeless people, then it becomes difficult to characterize it as anything less than a near total failure. At no time since the United States has been tracking the number of unhoused people have the numbers decreased appreciably. Nationally the number of people without sanctioned housing has remained relatively stable, with modest fluctuations, at approximately 300,000 people since the early estimates of the 1980s. In Seattle, like many other West Coast cities, numbers have slowly but steadily increased since the city began systematic counts in 2005. This is despite the city's valiant efforts to increase both temporary and permanent housing options, including sanctioned encampments.

As the numbers of unhoused continue to outpace efforts to displace and contain them, it is possible to see Seattle's homeless crisis as a crisis of property-based ideas of home and homelessness. Further, the encampments and newly formed tiny-house villages suggest an alternative—a way of thinking home beyond property as a space of care, commoning, and collectivity. Perhaps that is the real emergency. Perhaps this is also the real lesson of Tent City 3: that care, commoning, and collectivity can offer ways to radically undo the propertied presuppositions of personhood.

This point was driven home to me when I visited for research in 2017, amid the increasing crisis in housing prices and after the encampment legalization ordinance. The encampment ordinance created another tool for state management of marginality and reaffirmed rather than disrupted propertied citizenship. Concurrently, Seattle saw increasing sweeps and calls for containment. Yet residents who were in contact with sanctioned encampment residents were experiencing an encroachment of the ordinary of their own. While the current of criminalization, settler colonialism, and carceral care continues, other currents exist alongside that we might harness to consider home beyond property.

For officials and service providers, the importance of Seattle's long engagement with Tent City 3 and its spinoffs for making the self-governed camp a viable dwelling option emerged as the overarching theme. Everyone I spoke to attributed both the passage of the sanctioned encampment ordinance and the relative success of its implementation to Seattle's long history with encampments, and Tent City 3 in particular. By 2017, Seattle had lived with Tent City 3 for well over a decade. This persistence was enabled in large part by the lack of eventfulness of the tent city's presence. When faced with encampments, it is not uncommon for worried neighbors and antihomeless advocates to raise the specter of increasing crime rates, public nuisances, and safety concerns, but none of this ever manifested. Thus, with every return or move of the camp, the threat of these bogeymen became less and less tenable. In my original fieldnotes, I chalked this up to neighbors and critics simply coming to realize what people in Tent City 3 were telling them all along: that they were just "normal."

In 2017, however, these realizations of normality helped tent cities not only persist but proliferate. This came through particularly strongly in an interview I had with Cindy Roat, of Greater Seattle Cares, an organization that provides material support to Seattle area encampments. During our interview, she described a particularly contentious encampment move in the city of Shoreline, just north of Seattle proper. In this case, Camp United We Stand, a spin-off from Tent City 3, had lost its host and temporarily relocated to a parishioner's backyard. This move triggered a backlash, largely waged on the social media app Nextdoor, that Roat characterized as "horrible" and "vilifying." To her, the anger and vitriol largely came from a place of fear and lack of knowledge. It seemed like a "vision that they had of Shoreline being invaded by, like, zombie hordes of homeless drug addicts. It was like a scene out of a nightmare, and it was so *unrealistic*." While likely more restrained in tone than the Nextdoor conversations, a review of public comments submitted to the city affirmed Roat's characterization. Although some spoke of favorable past experiences with encampments, most comments repeated long-held, unfounded stereotypes of rising crime, visible drug addiction and mental illness, declining house values, and oddly, in a couple of comments, fears of sex slavery and child rape.

However, after a few months passed, Roat recalled, "Now that United We Stand has been around for a while, those attitudes do seem to be changing." Toward the end of the discussions with the city, Roat noticed that people were beginning to think of United We Stand campers as exceptional and not like "those other homeless." Small incremental victories like this were a common occurrence during my time at Tent City and even well before. When a camp arrived at a new location for the first time, there was resistance and even outrage. By the second or third time the camp arrived in that location, not only was there little resistance but the very few people who attended the mandatory community meetings mostly either spoke in support or offered to support or assist the tent city themselves.

George Scarola, director of homelessness for the City of Seattle in 2016–18, echoed Roat's experience. In reference to housed neighbors encountering encampment residents for the first time, he told me, "They are always surprised." He went on to explain that for most people the image they have is "frequently the ragged shoeless raving guy wrapped in a blanket." But, he explained, they show up at a community meeting and have no idea who is from the tent city and who is from the neighborhood. "So I think they are surprised at how ordinary [tent city residents] really are." This appeal to the ordinariness of tent city residents suggests that the politics of self-recognition I observed during my stay in 2006 was indeed encroaching. Such lowly appeals, in the context of propertied personhood, are radical. After twenty-three years in existence, the fact that meetings between encampments and their housed neighbors still have the capacity to be rendered normal is a small but meaningful rejection of the social division between homeless and homed. Rather than appearing as objects of charity, those without access to formal housing emerge from these encounters as simply normal.

It wasn't, however, the normalization of encampments that surprised me the most. It was the encroachment not just of the camps but of the practices of care, commoning, and collectivity that I observed in Tent City 3, which seemed to be proliferating. This also seemed to come as a surprise to Scarola. "It's amazing," he told me. "They [encampments] are like magnets for community involvement! People come out of the woodwork to do stuff." When I asked him why he thought that was, he explained that people wanted to do something to help other than "writing a check or donating a sack of clothes," but there wasn't much people knew to do. "[But then,] here is this group right in your neighborhood. . . . I think it's that simple. It's close, and people are very welcoming." In the months before my arrival, the fruits of the relationships between encampments and their host neighborhoods had been blossoming around the city. In the neighborhoods of Ballard, Interbay, and West Seattle, housed residents who had become familiar with the camp and its inhabitants had rallied and called upon the city to increase services, extend stays, and in the case of West Seattle, extend city support and recognition to a previously unsanctioned encampment.

Beyond the Crisis, Home

Within and against the exclusions of property, Tent City 3 persists. Between 2015 and 2022, amid the dual emergencies of visible poverty and the COVID pandemic, there was little mention of SHARE or Tent City 3 in the news. While Seattle was increasingly attuned to the habitations of the visibly poor, media reports about Tent City 3 became almost nonexistent, averaging about four per year despite the fact that the camp has throughout this time continued its intrepid march through Seattle, moving every ninety days, from church to university to community center. Further, while reports of unsanctioned encampments focus almost exclusively on public fears of disorder and criminality, media reports that mention Tent City 3 consist almost entirely of announcements of moves and new hosts. As it moves, it continues, through practices of care, commoning, and collectivity, to create homely spaces and subjects within and against propertied exclusion. Residents continue, through their ongoing interactions with hosts, to refuse homeless stereotypes and reframe recognition on their own terms. Indeed, as one of now many sanctioned encampments, the radicality of homeless refusal and collective homemaking has become ordinary.

Tent City 3 suggests a way of thinking home otherwise. Through their refusal of homeless subjectivities, residents create a sense and space of home within, against, and beyond the colonial logic of possessive property. Through practices of care, commoning, and collectivity, they create informal forms of homespace and belonging, and localized forms of governmentality. Beyond the space of the camp, residents refuse homeless stereotypes and seek recognition as equal participants in the construction of belonging. Taken together, these processes suggest a way of thinking home not as a bounded space of exclusion and segregation but as a place of openness, interaction, and negotiation. In the end, however, the practices of homemaking, citizenship, and governance of the tent city are both spatially and contextually contingent. While nearly all the tent city residents with whom I spoke highly valued the shared practices of care, commoning, and collectivity that enable the homespace of Tent City 3, few spoke of carrying those values or structures beyond tent city walls. Indeed, even if the desire was there, the possibilities are slim. Within the framework of the propertied home, escaping homelessness ultimately means participating in the very norms of precarity and exclusion that produce and maintain both homelessness itself and the normative ideals of propertied personhood.

The simple equation of home with private property and a cultural and policy environment that views access to private property as a single and unitary response to homelessness masks and enables the violence of displacement. Yet, in the United States, homelessness is defined exclusively in terms of one's relation or access to private or state-owned property. The idea that land can and must be owned to function as homespace has been the main weapon in the production and persistence of racialized settler colonial norms of social deviance and difference. Indeed, in the history of the settler colonial United States, the commodified home has been as much a weapon of exclusion, erasure, and dehumanization as it has been a space of shelter. Homelessness emerges not from a lack of shelter but from colonial processes of property making, normalization, and enforcement. Homelessness is the result of a myriad of unhoming processes through which the spaces, feelings, and bonds of home are undone through exclusionary practices of policing and the carceral spaces of homeless management.

To the extent that Tent City 3 and the myriad informal settlements in the United States and globally are considered exceptional, anomalous, dangerous, or deviant, the simple presence of these spaces does little to disrupt the settler colonial project of weaponized property relations. So, what does it mean to be at home in our dwellings, communities, and homelands? To do so requires envisioning an idea of home beyond property.

Thinking Home beyond Property—a Provocation

Thinking beyond propertied conceptions of home asks us to rethink the colonial binaries of formality/informality, home/homeless, and self/other. Rather than static, hierarchical, state-enforced boundaries that divide self from other and us from them, thinking home beyond property requires seeing legalized borderlines of ownership not as natural or necessary but as acts of domicidal power that forcibly displace people from normative boundaries of home. This demands rendering property porous—opening doors and tearing down the walls that support and sustain the settler colonial exclusions from home, hometown, and homeland.

Thinking home beyond property asks us to decenter the normative assumptions of the ownership model of property. For most contemporary city dwellers in the United States, the spaces of the settler colonial city appear as preinscribed through the binary division between those who have access to private property and those who do not, those who belong and those who do not, homeless and at home. Thinking about home beyond property requires reimagining these constructed dichotomies as spaces of possibility—as opportunities for homemaking.

The homemaking of Tent City 3 offers a possible starting point. Camp residents refused settler boundary-making through the creation of spaces, subjectivities, forms of belonging, and demands for recognition on their own terms within and against normative exclusions of possessive property. These were not structures or actions that occurred all at once or were ever universal or fully formed. Home is not a space but a process, one that unfolds slowly and continually through time. There can be no emergency homemaking or ending homelessness with a box, large or small. Home must be fostered, tended, and allowed. Within Tent City 3, care, commoning, and collectivity were tactics for creating an inclusionary homespace in a constantly evolving environment. These tactics may offer some lessons for thinking about home otherwise.

Thinking beyond the ownership paradigm requires recognizing that home is not something preexisting or predetermined. Thinking about home as a process and not a possession asks us to become homemakers rather than gatekeepers. Home, in its best sense, conjures feelings of security, belonging, agency, familiarity, and inclusion. Not all dwellings are like this. Many are sites of imprisonment, abuse, insecurity, and expulsion. Thinking beyond the ownership model requires attention, in both policy and practice, to making all homespace more homelike. This begins by foregrounding the universal collective necessity of home and homemaking in all its forms.

Residents of Tent City 3, deprived of the legal protections of property and dehumanized through carceral management, produced a homespace where they could reclaim a sense of autonomy, privacy, and security through practices of commoning. Foregrounding the idea of home as a making that occurs through practices of commoning enables reconsideration of the space of home—from one of exclusion, where the outsider arrives "as stranger or trespasser," to one of inclusion within the space of home, hometown, and homeland.[36] In Tent City 3, the production of a common homespace enabled participants to express and draw on their own knowledge, experience, and desires. In contrast to the right to exclude granted by the privatization of property, participatory commoning blurs the boundaries between home and away, us and them, self and other, potentially opening the door, so to speak, to a broader and more expansive conception of home.

As an unfolding and ongoing act of commoning, the homespace of Tent City was made possible through acts of care. Practices of giving and receiving care led residents to both reclaim a sense of themselves as human and develop a sense of affective belonging or feeling citizenship. In its best iterations, home is a place of care. Home is where we care and are cared for. Yet, within the bounded space of a propertied home, care is a private affair that has largely fallen upon the intersectional shoulders of women, the poor, people of color, and the colonized. Thinking home beyond property requires rethinking the hierarchical conditions of oppression and dependence that are created and make possible the ownership model of home.[37]

In the context of propertied norms of homelessness, care often operates as a disciplinary mechanism of carceral quarantine and recuperation. In Tent City 3, practices of care replaced pathology with multiplicity, lack with abundance, and need with gift. In their refusal of homeless pathology, residents built networks of care that resisted tropes of dependence. These practices drew on an assumption that all people were engaged in and capable of giving and receiving care. Rather than hierarchical models of those in need of care and those charged with care provision, acknowledging care as fundamental to the collective production of home shifts away from a focus on normative rehabilitation to care as unbounded, universal, and reciprocal.

To conceive of home not just as a space but as both product and productive of mutual care and respect requires thinking of both self and home as excessive: a site that transcends the polarity of self/other binaries but is also not fixed but always becoming.[38] Dignity, respect, equality, and inclusion are only attainable in spaces that account for multiplicities of identity and experience. Within an ownership paradigm, property-centric conceptions of law and planning construct and naturalize hierarchical spatial and social difference. Within and against this paradigm, Tent City 3 residents enacted governmental practices of negotiability that emerged in response to the transience of the camp and the everchanging multiplicity of its population, situations, and contexts. These practices articulated an art of governance that was democratic and contextually fluid so as to allow for maximum participation, tolerance, and respect for infinite difference in spaces and subjects of ongoing multiplicity.

Outside the tent city, residents encountered and resisted their property-based marginalization. In their refusal, they forged relationships of mutual recognition on their own terms. Through these relationships and the persistence of the camp itself, they contested their marginality and unsettled norms of propertied personhood, in time becoming ordinary. In the context of growing numbers of unhoused residents, the very ordinariness of Tent City 3 became a tool for shoring up the boundaries of the settler colonial city. Yet, in its persistence and normalization, the ongoing presence of Tent City 3 also exposes the incompleteness and deadly crisis of settler colonial hegemony.

Faced with the ongoing crisis of settler modernity, Tent City 3 offers a way of envisioning a more humane, expansive sense of home. The care, commoning, and collectivity practiced in Tent City 3 are neither radical nor esoteric. They don't require special degrees or training. They are practices of reciprocity, affection, and obligation that we participate in, and even relish, every day with friends, housemates, loved ones, coworkers, and family.[39] In attempting to outline a possibility of home beyond property, I have tried not to be prescriptive or linear. It is my hope that these provocations will contribute to existing conversations about what an anticolonial relationship between property, home, and personhood might be and how they might be produced within the house we all share together.

Notes

Introduction

1. Jeremy Waldron, "Homelessness and the Issue of Freedom," *UCLA Law Review* 39 (1991-92): 295.

2. Martin Heidegger, "Building Dwelling Thinking," in *Poetry, Language, Thought* (New York: Harper, 2001): 141-60; Sigmund Freud, *The Uncanny* (London: Penguin, 2003); Gaston Bachelard, *The Poetics of Space* (Boston: Beacon Press, 1969).

3. For instance, feminist scholars have long called attention to the reality that home, for women, has often been a site of marginalization and oppression. Betty Friedan, *The Feminine Mystique* (New York: Norton, 2001); Simone de Beauvoir, *The Second Sex* (New York: Knopf, 1953); Dolores Hayden, *The Grand Domestic Revolution: A History of Feminist Designs for American Homes, Neighborhoods, and Cities* (Boston: MIT Press, 1982). Stereotypes of femininity have placed on women the burden of the reproduction of men's labor while simultaneously denying women access to the public sphere. Mona Domosh and Joni Seager, *Putting Women in Place: Feminist Geographers Make Sense of the World* (New York: Guilford Press, 2001); Susan Hanson and Geraldine Pratt, *Gender, Work, and Space* (London: Routledge, 1995). Home has been a privileged site of exclusion in Western societies, where feelings of security and belonging are predicated on the subjugation, exclusion, and labor of gendered, racialized, and lower-class bodies and identities. Biddy Martin and Chandra Talpade Mohanty, "Feminist Politics: What's Home Got to Do with It?," in *Feminist Studies / Critical Studies*, ed. Teresa de Lauretis, 191-212 (Bloomington: Indiana University Press, 1986); Lynda Johnston and Gill Valentine, "Wherever I Lay My Girlfriend, That's My Home: The Performance and Surveillance of Lesbian Identities in Domestic Environments," in *Mapping Desire: Geographies of Sexuality*, ed. David Bell and Gill Valentine, 88-103 (London: Routledge, 2003); Nayan Shah, *Stranger Intimacy: Contesting Race, Sexuality and the Law in the North American West* (Berkeley: University of California Press, 2011).

4. Sara Ahmed, "Home and Away: Narratives of Migration and Estrangement," *International Journal of Cultural Studies* 2, no. 3 (December 1999): 329-47.

5. Mary Douglas, "The Idea of a Home: A Kind of Space," *Social Research* 58, no. 1 (1991): 287-307. See also Julie Botticello, "Lagos in London: Finding the Space of Home," *Home Cultures* 4, no. 1 (March 2007): 7-23.

6. "History—SHARE/WHEEL," SHARE/WHEEL website, accessed April 20, 2023, https://sites.google.com/sharewheel.org/index/about-us/history.

7. Seattle is also home to a number of sanctioned and unsanctioned encampments not run by SHARE/WHEEL. However, SHARE/WHEEL continues to operate the two camps operating under the Tent City name.

8. For important and meaningful exceptions to this exclusion, see Jessie Speer, "'It's Not like Your Home': Homeless Encampments, Housing Projects, and the Struggle over Domestic Space," *Antipode* 49, no. 2 (2017): 517–35; Teresa Gowan, *Hobos, Hustlers, and Backsliders: Homeless in San Francisco* (Minneapolis: University of Minnesota Press, 2010); Talmadge Wright, *Out of Place: Homeless Mobilizations, Subcities, and Contested Landscapes* (Albany: SUNY Press, 1997).

9. "General Definition of Homeless Individual," 42 U.S. Code § 11302, The McKinney-Vento Homeless Assistance Act As amended by S. 896 The Homeless Emergency Assistance and Rapid Transition to Housing (HEARTH) Act of 2009.

10. "General Definition of Homeless Individual," 42 U.S. Code § 11302.

11. Crawford Brough Macpherson, *Property, Mainstream and Critical Positions* (Toronto: University of Toronto Press, 1978).

12. Nicholas Blomley, *Unsettling the City: Urban Land and the Politics of Property* (London: Routledge, 2004), 2.

13. Waldron, "Homelessness and the Issue of Freedom," 299.

14. Walter I. Trattner, *From Poor Law to Welfare State: A History of Social Welfare in America* (New York: Simon and Schuster, 2007); Michael B. Katz, *In the Shadow of the Poorhouse: A Social History of Welfare in America* (New York: Basic Books, 1996).

15. Kathleen R. Arnold, *Homelessness, Citizenship, and Identity: The Uncanniness of Late Modernity* (Albany: SUNY Press, 2012); Leonard C. Feldman, *Citizens without Shelter* (Ithaca, NY: Cornell University Press, 2018).

16. Jessica Gerrard and David Farrugia, "The 'Lamentable Sight' of Homelessness and the Society of the Spectacle," *Urban Studies* 52, no. 12 (2015): 2219–33; Jessie Speer, "Urban Makeovers, Homeless Encampments, and the Aesthetics of Displacement," *Social and Cultural Geography* 20, no. 4 (2019): 575–95; Eric Goldfischer, "Diverting Eyes and Bodies: The Management of Homeless Visibility in New York City," *Metropolitics*, November 19, 2019, https://metropolitics.org/Diverting-Eyes-and-Bodies-The-Management-of-Homeless-Visibility-in-New-York.html.

17. Samira Kawash, "The Homeless Body," *Public Culture* 10, no. 2 (January 1998): 319–39.

18. Randall Amster, "Patterns of Exclusion: Sanitizing Space, Criminalizing Homelessness," *Social Justice* 30, no. 1 (2003): 195–221; Don Mitchell, *The Right to the City: Social Justice and the Fight for Public Space* (New York: Guilford Press, 2003).

19. Mariana Valverde, "Seeing Like a City: The Dialectic of Modern and Premodern

Ways of Seeing in Urban Governance," *Law and Society Review* 45, no. 2 (2011): 295. See also Rutherford H. Platt, *Land Use and Society: Geography, Law, and Public Policy* (Washington, DC: Island Press, 2004).

20. Isaac Rivera, Sarah Elwood, and Victoria Lawson, "Portraits for Change: Refusal Politics and Liberatory Futures," *Environment and Planning D: Society and Space* 40, no. 4 (August 2022): 637.

21. Patrick Wolfe, "Settler Colonialism and the Elimination of the Native," *Journal of Genocide Research*, December 21, 2006; Evelyn Nakano Glenn, "Settler Colonialism as Structure: A Framework for Comparative Studies of U.S. Race and Gender Formation," *Sociology of Race and Ethnicity* 1, no. 1 (January 2015): 52–72.

22. Eve Tuck and K. Wayne Yang, "Decolonization Is Not a Metaphor." *Decolonization, Indigeneity, Education, and Society* 1, no. 1 (2012): 1–40.

23. Anne Bonds and Joshua Inwood, "Beyond White Privilege: Geographies of White Supremacy and Settler Colonialism," *Progress in Human Geography* 40, no. 6 (December 2016): 721. See also Jessica Dempsey, Kevin Gould, and Juanita Sundberg, "Changing Land Tenure, Defining Subjects: Neo-Liberalism and Property Regimes on Native Reserves," in *Rethinking the Great White North: Race, Nature, and the Historical Geographies of Whiteness in Canada*, ed. Andrew Baldwin, Laura Cameron, and Audrey Kobayashi (Vancouver: University of British Columbia Press, 2012), 233–55.

24. John Stuart Mill, "Civilization," in *Collected Works of John Stuart Mill*, vol. 18, *Essays on Politics and Society*, ed. J. M. Robson (Abingdon: Taylor and Francis, 1996): 120.

25. Wolfe, "Settler Colonialism and the Elimination of the Native." See also Penelope Edmonds, *Urbanizing Frontiers: Indigenous Peoples and Settlers in Nineteenth-Century Pacific Rim Cities* (Vancouver: University of British Columbia Press, 2010); Blomley, *Unsettling the City*.

26. Nicholas Blomley, "Law, Property, and the Geography of Violence: The Frontier, the Survey, and the Grid," *Annals of the Association of American Geographers* 93, no. 1 (2003): 121–41.

27. Glenn, "Settler Colonialism as Structure," 52.

28. Tuck and Yang, "Decolonization Is Not a Metaphor," 5.

29. Edmonds, *Urbanizing Frontiers*.

30. Blomley, "Law, Property, and the Geography of Violence."

31. Patrick Wolfe, *Traces of History: Elementary Structures of Race* (London: Verso Books, 2016).

32. Audra Simpson, "The Ruse of Consent and the Anatomy of 'Refusal': Cases from Indigenous North America and Australia," *Postcolonial Studies* 20, no. 1 (January 2017): 21.

33. Bonds and Inwood, "Beyond White Privilege," 721.

34. *Seattle Is Dying | A KOMO News Documentary*, KOMO-TV, March 19, 2019, available on YouTube, https://www.youtube.com/watch?v=bpAi7oWWBlw&ab_channel=KOMONews.

35. Chris Herring, "The New Logics of Homeless Seclusion: Homeless Encampments in America's West Coast Cities," *City & Community* 13, no. 4 (2014): 291.

36. In doing so, I join a long and well-established ethnographic tradition that includes classic works like Jacob A. Riis, *How the Other Half Lives* (London: Macmillan, 2011); Nels Anderson, *The Hobo: The Sociology of the Homeless Man* (Chicago: University of Chicago Press, 1961); James P. Spradley, *You Owe Yourself a Drunk: An Ethnography of Urban Nomads* (Boston: Little, Brown, 1970); as well as more contemporary engagements with homeless squats and encampments in the United States, such as Wright, *Out of Place*; David A. Snow and Leon Anderson, *Down on Their Luck: A Study of Homeless Street People* (Berkeley: University of California Press, 1993); Gowan, *Hobos, Hustlers, and Backsliders*; Tuen Voeten, *Tunnel People* (Oakland: PM Press, 2010); Jason Adam Wasserman and Jeffrey M. Clair, *At Home on the Street: People, Poverty, and a Hidden Culture of Homelessness* (Boulder, CO: Lynne Rienner, 2010).

37. While these demographic figures give a fairly accurate picture of general trends in tent city demographics, this data is only a snapshot of a seasonally fluid population. This fluidity can lead to some skewed numbers. For instance, this count was conducted in January 2005. This timing may result in an overrepresentation of women, as many women-only emergency shelters operate only in the winter months. Location also represents a significant demographic variable, as there are typically higher numbers of youth present when the camp is located closer to either the university or neighborhoods perceived as friendly to "alternative lifestyles." Conversely, employment numbers tend to trend upward in summer, when more seasonal employment is available. SHARE/WHEEL does not refer to itself explicitly as a collective; however, in reference to the organizational structure and the practices of operations and governance, the term seems apt.

38. The consent decree under which the tent city operates forbids those under eighteen years of age.

39. PubliCola, "Most City Shelter 'Referrals' Don't Lead to Shelter, Police Preemptively Barricade Encampment against Protests, City Says It Can't Risk Handing HOPE Team to County," PubliCola, October 8, 2019, https://publicola.com.

40. Lauren Dunton, Jill Khadduri, Kimberly Burnett, Nicholas Fiore, and Will Yetvin, *Exploring Homelessness among People Living in Encampments and Associated Cost* (Washington, DC: US Department of Housing and Urban Development, 2020).

41. Rebecca Cohen, Will Yetvin, and Jill Khadduri, *Understanding Encampments of People Experiencing Homelessness and Community Responses: Emerging Evidence as*

of Late 2018 (Washington, DC: US Department of Housing and Urban Development, 2019).

42. Snow and Anderson, *Down on Their Luck*; Wright, *Out of Place*; Chris Herring and Manuel Lutz, "The Roots and Implications of the USA's Homeless Tent Cities," *City* 19, no. 5 (2015): 689–701.

43. For other recent examples of homeless refusal, see Rivera, Elwood, and Lawson, "Portraits for Change"; Goldfischer, "Diverting Eyes and Bodies."

44. Simpson, "The Ruse of Consent and the Anatomy of 'Refusal,'" 29.

45. Judith Butler, *Gender Trouble: Feminism and the Subversion of Identity* (London: Routledge, 2011), 33.

46. Audra Simpson, *Mohawk Interruptus: Political Life across the Borders of Settler States* (Durham: Duke University Press, 2014), 7.

47. Simpson, *Mohawk Interruptus*, 8.

48. Faranak Miraftab, "Insurgent Planning: Situating Radical Planning in the Global South," *Planning Theory* 8, no. 1 (2009): 32–50; James Holston, *Insurgent Citizenship: Disjunctions of Democracy and Modernity in Brazil* (Princeton, NJ: Princeton University Press, 2021).

49. Asef Bayat, *Life as Politics: How Ordinary People Change the Middle East* (Palo Alto, CA: Stanford University Press, 2013), 43.

50. Blomley, *Unsettling the City*; Sylvia Wynter, "Unsettling the Coloniality of Being/Power/Truth/Freedom: Towards the Human, after Man," *CR: The New Centennial Review* 3, no. 3 (2003): 257–337.

51. Speer, "'It's Not Like Your Home,'" 517.

52. Leilani Farha, *Report of the Special Rapporteur on Adequate Housing as a Component of the Right to an Adequate Standard of Living, and on the Right to Non-Discrimination in This Context* (Geneva: United Nations, 2018), 5.

53. Rolnick quoted in Farha, *Report of the Special Rapporteur on Adequate Housing*, 18.

54. Gillian Rose, *Feminism and Geography: The Limits of Geographical Knowledge* (Minneapolis: University of Minnesota Press, 1993); Bonnie Honig, "Difference, Dilemmas, and the Politics of Home," *Social Research* (1994), 563–97; Iris Marion Young, "House and Home: Feminist Variations on a Theme," in *Intersecting Voices: Dilemmas of Gender, Political Philosophy, and Policy* (Princeton, NJ: Princeton University Press, 1997); Sara Ahmed, *Strange Encounters: Embodied Others in Post-Coloniality* (London: Routledge, 2013).

55. Lorenzo Veracini, *The Settler Colonial Present* (London: Palgrave-Macmillan, 2015).

1. Home and Homelessness

1. Diane Brooks, "Seattle's Homeless Vote for Tent City—Street People Seek Alternative," *Seattle Times*, November 4, 1990, B3.

2. As many scholars have noted, visible appropriation of urban space by the unhoused is an important and valuable assertion of citizenship and inclusion. In this strain of scholarship, the ability of groups of unhoused people to stake a claim to public space goes hand in hand with an assertion of belonging, political recognition, and legitimacy. In this context, the visible presence of the camp and its residents become in and of themselves a political statement. See Neil Smith, *The New Urban Frontier: Gentrification and the Revanchist City* (London: Routledge, 2005); Leonard C. Feldman, *Citizens without Shelter* (Ithaca, NY: Cornell University Press, 2018); Don Mitchell, *The Right to the City: Social Justice and the Fight for Public Space* (New York: Guilford Press, 2003); Talmadge Wright, *Out of Place: Homeless Mobilizations, Subcities, and Contested Landscapes* (Albany: State University of New York Press, 1997); Susan Ruddick, "Heterotopias of the Homeless: Strategies and Tactics of Placemaking in Los Angeles," *Strategies* 3, no. 3 (1990): 184–201.

3. Brooks, "Seattle's Homeless Vote for Tent City."

4. For other examples, see Isaac Rivera, Sarah Elwood, and Victoria Lawson, "Portraits for Change: Refusal Politics and Liberatory Futures," *Environment and Planning D: Society and Space* 40, no. 4 (August 2022): 627–45; Margaret Marietta Ramírez, "Take the Houses Back / Take the Land Back: Black and Indigenous Urban Futures in Oakland," *Urban Geography* 41, no. 5 (2020): 682–93.

5. Evelyn Nakano Glenn, "Settler Colonialism as Structure: A Framework for Comparative Studies of U.S. Race and Gender Formation," *Sociology of Race and Ethnicity* 1, no. 1 (January 2015): 52.

6. Nicholas Blomley, "Law, Property, and the Geography of Violence: The Frontier, the Survey, and the Grid," *Annals of the Association of American Geographers* 93, no. 1 (2003): 121–41.

7. Mark L. Lazarus III, "An Historical Analysis of Alien Land Law: Washington Territory and State 1853–1889," *University of Puget Sound Law Review* 12 (1988): 232.

8. Josephine Ensign, *Skid Road: On the Frontier of Health and Homelessness in an American City* (Baltimore: Johns Hopkins University Press, 2021).

9. Ensign, *Skid Road*, 32.

10. Lisa Goff, *Shantytown, USA: Forgotten Landscapes of the Working Poor* (Cambridge, MA: Harvard University Press, 2016); Phoebe S. K. Young, *Camping Grounds: Public Nature in American Life from the Civil War to the Occupy Movement* (Oxford: Oxford University Press, 2021).

11. Penelope Edmonds, *Urbanizing Frontiers: Indigenous Peoples and Settlers in*

Nineteenth-Century Pacific Rim Cities (Vancouver: University of British Columbia Press, 2010); Heather Dorries, Robert Henry, David Hugill, Tyler McCreary, and Julie Tomiak, eds., *Settler City Limits: Indigenous Resurgence and Colonial Violence in the Urban Prairie West* (Winnipeg: University of Manitoba Press, 2019); Tim Cresswell, *The Tramp in America* (London: Reaktion Books, 2013).

12. Ensign, *Skid Road*.

13. Feliks Banel, "A Look at Seattle's Homeless 'Shacktown' History," *MyNorthwest .Com*, January 28, 2016, https://mynorthwest.com/330086/a-look-at-seattles-homeless-shacktown-history/.

14. Ensign, *Skid Road*.

15. Heather Dorries, David Hugill, and Julie Tomiak, "Racial Capitalism and the Production of Settler Colonial Cities," *Geoforum* 132 (2022): 263–70.

16. Michael B. Katz, *In the Shadow of the Poorhouse: A Social History of Welfare in America* (New York: Basic Books, 1996); Cresswell, *The Tramp in America*; Erika Lee, *America for Americans: A History of Xenophobia in the United States* (New York: Basic Books, 2019).

17. Quintard Taylor, *The Forging of a Black Community: Seattle's Central District from 1870 through the Civil Rights Era* (Seattle: University of Washington Press, 1994).

18. Megan Asaka, *Seattle from the Margins: Exclusion, Erasure, and the Making of a Pacific Coast City* (Seattle: University of Washington Press, 2022).

19. Susan Craddock, *City of Plagues: Disease, Poverty, and Deviance in San Francisco* (Minneapolis: University of Minnesota Press, 2000); Elizabeth Brown and George Barganier, *Race and Crime: Geographies of Injustice* (Oakland: University of California Press, 2018).

20. Rutherford H. Platt, *Land Use and Society: Geography, Law, and Public Policy* (Washington, DC: Island Press, 2004); Goff, *Shantytown, USA*.

21. Banel, "A Look at Seattle's Homeless 'Shacktown' History."

22. Nikhil Pal Singh, "The Whiteness of Police," *American Quarterly* 66, no. 4 (2014): 1091.

23. Young, *Camping Grounds*.

24. Young, *Camping Grounds*.

25. Todd DePastino, *Citizen Hobo: How a Century of Homelessness Shaped America* (Chicago: University of Chicago Press, 2003); Susan M. Schweik, *The Ugly Laws: Disability in Public* (New York: New York University Press, 2010); Edmonds, *Urbanizing Frontiers*.

26. Ensign, *Skid Road*.

27. Ensign's grounded history of Seattle echoes a vast body of scholarship illustrating that throughout US history, religious, charitable, and state responses to those who lack access to formal housing have overwhelmingly failed to focus on providing hous-

ing. Rather, following antecedents of seventeenth-century English poor laws and drawing on Christian, Benthamite, and Social Darwinist connections among labor, gendered domesticity, and morality, responses to poverty have focused on banishment and quarantine of the itinerant and precariously housed into the disciplinary and carceral spaces of poorhouses, workhouses, asylums, hospitals—and more recently, homeless shelters. As a result, the spatial management of the unhoused in public has long relied on constant and ongoing removal, displacement, and quarantine of unhoused bodies in the name of public safety, health, and morality. For a sample of this literature, see Jesse Walter Dees, *Flophouse: An Authentic Undercover Study of Flophouses, Cage Hotels, Including Missions, Shelters and Institutions Serving Unattached (Homeless) Men: A Sociological Study That Includes English Origins of Mass Relief, Samples of American Mass Relief and a Modern Investigation of Public and Private Policies in Chicago* (Francestown, NH: Marshall Jones, 1948); Anthony L. Beier and Paul Ocobock, *Cast Out: Vagrancy and Homelessness in Global and Historical Perspective* (Athens: Ohio University Press, 2008); Kenneth L. Kusmer, *Down and Out, on the Road: The Homeless in American History* (Oxford: Oxford University Press, 2003); Katz, *In the Shadow of the Poorhouse*; Jeff Rose, "Cleansing Public Nature: Landscapes of Homelessness, Health, and Displacement," *Journal of Political Ecology* 24, no. 1 (2017): 11–23.

28. Donald Francis Roy, *Hooverville: A Study of a Community of Homeless Men in Seattle* (Seattle: University of Washington, 1935), 7.

29. DePastino, *Citizen Hobo*; Frances Fox Piven and Richard Cloward, *Regulating the Poor: The Functions of Public Welfare* (New York: Vintage, 2012).

30. James Gregory, "Hoovervilles and Homelessness," 2009, Great Depression in Washington State Project, https://depts.washington.edu/depress/hooverville.shtml.

31. Dustin Neighly, "The End of Seattle's Hooverville," 2010, Great Depression in Washington State Project, https://depts.washington.edu/depress/hooverville_seattle_destruction.shtml.

32. For a more extended analysis of the relationship between Japanese internment and settler colonialism, see I. Day, *Alien Capital: Asian Racialization and the Logic of Settler Colonial Capitalism* (Durham: Duke University Press, 2016).

33. M. Christine Boyer, *Dreaming the Rational City: The Myth of American City Planning* (Boston: MIT Press, 1986); April R. Veness, "Home and Homelessness in the United States: Changing Ideals and Realities," *Environment and Planning D: Society and Space* 10, no. 4 (1992): 445–68.

34. Smith, *The New Urban Frontier*.

35. Smith, *The New Urban Frontier*. See also Jean-Paul D. Addie and James C. Fraser, "After Gentrification: Social Mix, Settler Colonialism, and Cruel Optimism in the Transformation of Neighbourhood Space," *Antipode* 51, no. 5 (November 2019): 1369–94; Robyn Burns and Lisbeth A. Berbary, "Placemaking as Unmaking: Settler

Colonialism, Gentrification, and the Myth of 'Revitalized' Urban Spaces," *Leisure Sciences* 43, no. 4 (February 2021): 1–17; Sara Safransky, "Rethinking Land Struggle in the Postindustrial City," *Antipode* 49, no. 4 (2017): 1079–1100.

36. Quoted in Timothy A. Gibson, *Securing the Spectacular City: The Politics of Revitalization and Homelessness in Downtown Seattle* (Lanham, MD: Lexington Books, 2004), 1.

37. Gibson, *Securing the Spectacular City*, 2.

38. Gibson, *Securing the Spectacular City*.

39. Robert Teir, "Restoring Order in Urban Public Spaces," *Texas Review of Law and Politics* 2 (1997): 255.

40. Gibson, *Securing the Spectacular City*; Don Mitchell, "The Annihilation of Space by Law: The Roots and Implications of Anti-homeless Laws in the United States," *Antipode* 29, no. 3 (1997): 303–35; Mike Davis, *City of Quartz: Excavating the Future in Los Angeles* (New York: Verso Books, 2006).

41. *Temporary Dwellings*, dir. Michael Regis Hilow (New York: Filmmakers Library, 1992).

42. Chris Herring and Manuel Lutz, "The Roots and Implications of the USA's Homeless Tent Cities," *City* 19, no. 5 (2015): 689–701; Wright, *Out of Place*.

43. Ensign, *Skid Road*.

44. Ronald Fitten, "The Bonds of Poverty—Tent City Knits Homeless into a Community," *Seattle Times*, December 3, 1990.

45. "Summitry for 1991: Start the New Year with Focus on Housing," *Seattle Times*, December 30, 1990, A18.

46. David A. Fahrenthold, "Eviction Notices Delivered to 'Jungle': We Won't Leave This Time without a Fight, Residents Vow," *Seattle Times*, July 3, 1998.

47. Share/Wheel v. City of Seattle, No. 49428-7-I, King County Superior Court, March 22, 2002.

48. Ruddick, "Heterotopias of the Homeless"; Smith, *The New Urban Frontier*; Wright, *Out of Place*; Chris Herring, "The New Logics of Homeless Seclusion: Homeless Encampments in America's West Coast Cities," *City and Community* 13, no. 4 (2014): 285–309.

49. Herring and Lutz, "The Roots and Implications of the USA's Homeless Tent Cities"; Giovanni Picker and Silvia Pasquetti, "Durable Camps: The State, the Urban, the Everyday," *Analysis of Urban Change, Theory, Action* 19, no. 5 (2015): 681–88.

50. Herring, "The New Logics of Homeless Seclusion"; Rebecca Cohen, Will Yetvin, and Jill Khadduri, *Understanding Encampments of People Experiencing Homelessness and Community Responses: Emerging Evidence as of Late 2018* (Washington, DC: US Department of Housing and Urban Development, 2019).

51. Wright, *Out of Place*; Jessie Speer, "'It's Not Like Your Home': Homeless En-

campments, Housing Projects, and the Struggle over Domestic Space," *Antipode* 49, no. 2 (2017): 517–35; After Echo Park Lake Research Collective, "Continuum of Carcerality: How Liberal Urbanism Governs Homelessness," *Radical Housing Journal* 4, no. 1 (July 2022): 71–94.

2. The Making of Homespace

1. Jessie Speer, "Urban Makeovers, Homeless Encampments, and the Aesthetics of Displacement," *Social and Cultural Geography* 20, no. 4 (2019): 575–95.

2. People often begin their time at the tent city in one of the larger congregate tents. For them, their cot or bunk becomes a temporary home until they are able and choose to move into a single or double occupancy tent.

3. Ananya Roy, "Dis/Possessive Collectivism: Property and Personhood at City's End," *Geoforum* 80 (2017): A1–11; Jessie Speer, "'It's Not Like Your Home': Homeless Encampments, Housing Projects, and the Struggle over Domestic Space," *Antipode* 49, no. 2 (2017): 517–35.

4. Thalia Anthony, "Settler-Colonial Governmentality: The Carceral Webs Woven by Law and Politics," in *Questioning Indigenous-Settler Relations*, ed. Sarah Maddison and Sana Nakata, vol. 1, *Indigenous-Settler Relations in Australia and the World* (Singapore: Springer Singapore, 2020), 33–53; Jean-Paul D. Addie and James C. Fraser, "After Gentrification: Social Mix, Settler Colonialism, and Cruel Optimism in the Transformation of Neighbourhood Space," *Antipode* 51, no. 5 (November 2019): 1369–94.

5. Douglas Porteous and Sandra E. Smith, *Domicide: The Global Destruction of Home* (Montreal: McGill-Queen's University Press, 2001).

6. Richard Baxter and Katherine Brickell, "For Home Unmaking," *Home Cultures* 11, no. 2 (2014): 134.

7. Adam Elliott-Cooper, Phil Hubbard, and Loretta Lees, "Moving beyond Marcuse: Gentrification, Displacement and the Violence of Un-Homing," *Progress in Human Geography* 44, no. 3 (2020): 492–509.

8. Addie and Fraser, "After Gentrification," 11.

9. Roy, "Dis/Possessive Collectivism."

10. Michael Simpson and David W. Hugill, "The Settler Colonial City in Three Movements," *Progress in Human Geography* 46, no. 6 (2022): 1322.

11. After Echo Park Lake Research Collective, "Continuum of Carcerality: How Liberal Urbanism Governs Homelessness," *Radical Housing Journal* 4, no. 1 (July 2022): 71–94.

12. Tony Sparks, "Governing the Homeless in an Age of Compassion: Homelessness,

Citizenship, and the Ten-Year Plan to End Homelessness in King County Washington," *Antipode* 44, no. 4 (2012): 1510–31; Piers Gooding, "Housing First and the Maddening Myths of Homelessness," *Parity* 31, no. 8 (2018): 31–32.

13. Don Mitchell, *The Right to the City: Social Justice and the Fight for Public Space* (New York: Guilford Press, 2003); Katherine Beckett and Steve Herbert, *Banished: The New Social Control in Urban America* (Oxford: Oxford University Press, 2009).

14. Beckett and Herbert, *Banished*; Sara Rankin, "Civilly Criminalizing Homelessness," *Harvard Civil Rights—Civil Liberties Law Review* 56, no. 2 (Summer 2021): 367–412.

15. Chris Herring, "Complaint-Oriented 'Services': Shelters as Tools for Criminalizing Homelessness," *Annals of the American Academy of Political and Social Science* 693, no. 1 (January 2021): 264–83.

16. Forrest Stuart, *Down, Out, and Under Arrest: Policing and Everyday Life in Skid Row* (Chicago: University of Chicago Press, 2016); Sara Rankin, "Hiding Homelessness: The Transcarceration of Homelessness," *California Law Review* 109 (2021): 559–613.

17. Leonard C. Feldman, *Citizens without Shelter* (Ithaca, NY: Cornell University Press, 2018); Kathleen R. Arnold, *Homelessness, Citizenship, and Identity: The Uncanniness of Late Modernity* (Albany: SUNY Press, 2012).

18. Ananya Roy, Terra Graziani, and Pamela Stephens, "Unhousing the Poor: Interlocking Regimes of Racialized Policing," Square One Project's Roundtable on the Future of Justice Policy, Columbia University, New York, August 25, 2020, https://squareonejustice.org/wp-content/uploads/2020/08/Ananya-Roy-et-al-Unhousing-the-Poor-1.pdf, 12; Judith Butler and Athena Athanasiou, *Dispossession: The Performative in the Political* (Hoboken, NJ: John Wiley, 2013).

19. Hannah Arendt, *The Origins of Totalitarianism* (Boston: Houghton Mifflin Harcourt, 1973), 296.

20. C. B. Macpherson, *The Political Theory of Possessive Individualism: Hobbes to Locke* (Oxford: Clarendon Press, 1964).

21. Ananya Roy, "Paradigms of Propertied Citizenship: Transnational Techniques of Analysis," Urban Affairs Review 38, no. 4 (2003): 463.

22. Roy, "Paradigms of Propertied Citizenship," 464.

23. Roy, "Paradigms of Propertied Citizenship," 463–64.

24. Roy, "Dis/Possessive Collectivism," A3; Stephen Przybylinski, "Realizing Citizenship in Property: Houseless Encampments and the Limits of Liberalism's Promise," *Political Geography* 91 (2021): 1–10.

25. Roy, "Paradigms of Propertied Citizenship," 476.

26. Brenna Bhandar, *Colonial Lives of Property: Law, Land, and Racial Regimes of Ownership* (Durham: Duke University Press, 2018).

27. Bhandar, *Colonial Lives of Property*.

28. Heather Dorries, Robert Henry, David Hugill, Tyler McCreary, and Julie Tomiak, eds., *Settler City Limits: Indigenous Resurgence and Colonial Violence in the Urban Prairie West* (Winnipeg: University of Manitoba Press, 2019); Sara Safransky, "Rethinking Land Struggle in the Postindustrial City," *Antipode* 49, no. 4 (2017): 1079–1100; Naama Blatman-Thomas and Libby Porter, "Placing Property: Theorizing the Urban from Settler Colonial Cities: Placing Property," *International Journal of Urban and Regional Research* 43, no. 1 (January 2019): 30–45.

29. Sara Ahmed, *Strange Encounters: Embodied Others in Post-Coloniality* (London: Routledge, 2013), 77.

30. Gaston Bachelard, *The Poetics of Space* (London: Penguin, 2014), 82.

31. Macpherson, *The Political Theory of Possessive Individualism*; Roy, "Paradigms of Propertied Citizenship."

32. Nicholas Blomley and Right to Remain Collective, "Making Property Outlaws: Law and Relegation," *International Journal of Urban and Regional Research* 45, no. 6 (2021): 915; Cheryl I. Harris, "Whiteness as Property," *Harvard Law Review* 106 (1993): 1709–91.

33. Doreen Massey, *Space, Place and Gender* (Hoboken, NJ: John Wiley, 2013); Linda McDowell, *Gender, Identity and Place: Understanding Feminist Geographies* (Cambridge: Polity, 2013).

34. Elizabeth Schultz, "The Fourth Amendment Rights of the Homeless," *Fordham Law Review* 60, no. 5 (April 1992): 1003–34.

35. Nezar AlSayyad and Ananya Roy, "Medieval Modernity: On Citizenship and Urbanism in a Global Era," *Space and Polity* 10, no. 1 (2006): 1–20.

36. Manuel Lutz, "Uncommon Claims to the Commons: Homeless Tent Cities in the US," in *Urban Commons: Moving beyond State and Market*, ed. Mary Dellenbaugh, Markus Kip, Majken Bieniok, Agnes Müller, and Martin Schwegmann (Berlin: Birkhauser, 2022), 102.

37. Lutz, "Uncommon Claims to the Commons," 103.

38. Silvia Federici, *Re-enchanting the World: Feminism and the Politics of the Commons* (Oakland, CA: PM Press, 2018); Stavros Stavrides, *Common Space: The City as Commons* (London: Bloomsbury, 2016); Julie Katherine Gibson-Graham, "The End of Capitalism (As We Knew It): A Feminist Critique of Political Economy," *Capital and Class* 21, no. 2 (1997): 186–88.

39. In truth, though rare, theft in the camp did happen. However, as Donna mentioned, it was almost never from the private space of tents. In the time I was there, a DVD player and a TV were stolen from the common TV tent, and a box of batteries and some sleeping bags went missing from the donations tent. But the only time I heard of a tent break-in it was the result of a personal dispute between campers.

40. This is not decolonization. Although the commoning practices of Tent City 3 residents occur both within and against settler colonial occupation, the tent city itself exists on stolen Indigenous land and does nothing to disrupt this relationship. Rather, this should be thought of as one example of commoning open up possibilities for decolonial futures.

41. Tessa A. Eidelman and Sara Safransky, "The Urban Commons: A Keyword Essay," *Urban Geography* 42, no. 6 (July 2021): 798.

42. Blatman-Thomas and Porter, "Placing Property."

3. Becoming a Good Camper

1. Audra Simpson, *Mohawk Interruptus* (Durham: Duke University Press, 2014), 109.

2. Simpson, *Mohawk Interruptus*, 176.

3. In using *becoming* here, I am drawing both on Nancy's notion of the singularity and on poststructuralist formulations of becoming as a process of subjectification that is always ongoing and never complete.

4. Sara Ahmed, *Strange Encounters: Embodied Others in Post-Coloniality* (London: Routledge, 2013), 94.

5. If someone had to be at work or up early for any reason, it was common practice to put their name on a list with a wake-up time at the EC desk. It was part of security duty to perform these wake-ups. Also, during my time in the camp, cell phones were relatively rare, and many relied on the camp cell phone kept at the EC desk. Campers could give out the number, and callers would leave a message with the EC on duty. It was security's job to either relay the message or bring someone to the phone if the matter was deemed urgent by the EC.

6. Silvia Federici, "Feminism and the Politics of the Commons," in *Uses of a Whirlwind: Movement, Movements, and Contemporary Radical Currents in the United States*, ed. Kevin Van Meter, Craig Hughes, and Stevie Peace (Oakland, CA: AK Press, 2011); Peter Linebaugh, *The Magna Carta Manifesto: Liberties and Commons for All* (Berkeley: University of California Press, 2009).

7. Jessie Speer, "'It's Not Like Your Home': Homeless Encampments, Housing Projects, and the Struggle over Domestic Space," *Antipode* 49, no. 2 (2017): 517–35.

8. Speer, "'It's Not Like Your Home,'" 1.

9. Michelle Daigle and Margaret Marietta Ramírez, "Decolonial Geographies," in *Keywords in Radical Geography: Antipode at 50*, ed. Antipode Editorial Collective, 78–84 (London: Wiley, 2019).

10. Jean-Luc Nancy, *Being Singular Plural* (Stanford, CA: Stanford University Press, 2000).

11. Nicholas Blomley, "Enclosure, Common Right and the Property of the Poor," *Social and Legal Studies* 17, no. 3 (2008): 311–31.

12. Judith Butler, *Bodies That Matter: On the Discursive Limits of "Sex"* (New York: Routledge, 1993).

13. Daigle and Ramírez, "Decolonial Geographies," 82.

4. Seeing Like a Tent City

1. Michel Foucault, "Governmentality," in *The Foucault Effect: Studies in Governmentality*, ed. Graham Burchell, Colin Gordon, and Peter Miller (Chicago: University of Chicago Press, 1991), 87–104.

2. Heather Dorries, "What Is Planning without Property? Relational Practices of Being and Belonging," *Environment and Planning D: Society and Space* 40, no. 2 (2022): 306–18.

3. Brenna Bhandar, *Colonial Lives of Property: Law, Land, and Racial Regimes of Ownership*, Global and Insurgent Legalities (Durham: Duke University Press, 2018); Heather Dorries, "Planning as Property: Uncovering the Hidden Racial Logic of a Municipal Nuisance By-Law," *Journal of Law and Social Policy* 27 (2017): 72.

4. Penelope Edmonds, *Urbanizing Frontiers: Indigenous Peoples and Settlers in Nineteenth-Century Pacific Rim Cities* (Vancouver: University of British Columbia Press, 2010); Ananya Roy, Terra Graziani, and Pamela Stephens, "Unhousing the Poor: Interlocking Regimes of Racialized Policing," Square One Project's Roundtable on the Future of Justice Policy, Columbia University, August 25, 2020; Dorries, "Planning as Property."

5. Naama Blatman-Thomas and Libby Porter, "Placing Property: Theorizing the Urban from Settler Colonial Cities," *International Journal of Urban and Regional Research* 43, no. 1 (January 2019): 30–45; Anne Bonds and Joshua Inwood, "Beyond White Privilege: Geographies of White Supremacy and Settler Colonialism," *Progress in Human Geography* 40, no. 6 (December 2016): 715–33.

6. Michel Foucault, Michel Senellart, François Ewald, and Alessandro Fontana, *Security, Territory, Population: Lectures at the Collège de France, 1977–1978* (New York: Palgrave Macmillan, 2009).

7. James C. Scott, *Seeing Like a State* (New Haven, CT: Yale University Press, 2008).

8. Glen Sean Coulthard, *Red Skin, White Masks: Rejecting the Colonial Politics of Recognition* (Minneapolis: University of Minnesota Press, 2014).

9. Ananya Roy, "Slumdog Cities: Rethinking Subaltern Urbanism," *International Journal of Urban and Regional Research* 35, no. 2 (2011): 233.

10. Christian G. Haid and Hanna Hilbrandt, "Urban Informality and the State: Geographical Translations and Conceptual Alliances," *International Journal of Urban and Regional Research* 43, no. 3 (2019): 551–62.

11. Leonard C. Feldman, *Citizens without Shelter* (Ithaca, NY: Cornell University Press, 2018).

12. Feldman, *Citizens without Shelter*, 17.

13. Feldman, *Citizens without Shelter*, 103.

14. Feldman, *Citizens without Shelter*, 103-4.

15. Arjun Appadurai, "Deep Democracy: Urban Governmentality and the Horizon of Politics," *Environment and Urbanization* 13, no. 2 (2001): 37.

16. Thalia Anthony, "Settler-Colonial Governmentality: The Carceral Webs Woven by Law and Politics," in *Questioning Indigenous-Settler Relations*, ed. Sarah Maddison and Sana Nakata (Singapore: Springer Singapore, 2020), 48. See also Coulthard, "Red Skin, White Masks."

17. Despite heated and ongoing debates about neighborhood orientation and the location of communal tents, these factors were, during my time in the camp, largely influenced by spatial constraints such as lot size and the location of roads, trees, fences, gates, or neighbors.

18. Dorries, "What Is Planning without Property?," 310. See also Ananya Roy, "Dis/Possessive Collectivism: Property and Personhood at City's End," *Geoforum* 80 (2017): A1-11.

19. Bhandar, *Colonial Lives of Property*, 200, quoted in Dorries, "What Is Planning without Property?," 308.

20. Dorries, "What Is Planning without Property?," 312.

21. As part of the broader SHARE/WHEEL consortium, each shelter and the two tent cities send one or two representatives per week to the SHARE/WHEEL "power lunch" board of directors meeting. The board is made up entirely of SHARE/WHEEL shelter and tent city residents. The main purpose of the board is to make funding and political strategy decisions that affect all the shelters and tent camps. However, it also provides an oversight function in which the board as a whole listens to, comments upon, and occasionally intervenes in the issues or decisions of a particular camp or shelter.

22. Foucault et al., *Security, Territory, Population*.

23. Bhandar, *Colonial Lives of Property*.

5. Community, Recognition, and Encroachment

1. Asef Bayat, "The Quiet Encroachment of the Ordinary," in *Life as Politics* (Palo Alto, CA: Stanford University Press, 2020), 14.

2. Bayat, "The Quiet Encroachment of the Ordinary," 56.

3. Bayat, "The Quiet Encroachment of the Ordinary," 61.

4. Ananya Roy, "Paradigms of Propertied Citizenship: Transnational Techniques of Analysis," *Urban Affairs Review* 38, no. 4 (2003): 463-91.

5. Iris Marion Young, *Justice and the Politics of Difference* (Princeton, NJ: Princeton University Press, 2011).

6. Leonard C. Feldman, *Citizens without Shelter* (Ithaca, NY: Cornell University Press, 2018), 91.

7. Glen Sean Coulthard, *Red Skin, White Masks: Rejecting the Colonial Politics of Recognition* (Minneapolis: University of Minnesota Press, 2014).

8. Feldman, *Citizens without Shelter*, 91.

9. Coulthard, *Red Skin, White Masks*, 31; Frantz Fanon, *Black Skin, White Masks* (New York: Grove Press, 2008).

10. For an extended discussion of refusal as reclaiming, from which I draw this argument, see Audra Simpson, "The Ruse of Consent and the Anatomy of 'Refusal': Cases from Indigenous North America and Australia," *Postcolonial Studies* 20, no. 1 (2017): 18–33.

11. Claudia Rowe, "Tent City Residents Are Homeless on Their Own Terms," *Seattle Post-Intelligencer*, December 11, 2004.

12. Claudia Rowe, "Homeless Advocate, City Lock Horns," *Seattle Post-Intelligencer*, April 12, 2006.

13. Rowe, "Tent City Residents Are Homeless on Their Own Terms."

14. Gayatri Chakravorty Spivak, "Can the Subaltern Speak?," in Cary Nelson and Lawrence Grossberg, eds., *Marxism and the Interpretation of Culture* (London: Macmillan, 1988), 82.

15. Liz Hunter, "Tent City through the Eyes of Kids," *Seattle Post-Intelligencer*, February 17, 2005.

16. Steven Mullet, "Mayors Forum: Tent City Experience Changes Attitudes in Tukwila," *Highline Times / Des Moines News*, August 2006.

17. Gayatri Chakravorty Spivak, *The Post-Colonial Critic: Interviews, Strategies, Dialogues*, ed. Sarah Harasym (London: Routledge, 2014), 383.

6. Home beyond Property

1. Committee to End Homelessness in King County, "A Roof over Every Bed: Our Community's Ten-Year Plan to End Homelessness," Homeless Hub, 2005, https://www.homelesshub.ca/resource/roof-over-every-bed-our-communitys-ten-year-plan-end-homelessness-king-county.

2. National Alliance to End Homelessness, *State of Homelessness: 2020 Edition*, accessed April 5, 2021, https://endhomelessness.org/wp-content/uploads/2022/09/StateOfHomelessness_2020.pdf.

3. Chris Glynn and Emily B. Fox, "Dynamics of Homelessness in Urban America," *Annals of Applied Statistics* 13, no. 1 (March 2019): 573–605.

4. National Alliance to End Homelessness, *Unsheltered Homelessness: Trends,*

Causes, and Strategies to Address, June 2017, https://endhomelessness.org/resource/unsheltered-homelessness-trends-causes-strategies-address/.

5. National Law Center on Homelessness and Poverty, *No Safe Place: The Criminalization of Homelessness in US Cities*, 2019, https://homelesslaw.org/wp-content/uploads/2019/02/No_Safe_Place.pdf.

6. Maria Foscarinis and Eric Tars, "Tent City, USA: The Growth of America's Homeless Encampments and How Communities Are Responding," in *Public Space / Contested Space*, ed. Kevin Murphy and Sally O'Driscoll (London: Routledge, 2021), 224–40.

7. Edward B. Murray, Sally J. Clark, and Steve Walker, *2014 Report of Accomplishments* (Seattle: City of Seattle, 2014).

8. Based on a ProQuest News search of Seattle area newspapers for the terms *Seattle*, *encampments*, and *homelessness* conducted on June 15, 2022.

9. Rebecca Finkes, *City Sanctioned Homeless Encampments: A Case Study Analysis of Seattle's City-Permitted Villages* (Columbus: Ohio State University, 2019).

10. City of Seattle, Transitional Encampment Ordinance 123729 (2011).

11. City of Seattle, An Ordinance Relating to Land Use and Zoning; Amending Sections 23.42.054, 23.54.015, 23.76.004, 23.76.006, 23.76.032, and 23.84A.038 of the Seattle Municipal Code; and Adding New Section 23.42.056; to Permit Transitional Encampments for Homeless Individuals as an Interim Use on City-Owned or Private Property, Pub. L. No. City 124747 (2015).

12. Chris Herring, "The New Logics of Homeless Seclusion: Homeless Encampments in America's West Coast Cities," *City and Community* 13, no. 4 (2014): 285.

13. Herring, "The New Logics of Homeless Seclusion," 303.

14. Daniel Beekman, "Task Force Wants More Tent Cities for Homeless," *Seattle Times*, December 19, 2014.

15. Daniel Beekman, "Officials Say More 'Sweeps' of Homeless Camps in the Works," *Seattle Times*, December 21, 2015.

16. Edward B. Murray and Catherine Lester, *Homeless State of Emergency Implementation Plan*, City of Seattle Human Services Department, February 2016.

17. Samantha Batko, Alyse D. Oneto, and Aaron Shroyer, *Unsheltered Homelessness* (Washington, DC: Urban Institute, 2020).

18. Ashley Archibald, "Seattle Issues $1 Million Contract for Homeless Sweeps," *Real Change News*, June 24, 2017, http://www.realchangenews.org/news/2017/06/14/seattle-issues-1-million-contract-homeless-sweeps.

19. Vernal Coleman and Christine Clarridge, "Seattle Evicts Final Holdouts from Troubled Jungle Camp," *Seattle Times*, October 12, 2016.

20. Sara Rankin, "Hiding Homelessness: The Transcarceration of Homelessness," *California Law Review* 109 (April 2021): 559–614.

21. Rankin, "Hiding Homelessness," 559.

22. Kevin Schofield, "A Timeline of the Navigation Team," *Seattle City Council Insight* (blog), October 18, 2019, https://sccinsight.com/2019/10/17/a-timeline-of-the-navigation-team/.

23. Jessie Speer, "The Rise of the Tent Ward: Homeless Camps in the Era of Mass Incarceration," *Political Geography* 62 (2018): 160–69.

24. Daniel Wu, "When a Homeless Encampment Was Cleared, No One Went to a Shelter: The Reasons Are Complicated," *Seattle Times*, August 19, 2021.

25. Rankin, "Hiding Homelessness"; Erica Barnett, "City's Outreach Partner Disengages from Navigation Team as City Removes More Encampments without Notice," *PubliCola*, May 20, 2019, http://publicola.com/2019/05/20/citys-outreach-partner-splits-from-navigation-team-as-city-removes-more-encampments-without-notice/.

26. Nicholas Blomley, "Urban Commoning and the Right Not to Be Excluded," in *Commoning the City: Empirical Perspectives on Urban Ecology, Economics and Ethics*, ed. Derya Özkan and Güldem Baykal Büyüksaraç (London: Routledge, 2020), 89.

27. Jean-Paul D. Addie and James C. Fraser, "After Gentrification: Social Mix, Settler Colonialism, and Cruel Optimism in the Transformation of Neighbourhood Space," *Antipode* 51, no. 5 (November 2019): 1369–94.

28. Dae Shik Kim Jr. and Guy Oron, "Seattle Destroyed Homeless Encampments as the Pandemic Raged," *The Nation*, April 2, 2020.

29. Ananya Roy, "Emergency Urbanism," *Public Books* (blog), November 24, 2020, https://www.publicbooks.org/emergency-urbanism/.

30. Naama Blatman-Thomas and Libby Porter, "Placing Property: Theorizing the Urban from Settler Colonial Cities," *International Journal of Urban and Regional Research* 43, no. 1 (January 2019): 30–45.

31. Sydney Brownstone, "Tension over Visible Homelessness Has Risen in Seattle—and the Country," *Seattle Times*, August 22, 2021.

32. Rebecca Cohen, Will Yetvin, and Jill Khadduri, *Understanding Encampments of People Experiencing Homelessness and Community Responses: Emerging Evidence as of Late 2018* (Washington, DC: US Department of Housing and Urban Development, 2019).

33. Scott Greenstone, "221 Homeless People Have Died in Seattle since Last Winter, One of the Highest Numbers on Record," *Seattle Times*, November 23, 2021.

34. "Homeless Deaths Investigated by the King County Medical Examiner's Office," King County website, accessed September 29, 2022, https://kingcounty.gov/depts/health/examiner/services/reports-data/homeless.aspx.

35. Nicholas Blomley, "Law, Property, and the Geography of Violence: The Frontier, the Survey, and the Grid," *Annals of the Association of American Geographers* 93, no. 1 (2003): 121–41.

36. Silvia Federici, *Re-enchanting the World: Feminism and the Politics of the Commons* (Oakland, CA: PM Press, 2018), 77.

37. For an extended discussion of what this might look like, see J. C. Tronto, *Caring Democracy: Markets, Equality, and Justice* (New York: NYU Press, 2013).

38. See, for instance, Kathleen R. Arnold, *Homelessness, Citizenship, and Identity: The Uncanniness of Late Modernity* (Albany: SUNY Press, 2012).

39. Michelle Daigle and Margaret Marietta Ramírez, "Decolonial Geographies," in *Keywords in Radical Geography: Antipode at 50*, ed. Antipode Editorial Collective (London: Wiley, 2019), 78–84.

Index

Addie, Jean-Paul, 50
Agamben, Giorgio, 96
Ahmed, Sara, 58, 72
AlSayyad, Nezar, 63
Anthony, Thalia, 102
antihomeless laws, 20, 35, 36, 41, 52, 57, 125
Appadurai, Arjun, 101
Arendt, Hannah, 53, 119

Bachelard, Gaston, 59, 60, 63–64
bars (banishment orders), 108, 109–11, 113
Baxter, Richard, 48–49
Bayat, Asef, 119
"being-in-common" (Nancy), 86
Bhandar, Brenna, 106
Blomley, Nicholas, 12, 16, 60, 64, 145
Bonds, Anne, 16
Brickell, Katherine, 48–49
Butler, Judith, 22, 92
Byers, Tom, 43

camp governance. *See* executive committee (EC); rule creation and enforcement; self-government
camping, recreational, 34
camp legalization, 137–41
camp maintenance, 73, 83–85, 105
camp meetings, 97–101, 105, 113
camp permits, 43
camp sweeps, 20, 42, 142, 143–44, 146, 147
camp tours, 102–3

Camp United We Stand, 150–51
Camp Unity, 139–40
care ethic, 69–70, 77–78, 84, 85, 89, 111, 114, 151, 155
care work, 73, 75, 76, 78, 81, 83, 84
Cherry Hill Baptist Church (Seattle), 1, 18, 90, 99
Chinese Americans, 32
churches, 19, 122, 123–24, 139, 140. *See also* Cherry Hill Baptist Church (Seattle); Saint Mark's Cathedral (Seattle)
citizenship, 75, 76, 80, 84–86, 90–92, 103, 113, 116; propertied, 53, 59, 62, 91, 149. *See also* "feeling citizenship" (Simpson)
Citizens without Shelter (Feldman), 96, 125
city council, 104, 121, 129, 140
codes of conduct, 5, 71, 78, 100, 110–11, 113
codes of honor, 65
code switching, 125
colonialism. *See* settler colonialism
commons and commoning, 64–69, 76, 78, 91, 92, 145, 151, 154–55
community, 86, 120, 127–31
community credits, 120–22, 123, 128–30
consent decrees, 3, 43, 62, 63, 109, 120, 139, 160n38
Coulthard, Glen, 126
court decisions, 43
COVID-19 pandemic, 4, 138, 145–47
criminalization, 20, 35, 36, 41, 52, 57, 125

Index 177

Daigle, Michelle, 92
decolonial struggles, 26, 75, 92, 169n40
decoration of tents, 46, 48, 49, 57, 81–82
dehumanization, 13–14, 16, 20, 28, 36, 52, 54, 74; of Black and Indigenous people, 75
demographics, 19
demolition of camps, 20, 42, 142, 143–44, 146, 147
Dignity Village (Portland, Oregon), 43, 94
"domicide" (word), 48–49
donations coordination, 85
Dorries, Heather, 106–7
drugs. *See* illicit drugs; medications

Edmonds, Penelope, 16
Eidelman, Tessa, 67
encampment legalization, 137–41
encampment permits, 43
encampment sweeps, 20, 42, 142, 143–44, 146, 147
enclosure of public land, 34
Ensign, Josephine, 30–31; *Skid Road*, 36
ethic of care, 69–70, 77–78, 84, 85, 89, 111, 114, 151, 155
eviction of camps, 20, 42, 142, 143–44, 146, 147
evictions from camp, 108, 109–11, 113
exclusion, 12, 32–33, 135–36
executive committee (EC), 107–10, 112, 115

Farha, Leilani, 25–26
"feeling citizenship" (Simpson), 70, 76, 77, 78, 81, 91, 92, 120, 155
Feldman, Leonard, 96, 125
food supply, 86–88
Foucault, Michel, 95, 101; *Security, Territory, Population*, 115
Fourth Amendment, 61, 62

Fraser, James, 50
freedom of movement, 55–56, 57, 146

gentrification, 18, 40, 140, 148, 149
gift economy, 89–91
Glenn, Evelyn Nakano, 16, 30
governance, urban, 39, 94–95, 115
governmentality, 101–4, 111, 112, 113, 115
Greater Seattle Cares, 150–51

healthcare, 89
Herring, Chris, 17, 52, 142
home (concept), 3–4, 5, 12, 58, 59–60, 63, 152–56
"homeless" (word), 11, 13, 14, 35
homeless shelters, 20, 28, 55, 58, 65, 97, 138, 146, 164n27; compared to Tent City, 72; in "continuum of carcerality," 51–52; funding, 143; refusal of, 56
homemaking and homespace, 47–68, 73, 81–82, 92, 129, 133–34, 154. *See also* decoration of tents
Hoovervilles, 33, 36–38, 42, 44
hotel rooms, 146
housing vouchers, 146
Hugill, David, 51
Hunter, Ted, 43

illicit drugs, 109, 115
Indigenous people, 30, 31, 32, 42, 44, 56, 70, 75
infantilization, 14, 55, 72
informal governance, 93–117
Inwood, Joshua, 16

Japanese American internment, 38–39
Jungle (Beacon Hill), 143–44

Kawash, Samira, 14
Kikisoblu, 31, 32, 42

kitchen tent and kitchen work, 6, 7, 76, 77, 85, 86, 87, 94; coordinator, 73, 83, 87

law enforcement, 28, 52, 61–62
laws, antihomeless, 20, 35, 36, 41, 52, 57, 125
legalization of encampments, 137–41
Low-Income Housing Institute (LIHI), 140
Lutz, Manuel, 64

Macpherson, C. B., 53, 59
maintenance, 73, 83–85, 105
Marchand, Michelle, 96–98, 121, 129
McGinn, Mike, 139
medications, 88–89
meetings, weekly, 97–101, 105, 113
mental illness, 84–85, 114; transcarceration and, 144
Mill, John Stuart, 15
Mohawk sovereignty, 70
move master position, 104–6
Mullet, Steven, 135
Mullins, Mark, 27
Murray, Ed, 140, 143

Nancy, Jean-Luc, 69, 86
Native Americans, 30, 31, 32, 42, 44, 56, 70, 75
Neighly, Dustin, 38
Nextdoor, 150
Nickelsville, 140
nursing care, 89

One Thousand Homeless Men (Solenberger), 35
other (role), 125, 126, 131–33, 143

paid employees, 97–98
pathologizing of homelessness, 36, 52, 72, 75, 88, 91, 133

permits, 43
personhood, propertied. *See* propertied personhood
policing, 28, 52, 61–62
poorhouses, 31, 36, 164n27
Porteous, Douglas, 48
privacy, 58–64, 66, 68; tours and, 103
private property, 12–13, 29–30, 32, 53, 59, 145, 153; Fourth Amendment and, 61; security, 64–65. *See also* right to exclude
propertied citizenship, 53, 59, 62, 91, 149
propertied exclusion, 12, 32–33, 135–36
propertied personhood, 25, 50, 53, 119, 125–26, 136, 138, 142–43, 145, 146, 153; racialized, 16; resistance and refusal, 58, 67, 68, 118, 156
property, private. *See* private property
public land: enclosure, 34

racial demographics, 19
racialization, 15, 16; housing, 30, 31, 32–33
Ramírez, Margaret Marietta, 92
Rankin, Sara, 144
recreational camping, 34
refusal, 21, 45, 118, 154, 155, 156; of homelessness, 35–36, 48, 54–58, 73, 86, 119–20, 131, 135, 144; of housing vouchers, 147; of stereotypes, 152; of subjectification, 126–27, 131–32, 136, 152
removal of camps, 20, 42, 142, 143–44, 146, 147
right to exclude, 16, 29, 64, 66, 67, 148
right to have rights, 53, 119
Roat, Cindy, 150–51
Rowe, Claudia, 132
Roy, Ananya, 50, 53, 59, 63, 119, 146, 174n29
Roy, Donald, 36–37

rule creation and enforcement, 111–16

Safransky, Sara, 67
Saint Joseph's Catholic Church (Seattle), 19
Saint Mark's Cathedral (Seattle), 1, 18, 87
"sanitation sweeps," 20, 42, 142, 143–44, 146, 147
Scarola, George, 151
Scott, James: *Seeing Like a State*, 95
Seattle City Council, 104, 121, 129, 140
Seattle Housing and Resource Effort (SHARE), 5–6, 19, 27, 41–44, 121, 131–33; Marchand, 97; media coverage, 152; Nickelsville, 140; problems and, 109; weekly "power lunch," 110, 171n21
Seattle Is Dying (documentary) 17–18, 27, 42, 148
Security, Territory, Population (Foucault), 115
security duty (Tent City 3), 71, 75–81
Seeing Like a State (Scott), 95
self-government, 93–117
settler colonialism, 15–18, 22–23, 26–45, 48, 53–54, 56, 115–19, 126, 137–38, 147–54; Addie and Fraser on, 50; Anthony on, 102; governance, 95; rejection and alternatives, 66–67, 70, 136; sanctioned shelter spaces and, 141, 143, 145; Simpson and Hugill on, 51
Shacktown (Seattle), 32, 33, 35, 36, 37, 42
shantytowns, 30–31, 32, 33, 35, 42, 44
SHARE. *See* Seattle Housing and Resource Effort (SHARE)
shelters. *See* homeless shelters
shoppers and homeless people, 41, 42
Shoreline, Washington, 150
Sidran, Mark, 41

Simpson, Audra, 2, 69, 70
Simpson, Michael, 51
Singer, Jeffrey, 12, 13
Skid Road: On the Frontier of Homelessness in an American City (Ensign), 30–31, 36
Smith, Neil, 40
Smith, Sandra E., 48
Solenberger, Alice: *One Thousand Homeless Men*, 35
Speer, Jessie, 81
Spivak, Gayatri, 133, 136
state, 91, 95–96; violence and surveillance, 51
statistics, 149; demographic, 19
stereotypes, 14, 72, 94, 126, 130, 151, 152
substance abuse, 84
surveillance, 51, 61, 68, 106, 115
sweeps and evictions, 20, 42, 142, 143–44, 146, 147

Tenke, Howard, 27, 28, 36, 44
Tent City 1, 27, 40, 41–42, 142
Tent City 2, 42–43
Tent City 4, 132
tent city citizenship. *See* citizenship
Tent City Code of Conduct, 5, 71, 78, 100, 110–11, 113
tent city governance. *See* executive committee (EC); rule creation and enforcement; self-government
tent city maintenance, 73, 83–85, 105
tent city tours, 102–3
tent city weekly meetings, 97–101, 105, 113
"tent commons," 64–68
tent decoration, 46, 48, 49, 57, 81–82
tent maintenance and tent master position, 73, 85, 105

tent names and naming, 46, 47–48, 57, 58–59
theft, 64–65, 82, 168n39
tours, 102–3
town planning, 115
transcarceration, 144
Transitional Encampments Ordinance, 140
Tukwila, Washington, 135

"unhoming," 48–49, 50–54, 57, 88, 125, 146, 153
United We Stand. *See* Camp United We Stand
urban governance, 39, 94–95, 115

Veracini, Lorenzo, 26
vouchers, housing, 146

weekly meetings, 97–101, 105, 113
West Seattle, 152
WHEEL. *See* Women's Housing and Enhancement League (WHEEL)
white supremacy, 31–32
Wolfe, Patrick, 16
Women's Housing Equality and Enhancement League (WHEEL), 5–6, 19, 43, 171n21; Marchand, 96–97
World War II, 38–39

Printed in the USA
CPSIA information can be obtained
at www.ICGtesting.com
CBHW030905050924
13595CB00001B/1